The Executive's Guide to Customer Relationship Management

Retention • Loyalty • Profit

SECOND EDITION

PAUL ANDERSON
AND
ART ROSENBERG

Doyle Publishing Company, Inc.

Published by
Doyle Publishing Company, Inc.
5206 FM 1960 West, Suite 107
Houston, Texas 77069 USA
1-800-457-6459
www.doylepublishing.com

Publisher's Cataloging in Publication
Anderson, Paul, 1964-
    The executive's guide to customer relationship management : retention - loyalty - profit -- second edition / Paul Anderson and Art Rosenberg.
        p. cm.
        ISBN 0-9653359-4-1
        1. Call centers -- Computer network resources. 2. Internet (Computer network) 3. World Wide Web (Information retrieval system) 4. Internet telephony. 5. Customer services. I. Rosenberg, Arthur M., 1928-   II. Title.

    HE 8788.A64 1999   658.8'4   99-85843

Cover design by Decoz
Edited by Kay Morton
Printed in the United States of America
First printing: 2000

About the Authors

PAUL ANDERSON is a Houston, Texas based writer, author and consultant who writes about and works with clients to develop strategies that take advantage of new communication technologies in this emerging age of access and information. In addition to consulting with industry leaders, Mr. Anderson has written and authored numerous reports, white papers and articles and has participated in many conferences on the technologies of customer relationships. Mr. Anderson is the author of the best selling book; "A Call From the 21st Century, The Technology of Customer Contact," currently going into a second printing. Paul can be reached at (713) 937-4125 or paulvanderson@cs.com.

ART ROSENBERG is from Santa Monica, CA and is a product/market planning expert, writer, and application consultant for call center and messaging technologies, having been involved in the development of the earliest attempts to automate call center operations in the late '70s with Delphi Communications Corp. Many of the "new" innovations being trumpeted by the industry were implemented for Delphi's call center services using their pioneering integrated multimedia system, including skills-based routing, screen "pops", multilevel desktop application displays, voice and text messaging, fax response, "blended" inbound/outbound call handling and others. Art consults and writes on a variety of customer technology issues and can be reached at (310) 395-2360 or artr@ix.netcom.com.

Both Art and Paul have contributed numerous articles on leading edge call center technologies and applications to such publications as *Business Communications Review, Voice Processing Magazine, Telephony, CommunicationAge, InterFace, TeleProfessional, Call Center Magazine* and others. Both have extensive portfolios consisting of white papers, research reports, and conference participation presentations for such technology information providers as Gartner Group/DataPro and Probe Research.

Table of Contents

The Executive's Guide to Customer Relationship Management

Retention • Loyalty • Profit

Chapter Five - Technical Intimacy and the Art of Customer Loyalty   91

Popularized by the books The Loyalty Effect, The One to One Future and others, this chapter explores the impact that 1:1 marketing, relationship marketing, customer intimacy and data mining will have on the call center. Enterprise Relationship Management applications and software is no longer just available to Fortune 1000 companies and its benefits are quickly being assimilated into more call center operations. Also discussed are the application database servers that comprise the "back office" for call center operations, as well as the issues related to customer privacy and authentication.

Chapter Six - Call Center Humanware: White Collar Slave or
Gold Collar Worker?   117

While the trend has started changing recently, most technologists tend to neglect the agent as a crucial and strategic piece of the customer technology picture. It is in the technology of "humanware," the agents and customer service representative, that most customer loyalty battles will be won. The new breed of articulate, educated, and responsible "agent", the remote environments they will work from, and the technologies that will empower them to be more effective and efficient are put into perspective. In the rush for control of this moment we may be creating a threat to ourselves or a near perfect boon to global enterprise. Is it humanware or human being? White collar slave or gold collar worker?

Chapter Seven - E-business and Customer Relationship Management   143

The world of e-commerce and e-business is in an evolutionary (or maybe revolutionary) learning mode, and traditional customer telephone interactions are being supplanted by internet-based alternatives. The problem is that no one really knows exactly what the "customer" will expect in the new communications environment of the world wide web.

Chapter Eight - Taming Chaos: When Neural Networks Meet
Customer Service   169

Running parallel to the information revolution, is the relationship evolution. This evolution demands that stimulating and garnering the future value of customers now requires executing every customer service event with bias, preference, discretion and prejudice. Technology can now be leverage to turn the enterprise away from inefficient, deeply embedded and institutionally persistent ways of fulfilling service demands. Traditional call center technology is designed around substituting transactional activity for branding achievement. Efficiency no longer equals effectiveness. The technology enabled arbitrage of customer events, enterprise human resources and every media channel can now be prioritized - not by age, but by value. At its core, taming the true chaotic nature of customer and agent events, both in the timing and media, requires new tools, applications and technologies.

Chapter Nine - The Informal Call Center and Relationship
Communications   193

While "formal" call center operations and technologies traditionally deal with dedicated call-handling workgroups, this chapter defines and discusses the "informal" call center as a practical way to involve anyone within the enterprise with customer relationship management. While this concept is being implemented by consolidating and centralizing all customer-related information and interactions through back-office database servers, multimedia communication contact control is also being expanded at the individual user level, or "The Call Center of One." In particular, the rapid growth of public two-way messaging via the Internet will expand the role of personal unified message/call management (UM/CM) technologies for "informal" call center activities in the small enterprise, as well as for integrating with the call/message routing technologies of "formal" call center departmental workgroups.

Chapter One
Embrace the Changing Edge

Introduction

We are taking part in the most extraordinary revolution in history. It is a technology revolution that has borne the age of multimedia; an age where the barriers of time and space no longer exist. It is an age where people from opposite sides of the world will soon be able to communicate face to face, just as if they lived next door to each other.

New networking capabilities, technologies that enable connectivity and bandwidth as well as the standards that drive new applications, are coming together in an environment of upwardly spiraling processing power and deepening technological penetration. Any number of converging technologies are contributing to this pace of change. There must be a dramatic fundamental change happening when toothpaste commercials now have world wide web addresses.

Technology is creating new interfaces, seams and edges on the peripheral, of which enterprises must adapt to or face the challenge of losing contact with their customers to the competitor that does. The internet is an excellent example and, while those sages and prophets of the internet have been fascinated by its property of having no edge, it does in fact have an edge. It is that boundary between those who are connected and therefore are valuable to the enterprise and those who are not connected and therefore are not relevant. The edge is a perilous place; it's the juncture where your enterprise network meets the great wide-open public network.

This fundamental change obviously has not escaped influencing the enterprise call center. Microsoft has a marketing message that says that information technology is increasingly forming the enterprises "digital nervous system." For the most part, the closest an enterprise can get to it's customers is the call center. This makes the call center the nerve endings of this "digital nervous system," the sensory inputs of the enterprise's "digital nervous system." As such, the call center is growing to become essential to the support of a customer's life cycle through the stages of acquisition, service and retention.

We should consider that the evolution of technology is primarily about the evolution of interfaces and that the call center, as the single most important locus of customer interaction and collaboration, is where we can witness the pragmatic application of the digital revolution. If it is not being used in the call center, it's probably not (yet) a significant technology.

The real struggle with enterprises today is not over information and the technology that creates it, but over relationships. When we design networks and customer interfaces for the enterprise, are we designing them to manage important information, or to manage important relationships? With the exception of those dependent on or responsible for the enterprise's customer relationships, it was not too long ago that information (data and the reports it generates) was more important than the relationships. But customer relationships too are vulnerable to the evolutionary influence of technology and we now see that technology executives are trending toward making their information systems more extroverted, with customer communication becoming the highest priority and customer satisfaction being the paramount justification.

Enterprises with extroverted-oriented information and communication systems are more successful and have greater productivity when compared to "introverted" companies. The extroverted company's productivity is growing comparatively faster as well.

Extroversion requires more accessible and open systems. Those executives that are evolving at the pace of technology know that they too must constantly work on integrating information systems and interfaces across the entire enterprise, dissolving previously impervious boundaries – those edges that have traditionally separated customer service from the rest of the business. The existence of this dichotomy is evident in the familiar gap between the data and the telecom disciplines.

Enterprise extroverts view the call center as a tool for increasing revenue by improving customer satisfaction; identifying and gaining new customers, enhancing the quality of the company's products and services and competing with speed by increasing enterprise responsiveness. In contrast, the old introverted model was one of customer service that put much more value on improving management's control of information flow, saving on labor (agents) resources and lowering manufacturing costs. Extroverts use call centers to improve their relationships with customers through the constant rapid redesign of business processes, while the introverts tend to be associated with little organizational change.

There has been a slew of studies, articles and reports in the past several years empirically demonstrating that US companies lose one-half of their customers every five years (known commonly in some industries as churn). The most successful strategy for reducing customer churn is to make it easier for customers to engage and communicate with your company. Accumulating this experiential knowledge is driving competitive companies to extend customer engagements into extended customer relationships. The emerging view is that "extended customer relationships" now means the length of the customer's life cycle, expressed in the concept of a customer's "life-time value." Personalization, customerization, one-to-one marketing and relationship marketing are the buzz words of this emerging view.

Personalization is the integration of relevant customer databases to centralize all of an enterprise's content, policies and strategies to identify, generate and exploit new revenue streams from existing customers. The new power of technology increasingly allows enterprises to customize and personalize the experiences its customers have with the company.

The telephone has been the traditional interface of customer engagements for at least fifty years. Because of the deep institutional permanence of the telephone, many believe that it will be some time before the telephone will go away or even that its importance will diminish. This is not to say that the enterprise should ignore or discount the ever-growing importance of emerging interactive technologies. There is certainly an acute need, where there may not have been one in the past, to be increasingly aware of these emerging interactive technologies. Some will grow to be significant (for example, the internet) and some will fade into obscurity in spite of their hype (for example, Apple's Newton).

Knowing which technologies are potentially significant and those that are not is explicitly relevant to the business that you are in. As we evolve from the age of reactive customer service to the age of collaborative engagements, strategic decisions based on observations from the peripheral of the call center become increasingly more important.

From the Peripheral

To customer service executives, understanding the peripheral has had little importance since, for the most part, the telephone was the principle device used for customer engagements. The new age of access demands an understanding of, obviously, more than just the telephone (the internet really changed this one). Because interactive technologies are so temporal and fluid, but increasingly influential, one of the most valuable skills an executive can develop is the observation and understanding of the ever-widening peripheral influences of the call center. Management decision-makers rarely have the time to observe and examine all of the influencing technologies surrounding the periphery of the call center, but they no longer have the option of ignoring it either. Ignorance is a misunderstood word. It is not a synonym for stupid; it simply means lack of awareness.

The word "peripheral" itself is unique to information technology. There is no such thing as travel, food or shipping peripheral. It is from the peripheral that we find the basis for the way we do everything, from watching home entertainment, doing to our banking, handling our voice and printed communications or finding our way from city to city. Looking around the next curve, there are certain things happening on the horizons, the periphery, that will have profound impact on the way we do business.

We use the periphery to define what we are aware of without attending to expressly. For example, ordinarily when we drive, our attention is focused on the road ahead of us, the radio, a passenger, a car phone conversation, children in the back seat or the obnoxious slow driver in the left lane. Rarely do we concentrate on the noise of the engine. However, any unusual engine noise is immediately noticed, demonstrating that we are not so far from immediately noticing the noise in the periphery.

It should be made clear that "on the peripheral" is anything but "on the fringe," "insignificant," "inconsequential" or "unimportant". The danger with the evolutionary speed of technology's influence is in underestimating that what is on the periphery at one minute may be in the center the next.

Often customer service executives are so enchanted by the volume of information that an enterprise's information systems generate - and for most that's about all it generates so far – that they have neither the mind nor the time for observations of the peripheral. Peter Drucker has been warning executives for a long time about the dangers of being mesmerized by technology and the data it generates: "All great changes in business have come from outside the firm, not from within. But because saving time (creating a relationship) is an eternality, not capable of easily being measured in any of the typical productivity data, many experts and operational managers are missing the profound impact of technology."

Small jets are doing to the airline business what PCs did to mainframe computing, fractional horsepower machines did to turbines, mini-mills did to steel, cellular is doing to telephony, mutual funds are doing to centrally managed pension plans and what coming mini-generators will do to massive power plants. It is about power moving away from the machine-age center toward individuals of the microchip era (Forbes Magazine 6/97). In a couple of short years, the personal computer will be where a Silicon Graphics workstation is today. For example, the animated movie Toy Story was developed using 50 Silicon Graphics workstations. The same movie would have taken 47 years to render on a single Pentium chip today.

Increasingly, to understand what will be important next, one must pay attention to more fields of technology at the same time: chips, modems, PCs, software, fiber, satellite, internet, wireless and new applications such as electronic commerce. When it comes to call centers, it is the peripheral that is expanding; customers and callers are coming from all sides and faster than ever. Which of all of the peripherals should we follow if we are to know about the future? Some are predictable, some are wildcards. An example of an unanticipated wildcard with the new digital television (HDTV) is the problem, not with the technology (it looks great), but in the Sisyphan effort to build the broadcast towers. Quite literally, they could have seen the problem that there were not enough television towers and crews in the country to erect them, creating a huge backlog and most likely causing a failure of television stations to meet their mandated deadlines.

Even customers themselves loom as significant influences from the peripheral. Not so long ago, the customer call was a predictable metric defined by an Erlang value, but today it's no longer the call center that is increasingly digital, it is now the customer as well. The digitization of the customer is a penetrating factor influencing how businesses will perform and compete. How many call center executives are aware that in many US ghettos and housing projects, television penetration is greater than telephone penetration? If your customers live in ghettos, then you need to learn how to communicate with them through their televisions.

There are plenty of influential issues on the peripheral, some more influential than others. While an issue or technology may indeed be on the peripheral, until the number of people using a new technology reaches a critical mass, there are few real advantages to users (internet-based telephony, for example). Your telephone would be useless if you were the only one who owned one. The internet, television and radio would be useless without content; automobiles would be useless without paved roads and gas stations. But good content, highways and technologies don't occur until a critical mass of customers are ready to use them.

The use of language is another of the more underestimated peripheral influences. Language is certainly important to the call center because it is the most fundamental of tools that we use in call centers. There are two to three thousand languages spoken around the world, not including the strange language spoken by teenagers. Interestingly, almost one-quarter of all the English language has been created in the last 25 years, most of it having to do with information and technology. Ubiquitous words about the paradigm like interactive, virtual, models, feedback, infrastructure, and the internet fill, as Peggy Noonan is quoted later, "Our tribal language of jargon." The word "peripheral" itself is a relatively new word.

Even Microsoft Windows 95 itself now have its own dictionary definition. The definition of Windows 95: *noun.* 32-bit extensions and a graphical shell for a 16-bit patch to an 8-bit operating system originally coded for a 4-bit microprocessor, written by a 2-bit company that can't stand 1-bit of competition.

Language's influence on the business of call centers is significant and it tends to be inadequate to describe the importance of the langauge of the customer because executive management themselves are so saturated with jargon and acronyms, they simply can not hear. It is difficult to overlook the communications technology industry's particularly blatent penchant for developing new acronyms: TCP/IP, ACD/PBX, HTML, SMDR, SQL, LAN, WAN, SCSI, ATM, ADSL, ISDN, POTS and CTI to name a few. Using more elaborate and complex combinations of letters with catchy and zippy, "cadences of poetry is our industry's equivalent of a good old fashion pissing contest."

Peggy Noonan, a prominent White House speech writer, wrote in her recent book, "Simply Speaking," that, "The thing that has replaced accents in America is professional jargon, the shorthand language of shared knowledge. If you've ever seen ER, you've seen a good example of pure dialect, not of our tribe, but of our profession. Because our profession now is our tribe."

Observations from the peripheral demonstrate that even the Microsoft product PowerPoint is evolving from being a noun to being an adjective. Increasingly, it is used in reference to "powerpointing" observations, products or organization. When someone refers to "powerpointing" their comments, they do not necessarily mean to pull out their laptop and visually demonstrate their point, they are referring to using PowerPoint as a substitute to expand upon. One of the characterizations of "powerpointing" is a proclivity of call center technology vendors to promote the "powerpoint product," which, like the distinction between software and vaporware, often theatrically demonstrates products or services that do not yet exist.

History's Perspective

One of the most underestimated of the call center's peripherals is the one directly behind us - history. Along with the 35 year durability of Moore's Law, there also appears to be a certain amount of truth to the African proverb that says, "If you know your history, the future will trouble you."

1997 was the third decade of the PC, the 25th year of the microprocessor and the 50th year of the electronic computer. In 1975, there were only 300,000 computers on the planet. Today, we produce twice that many computers every week, or two every second. A 300 megahertz chip is worth more than its weight in gold. A program sold by Microsoft weighs nothing at all (Windows NT creates a profit of $90) and can be shipped instantly to any point on the globe. In contrast, the telephone is a 123 year old device that still dominates the interface landscape.

In the 1960's and 1970's, we ran businesses with big iron (mainframes) and batch processing, taking advantage of the capability to store and retrieve large amounts of data. In the 1980's PCs emerged, giving enterprise managers quick access to critical data and the ability to analyze, reorganize and process data much more quickly and effectively.

What history has to teach us in the call center business is that the staying power of the telephone can be attributed to the fact that we are, on a cultural whole, much more pragmatic than the popular media would have us believe. When the phone company first introduced touch tone calling, they charged a stiff premium; we bought it anyway. Now try taking somebody's touch-tone away from them. What would they have to pay you not to go back to rotary dial?

Answering machines were considered "insulting" by many in the 1970's, but by 1987 people were evenly split on their worthiness, this change took ten to fifteen years. Today, two-thirds of US households have them. It took eight years for credit cards to be embraced by consumers in the market place. In contrast, the internet has only been used as a sales medium for the past several years at most. First came email, and now the internet carries more messages than the postal service carries letters.

The first major step in increased data network access for the consuming public occurred over twenty years ago with the automatic teller machine and, for the first time, the general public came into direct contact with a computer-based application near and dear to their hearts, or more accurately their wallets. However, still today customers must travel to the ATM terminal and hope that the network is operating.

The transitory nature of the transistor is responsible for the fact that critical technologies that would have been meaningless 50 years ago (cellular services, fax machines, color printers, modems, internet service providers, music on hold, laser pointers, video conferencing), are now in the forefront of customer and enterprise engagements. Just as technologies evolve to the forefront, they dissolve into obscurity as readily. The VCR is a dying technology (being killed by DVD) as is the fax and paper checks. Just as assuredly, the cellular phone and the PC will die eventually.

One of the consistent lessons of technological innovation is that the emergence of standards stimulates both uptake and investment. In the early part of this century, convergence on voltage and current standards "sparked" an explosion in electrical devices and usage. Similarly, wireless communication standards created the rapid growth of cellular phone users in the early 90's. Standards today such as HTTP (Hyper Text Transfer Protocol), HTML (Hyper Text Markup Language) and IP (Internet Protocol) are driving the rapid growth of the internet.

The fact that the phone is over 120 years old testifies that the telecommunications industry's speed of change has been glacial. The fact is that it has only been relatively recently that our ability to manipulate data has exceeded our ability to communicate. Unable to no longer ignore pervasive competition, new legislation, new technologies and new customer demands, the telecommunications industry is having to rethink every assumption it ever made. One of the great historical ironies of the information age is that many of the telecommunications networks that the internet depends on are built upon industrial-age networks of railroad track and oil pipeline right of ways.

Knowledgified Customers

The most profound influence of technology on the enterprise has been the profound influence it has had on it's customers. Enterprise is increasingly finding themselves selling into an infomated world. Because of the fundamental availability of information, customers know more about you than they ever have before and they come to every transactions more "knowledged-ified."

The broad historical perspective establishes that power is now shifting from the enterprise to the customers and that technology, particularly the internet, is giving every customer the ability to survey the market place and make optimal purchases. Now enterprises are answering to empowered and smartened customers talking to equally skilled advisors.

What the internet does is enables is the availability to the customer of a vast supply of research and internal information on every imaginable item one would want to purchase. Retailing of every sort has gone from an information-scarce to an information-rich environment.

As interaction cost falls, goods and services providers will go directly to consumers or the consumers will do their own searching. In a single hour today, we can accomplish tasks that would have taken most of the day under the previous generation of interaction paradigms, such as buying a car or book. The savings that atom-based companies gain by bypassing traditional channels are more compelling than the enhanced services that characterize most on-line bit-based offerings. In the case of books (Amazon.com), PCs (Dell) and cars (AutoQuote), consumers directly benefit from the real costs that are taken out of the distribution system. Consumers today can rent cars, buy airline tickets and check in and out of hotels with little or no human contact. The internet and intranets have put meaningful technology power directly in the hands of employees, customers and business partners.

As the value customers derive from searching declines, intermediaries will have to enhance other aspects of their role, or create new roles to play. Some will build businesses around pure transaction channels; Charles Schwab is an example of this. Unlike the single call, or one-shot transaction, call centers are at the forefront of the emerging complexity of customer engagements (they are knowledgified now) and the demand for tiers of service (airline frequent flier programs) and preferential treatment for various classes of clients and customers.

In bit-based (information) businesses such as banking, finance and on-line entertainment, especially those supported by advertising, there is very little consumer cost to be reduced. The conclusion is that internet-based systems compete mostly on convenience and functionality. In bit-based businesses such as stock brokerages and travel services, the only thing that has been really replaced is the telephone call (ironically in fact it still being made via dial-up modem), essentially eliminating a customer service agent. The elimination of the middleman (an infomediary) creates lowered costs. Lower prices, not enhanced service, drive the demand. The customer's real electronic benefit can be found when buyers can save money.

Customer service-focused organizations are losing control of information technology because technology is no longer just a way to automate back-office processes or collect data; it has become a part of every enterprise's products and services, from the initial design stage to the customer service, support and retention. Customer interactions with the call center and all of the other types of self-help applications and mediums such as the internet, email and IVR make up the consumer's entire impression of the enterprise. Even though the amount of time saved and the ability to shop prices worldwide is a valuable resource, customer service is definitly lacking. Networking and telecommunications have matured and so have expectations. Smart shoppers are learning to identify and separate those that can service them – knowledgeably – or eventually these companies will perish.

It does not take much to realize that a satisfied customer is more likely to become a repeat customer, but until recently, technology that could significantly improve customer satisfaction was either unavailable or because of costs and complexity, limited to the very largest of formal call centers.

The new span and power of technology 'databases' makes it possible for every enterprise to remember each customer as readily as the customer can remember an enterprise. This is now easy to accomplish because the power of the processor brings the ability to remember each transaction and customer's preferences. Using multimedia server technology, these next generation systems can consolidate the connection, identification, management, routing and retrieval of virtually any type of customer contact, – voice, fax, email, or internet-based communications – into a single seamless process.

The key to management success in this age of access lies is spotting and analyzing key shifts in communication technology and then adapting and translating those changes into better ideas for helping your employees and customers improve core business functions. The challenge is understanding how communications technology is used to create stronger customer relationships - providing the best possible experience at the least expense to the enterprise.

Management

The economies of enterprise computing have, in the past five years, turned from struggling with scarcities of processing power, bandwidth and distribution to integrating with a networked society that is structured around flows of capital, information, technology, organizational interaction and relationships. Within a short period of time, many enterprises will face an embarrassment of having more information than they know what to do with and in the bloodthirsty business arena, it's either be in control of your information flow or get crushed under it. To avoid this, successful call center managers must increasingly become business managers, technical wizards, corporate team players, budget masters, long-term planners, educators and promoters. The new generation of call center managers must increasingly also deal with the pressures of budget cuts, mergers, downsizing, outsourcing and ever increasing workloads.

One of the most significant issues surrounding the enterprise's evolution into the new age of customer relationships does not lie with technology or the information access that it enables, it lies more often than not with the senior management. It is management style that is the most difficult to change in an enterprise because it involves altering ingrained, often institutionalized behaviors. Senior executives have no interest in changing what has made them successful and usually there is no one around to tell them to do it differently or that they must change. Those managers who anticipate and understand the fundamental nature of the changes ahead and actively reshape their business models in response will best be in place to exploit the opportunities. Those that do not will face a difficult transition from the legacies of the past to the intimate realities of the future. Anticipation is often said to be the basis for opportunity.

One of the impediments to management change is competitive uniphobia - a term coined by Watts Wacker in his book The Five Hundred Year Delta. Competitive uniphobia is fixation on competitive situations that, by their very character, are transitory in nature. Unlike the peripheral issues expounded on earlier, competitive paranoia is a useless exertion, with the exception of understanding how competitors themselves are using technologies to enable greater customer access. Looking at the competitive landscapes, particularly in the recently deregulated industries such as banking and utilities, an enterprise has no way of knowing who its competitors are, or will be, or what information about them it will need; it makes much more sense to focus on describing the competitive information the enterprise has today. Barnes and Noble never anticipated that an inventory-less company called Amazon.com would emerge as their chief competitive threat.

An implication of the technology revolution is the evolution of managers from infrastructure managers to information managers. This is a major cultural change for call center managers and customer service chain executives. In the past, managers managed the differences between data and information, now the paradigm is the difference between information and intelligence. Although many customer service managers try to relate the long term value customer relationships to revenue, asset deployment and operational costs, these are poor surrogates for the real implications of the "life-time value" of customers.

Describing and understanding any enterprise's current information environment can be a daunting and major undertaking. Describing who has what information, the various sources of information, how information and knowledge are used in work processes and an organization's intentions and objectives for this information is an essential task for competing. The rapid change and "growth" of an enterprise's information resources is becoming almost organic in its nature. In fact; new schools of thought express that information technology must be managed "ecologically" - growing, permutating and always in flux. By inference, the ecology of information becomes the ecology of relationships.

Information ecology is an abstract management metaphor, but a good one given the growing interconnectedness of the enterprise's information environments. As biological ecologies thrive on species diversity, so information ecologies thrive on information diversity. Still, true information integration won't happen without major changes in management approaches and organizational structure, particularly in the age of relationship management (a.k.a. one-to-one marketing). In fact, enterprises that wish to truly meet their customer's needs should not be directing people to any particular type of information, they should combine all of the information media available.

Another increasing characteristic of successful call center managers and customer service chain executives will be a trait (again framed by Watts Wacker) of intelligent disobedience. Intelligent disobedience is what seeing eye dogs are taught; essentially that they are to obey unless they have a better idea. Intelligent disobedience is not only a characteristic of the new generation of managers, but as an executive, the challenge will be in allowing a certain amount of intelligent disobedience in employees and agents. How many of us have had, from our perspective, exceptional customer service based on an agent or employee making a decision that probably was in infringement of a certain policy or procedure?

The opposite of embracing the search for intelligence in the mountains of information an enterprise can generate is avoiding it. Substituting activity for achievement, or discorporation, is a growing phenomenon where managers spend their days in "static observation mode" scrolling through screenfuls of data and management reports, bit by digital bit, searching for nuggets of revelvancies between call traffic, agent staffing, skills, trunks and trends.

Intelligent management, as opposed to informed management, distinguishes the difference between knowing how to effect a result and spending time achieving a result (substituting activity for achievement). As an example, there is a difference between knowing the formula to calculate how many golf balls it takes to fill an Olympic size swimming pool and exploiting other resources to do it for you (consultants, vendors, et al.). If calculating the number of golf balls in the pool is not your core competency, then you do not have to know that the diameter of the golf ball is 1.68 inches, that the radius is 0.84 inches, that a golf ball's volume is 2.48 cubic inches, or even that the densest packing of spheres possible is 74 percent. All you need is the answer of 68.28 million.

Rapid Prototyping

Complaining that technology changes fast is like complaining that rocks are hard; it's true but useless. It is also a little like expecting a bull not to attack you because you are a vegetarian. The future belongs to the organization that aggressively manages what they are not aware of, change. And just keeping up is not fast enough anymore. Today, an enterprise's ability to take advantage of the rapid hyper-evolution can be the most significant factor determining the enterprise's ability to keep up and compete with faster more nimble competitors. Take the idea of being open for business 24 x 7 x 365; not too long ago, this symbolized extreme competitiveness. Today, it is the norm for the blistering pace of a world open for business 24 hours per day.

Business is fast becoming a rapid feedback loop. Information sharing is what technology enables. Information from the feedback loop provides the ability to move quickly to offer new services and to unify whole enterprises, customers and vendors. What a free market does is allow people to make the cheap, fast mistakes necessary when developing complex systems and lifetime relationships. Information, unless it produces action, is overhead and one of the defining traits of a manager prepared to face the challenges of the 21st century call center will be the ability to adapt to the accelerating pace of change by discarding obsolete ideas.

Much of the current mindset about the organization of enterprises is inherited from an age of mass production and, in an interconnected world' small changes can quickly work their way through the entire system. Sampling and market tests, for example, are increasingly becoming limited, if not useless, because there is no way that all of the (new) variables that exist in the real world can be touched. In fact, one of the concepts that will drive the role of call centers in the future will be the idea of "pure response" marketing. Pure response marketing is the concept of near-instantaneous input of customer information, reactions and feedback into the enterprise's information systems.

Consider the speed of the stagecoach versus the train, versus a car, and now the space shuttle traveling at 36,000 mph. Jim Taylor, Gateway 2000's visionary, estimates that innovation in digital technology gets produced somewhere on average every three seconds. Product development approaches such as iterative prototyping and rapid application development are just as applicable to customer service initiatives as they are to develop-ing widgets. Tom Peters makes the observations that the revolution of the last 25 years created the phenomena of Staples, Blockbuster, Home Depot, Circuit City and Wal-Mart, and it is his observation that these enterprises were born out of the competitive complacency of their traditional rivals. But, he astutely asks, "Do you think that the next 25 years are going to be more mellow than the last?"

Falling interaction and communication costs enable enterprises to execute strategies based on the concepts of mass customization. Not only will finding and reaching new customers become simpler, but tailoring products and services for them will be easier, faster and cheaper.

Look What the Net Has Dragged In

The internet is the technology that has emerged to be the one with the greatest earth-shrinking potential.

As we enter the first decade of the internet, we find that more than one trillion bytes of information (equal to 60 million typed pages) are posted on the internet each month. Internet traffic grows a hundred fold every 1,000 days. At the time of printing, the record for most web page hits in one week was from CNN Interactive, Atlanta, who said that its servers delivered 59.6 million individual page hits from August 30, 1997, to September 6, 1997 the week following the death of princess Diana. In one hour alone, CNN Interactive servers delivered one million page impressions. The number of internet users will grow by another 100 million in 1998.

According to a Booz, Allen & Hamilton study, a traditional bank transaction costs $1.07; the same transaction over the web costs about 1 cent. A traditional airline ticket transaction costs $8.00 to process, an electronic ticket cost of just $1.00. Federal Express loses money everytime they have to take a package tracking call. They actually make money when a customer uses the web-based tracking system. A personalized version of Time Magazine is available on-line to subscribers in Australia. Today, it only costs a few cents to create and deliver; in 1987 it would have cost $5.00 and taken four days.

Manual Castrell (author of The Information Age: Economy, Society and Culture) has defined the advance of the internet as "Rapture of the Net," "wherein this mystical network becomes a general purpose solution for social and cultural problems, a gateway to paradise. We're going to fix schools, reinvent government and link the world in an orgy of mass communication - and get rich in the process." The internet's growth will accelerate as computer prices fall and, although it is now dominated by American users, it will quickly acquire a more global reach. The span between nodes on the net is irrelevant since the speed of light essentially erases distance.

On the other pragmatic side, if you ignore the fact that after 125 years most of the 5 billion people on the planet still do not have telephones, adding on internet users could take decades. Some experts expect that the growth of the internet will in fact slow drastically and that by the year 2005 the internet's impact on the economy will prove to be no greater than the fax machine or Palm Pilot.

Solutions to the low bandwidth of ordinary telephone lines must emerge before the internet becomes the main medium for communications and contact. The battle is on between ISDN, ADSL or cable modems to supply high-speed net connectivity to the home.

Industry analysts and experts predict that web-based support will soon be the dominant means of customer service support. According to one of the leading internet analyst firms, Jupiter Communications, the internet will become a common method of customer support and they predict that by the year 2002, an estimated 50 percent of all on-line sites will use on-line support to augment their telephone customer service efforts.

As of March 1998, 15 percent of all call centers were web enabled. Some analysts estimate this number will double every year for the next several years. However, polls and surveys of Fortune 1000 enterprises indicate that most are not ready to integrate the internet into their call center operations. They do believe that the internet will grow to be a significant part of revenues and interactions in a few short years.

Strategic Danger Points

Technological progress is bringing about a massive increase in interactive capability. All modern forms of interactions – whether they be as simple as writing a letter or as complex as solving a customer problem in a call center – are being influenced by computing and communication technologies. The last several decades have brought remarkable innovations, but many feel that modern technology has failed to exploit opportunities to increase the quality and quantity of customer interactions and reduce their costs.

Information and data in the right hands at the right time can have a powerful effect. The same information misinterrepted or misapplied can be unuseful. How many useless web sites are languishing out there because someone got techno-duped into paying for them? There is an insidious side to technology and that is it often dupes us into changing our habits and overlooking common sense. Why use the internet for service if the ISP is always busy? The phone always works.

Investments in leading edge technology often reduce the very reliability and convenience that the "silent majority" of customers sorely desire and need. In fact, the majority of customers are often overlooked in the unimobileteledigicomlink babble of the more vocal, activist, functionality hungry customers. In satisfying this group, enterprises can pass up the opportunity to provide more of the reliability and convenience that mainstream users desire.

Too much technology can turn off customers. Systems that offer functions users don't really want and lack the qualities they find important, frustrate users. Not long ago, customers frequently complained that automation was putting businesses out of touch. Slow, unwieldy automated voice response systems were the biggest source of complaints. One of the risks from the rapid growth of technology is ignoring the significant proportion of the population, is in fact "down-teching." Add technology too rapidly and the enterprise runs the risk of frustrating a customer base used to personal service.

It is easy to have an appreciation of the potential of technology, but it is a problem when managers ignore what happens when technology misuses its potential. Take IVR as an example. In call centers the balance must be found that juggles the efficiencies of long menus versus the anger of customers stuck in them.

According to Forrester Research, Inc. in Cambridge, Mass., companies can trim 43 percent off their customer service and call center labor costs by offering some service on-line. In comparison, without internet-based solutions, the same cost will likely rise by 3 percent.

Using internet technology to reduce the costs per call or increase the number of calls handled reads well, but it is short-term thinking. The reality of this model is that it pushes the support and engagement burden back on the customer. The fact is that internet support does not necessarily reduce costs. Customers forced to exchange email with a product support person often takes weeks, when the issue could have been resolved in a fewer number of telephone calls. The individual transaction cost may be lower, but the frequency of contact is high.

Techno-duping (save a whopping 43 percent!) avoids focusing on customer satisfaction, not cheaper resolution. Competitive advantages no longer lie in saving a few dollars, but in fostering loyal customer relationships. If companies truly want to reduce their support costs, they should make products that need less support.

One of the pervasive, but often ignored issues in this age of access, is the underestimated craving of people for social interaction and contact in all of their engagements. One of the failures (or perhaps unanswered questions, since electronic commerce hasn't been around that long) of electronic commerce has been to faithfully recreate the social aspects of the traditional retail buying experiences. Barnes and Noble's competitive success against Amazon.com today lies in their offering of coffee shops and lounges, not in their book selection.

Understanding this characteristic of human nature, the striving to make technology more "intimate" is leading to some pretty humorous results. Researchers at Bell Labs have developed a Web page that turns yellow and crinkles in front of your eyes – just as a piece of loose leaf paper would after being handled by thousands of human hands. Algorithms automatically "age" the Web page based on the amount of traffic it endures. "Web pages are touched every day by thousands of people and there must be a way to convey the age of the page itself (using counters)," said Doree Seligmann, co-developer of the virtual paper. The Web desperately needs "signs of life and interaction in order to become more engaging." How do you intend to fill your customer's need for familiarity and intimacy? Or, are you avoiding it?

The Future

The trouble with the future, someone observed, is that there are so many of them.

The further ahead that communication technology futurists and experts project their minds, the deeper their insights are thought to be. Futurists would rather not predict what will happen next year. They prefer to think further, to a safer distance ahead, twenty, fifty or a millennium ahead. If they think far enough into the future, they are called, reverently, visionaries.

Futurists have a great line of work, they get paid to make broad generalizations, wild assumptions and baseless conclusions and all they have to do is be right about 20 percent of the time to be taken seriously. If only call center managers and customer service executives had that kind of luck or clout; If only 20% of your application attempts worked, you wouldn't be taken very seriously would you?

As we look to the 21st century, many of us try to identify trends that will have a major impact on every enterprise. The phenomenas that will change society as a whole – the aging of the baby boomers, new media like the internet and wireless phones, information delivery systems such as satellites – are surrounding us as influences. Rapidly falling communication costs will create equally rapid changes in the relationships between companies and their customers. As inexpensive communication becomes ubiquitous, geographic barriers between and among people, businesses and governments will diminish, opening up new commercial and social opportunities.

We have entered an era when an enterprise's anticipatory reactions are no longer governed by the domino effect, but by the "slinky theory" - a theory based on the premise that at any given moment society is either contracting toward consensus or expanding toward the exploration of endpoints. Unfortunately, " The shortest path between two points is always under construction." (Noelie Alito)

A whole new section of the global economy will see the communication capacity grow, as basic technologies such as PC and telephone service penetrate more deeply over the next decade. "A convergence of technologies is set to increase our capacity to interact by a factor of two and five in the near future. This enhanced interactive capacity will create new ways to configure businesses, organize companies, and serve customers, and have profound effects on the structure, strategy and competitive dynamics of industries." (McKinsey Quarterly)

Growing standardization will also encourage the integration of many technologies into the processes and methods of customer interactions. Just as the expansion in transcontinental railroad transportation compelled US railways to standardize track size in the early 1900's, the extra traffic created by lower interaction costs will force the emergence of new communication and information standards in the new millennium.

The general public will scarcely recognize that a revolution is underway because capabilities will come slowly and incrementally. The likely "revolutionary" technologies include ISDN, Asynchronous Transfer Mode and wireless. Local, long-distance, paging, cellular, entertainment and electronic commerce and internet access services which were at one time provided by different companies are now increasingly being provided by all types of telecommunications companies.

An example of the linear, pragmatic evolution of technology is movement of IVR toward ever more complicated and natural applications, of which the most natural is speech recognition. Speech driven autoattendant is certainly one of the killer applications of voice technologies. The next logical permutation after this is natural language recognition. Imagine what happens to the global opportunities when an enterprise can take calls from anywhere in the world and language is no longer a barrier to doing business.

In this new information age, information is currency and the discipline most likely to benefit from the emergence of the intimate transactional technologies is consultative support and service. "Infomediaries," which is exactly what agents in a certain context are, cater to the awareness that the time value, the financial value, and the relationship value of the next call is extremely important to the enterprise. This awareness alone, for management astute enough to embrace it, will drive the call center from the peripheral (there's that word again) to the center of corporate strategy; from cost centers to revenue centers, as the cliché goes.

Opportunities with intimate customer relationships and the call centers that serve them are sometimes difficult to anticipate, plan or foresee because many company's and enterprise structures today are still very much based more on assumptions about enterprise organization, than on the economics of interactions and communications (Egghead Software is an excellent example of this shift; closing nearly 50 stores to do business entirely on-line).

Anticipation is the basis of opportunity and, with each hard-won insight, the pragmatic manager will pause just long enough to plot a new course, designed to take advantage of what has just been learned. If you focus on too distant a goal, you may find an obstacle blocking the path that didn't appear on the map - better to follow the contours of the terrain. This is the critical function of having the enterprise enabled with technologies that make relationship and pure response marketing possible.

Conclusions

The effective use of technology is the price of admission to successfully compete in the next century. Managers and executives of customer-focused enterprises can either evolve by a thousand cuts, or experience revolution by big bang (fired). Adapting "out-of-the-box" thinking is absolutely necessary to become competitive in the new information era. Customer service decision makers must take risks when stepping outside of the usual paradigm of the "box" - because what is working today, won't necessarily work tomorrow.

The role of call centers will morph from simple large scale telephony exchanges to customer interaction centers surrounded by touch points of different devices. Enterprise call centers must adapt to a new stream of customer transactions that originate in cyberspace.

The tradeoffs that shape economic activity-enterprises trading off specialization against interaction costs, customers weighing current selections against further search costs, enterprises considering alternative configurations - will each find a new balance point.

The greatest evolutionary change for customer technology managers will come with the recognition that there is a fundamental difference between managing an information system and running an information ecology, just as there is a difference between operating a grape press and making wine.

Call centers are one of the few business disciplines that have delivered on the promise to improve productivity, information immediacy, raise the standards of customers service and meaningfully increase revenue. The future of communications is in direct and instantaneous contact with your customers and the public. It is certain that, with technology, we can boost social responsibility and consumer loyalty at the same time. Successful companies will drive toward customer enlightenment, not just enterprise enrichment; people, not profits.

"Manifest simplicity, embrace change, reduce network downtime."
The Tao of the Router
- computer ad

Chapter Two
The Decade, Demographics and Devices
of the Technologies of Call Centers

Introduction

"It was not so long ago that people thought that semiconductors were part time orchestra leaders and microchips were very, very small snack foods."
– Geraldine Ferraro

The modern world's economy is in the early stages of profound changes. Two centuries ago, dramatic changes in the economy, precipitated by innovative developments in production and transportation, ignited the industrial revolution. Today, an upheaval of even greater proportions is about to be brought on by unequaled changes in the economics of communication and interaction - although it is not so much the changes, as it is the fusion that is occurring. The fusion (the call center industry's equivalent word is convergence) is happening between the power of computing and the bandwidth communication. What makes the digital revolution so perverse is its immensity.

The heat of this "fusion" demonstrates that we are no longer in the age of Aquarius. In fact, as Watts Wackers describes in his book, The Five Hundred Year Delta, this is the Age of Access. The Age of Access - a period we are already in, an era in which connectivity drives the access of everyone and everything and everyone to everyone. Access and connectivity are what call centers are about, not necessarily what they do.

There is an innovation in digital technology every three seconds. The result is that the price performance of modems is improving at 55 percent per year, fiber optics are proliferating at a pace of thousands of miles per day and television-quality bandwidth is being drawn out of plain old copper telephone wires. From mainframes to the desktop to networked computing of the 90's, incremental improvements in connectivity and bandwidth technology over the next ten years will exponentially multiply the interactive power of networks.

To avoid "paving the cow-path", the lure of "techno-duping" and the dichotomy of "good intentions, bad results", this chapter examines the underestimated influence on customer service and call centers by the advance of technology and the changing face of demographics. No longer the cliche "island in the enterprise", call centers' influences now come from the peripheral more than ever. Influences such as one-to-one marketing, the internet, Microsoft, core competency, 2¢ per minute long distance rates, wireless, PCs, customer demographics and many others.

Today, when we take a closer look at the misalignment between the technologies that are being used and the technologies being hyped, it becomes a critical, but often overlooked, practice to align business practices with new technology. What the executive strategists don't get, but that the operational managers responsible for the day to day operations of an enterprise's customer service function do, is a fundamental understanding of the economics and effects of changing demographics on who your customers are and, most importantly, how they will communicate with you over the coming years.

To baseline this perspective and bring some consistency to a market fraught with hype, if any particular technology is not found in a call center or is specifically being used to facilitate customer contact and access, chances are that it is not yet a commercially pragmatic technology.

Call Centers Are an Intellica

The biggest challenge of customer service chain executives today is maintaining *intellica* (en-'tel-Í-ka) a Latin term that is defined as the point between potentiality and actuality. This is what the call center has evolved to, the junction of old and new, past and present. Intellica is the point between smoke signals and internet telephony. Intellica is the point between rotary calls (of which there are still a substantial population in North America) and voice recognition.

On the potentiality side of the customer engagement is new technology; functionalities such as skills-based routing, IVR, the internet, IP telephony, workforce management, reporting and others. On the actuality side of the equation is the requirement for transactional efficiencies, speed of answer, quality of service levels, human resources, budgets, lines, ports and trunks. Intellica is the point between vendor push and customer pull. Your awareness of being your enterprise's "intellica" is an important and significant part of the evolution of your call center.

In spite of the blistering pace of change of a world open for business 24 hours a day, call centers seem to have the most pragmatic approach to the implementation of new technology, mostly because there is an embedded, intrinsic hesitation to experiment with customers. Managing for intellica is intimidating, and the unease it generates probably accounts for, more than any other factor, the perception of a slow adoption of technology in call centers. This "dis-ease" can't be measured, but we would agree that it is there.

Often, it seems as though industry has lost touch with the realities of running the enterprise. Call centers are in the unique position of having their feet in two worlds, the world of the pragmatic, functional and practical requirements of running the enterprise call center and the other foot in the future – the near future as well as the distant future.

Call centers used to be fairly isolated from the enterprise, an "island onto themselves." Now, as the intellica of your organization, the call center is the test and implementation bed for all sorts of progressive activities, strategies, applications and technologies. Some of these influences come from outside your company and you have little or no control over them; the internet and the growth of wireless are two examples. The redefinition of your enterprise core competency (although I will point out that your core competency, if you have not realized it already, is caller care) and one-to-one relationship marketing are examples of internal influencers.

As an intellica, the enterprise's call center is precisely where the rubber hits the road. If there were ever a front door or front counter to your company, the call center is now it. Call centers are, without question, at the heart of today's consumer-focused enterprise. The three or five minutes that a customer is engaged with your enterprise represents the "moment of truth"; the moment that if your customer's needs are not met expeditiously and professionally, your company stands to sacrifice quality in the customer relationship.

Those companies that have caught on to the "intellica" role of call centers realize that call centers are the closest that companies can get to their customers and the markets that they serve. The enterprise call center is the place where the practical implementation of the forward looking vision for today's customer engagements occur, because it already is the most critical point that an enterprise has to its customers.

The Uncertain Definition of "Call Center"

The term "call center" has devolved to meaninglessness and we have used it as jargon of convenience for so long now – more than twenty-five years – that it is just not worth trying to change, as technology in general has a deeply embedded collective agreement on this term. From time to time we see an attempt to change it into customer interaction center, or customer relation point, or contact center or various other terms. At this point, it's a term that's just too hard to change; some have tried using descriptors such as transaction center, information center, communication center, enterprise communications point, multi-media access center, casual or informal call center, customer care center and so on. Since everyone here today is in the business, we'll use it, but let's agree that it encompasses so much more now.

The term "call center" today simply does not fit what it now tries to define, which is the collective engagement of different media to effect technically intimate transactions with your customers. Today, the term "call center" conjures up a denotation of something formal and structured, high volume or high turnover, even though we would agree it rarely is any more. "Informal," "knowledge-based" and "casual call" centers are recent terms used to attempt to define these types of engagement "activities." It is consistent that the further from "formal call center" you get, the blurrier the definition of call center.

Call centers are now defined by what they do, not what they are. Do you have:

> Contact Management?
> Collaboration?
> Customer Service?
> Distributed "Net-workers"?

Any one of these enterprise functions uses CTI technology and applications developed from formal call center environments.

The Increasing Value of Time

Customers have become so used to the efficiencies created by technology that they are now impatient if a company's agent doesn't know everything about their histories and transactions as soon as the agent answers the phone. Consumers do not want to waste time not communicating meaningfully - you better have something meaningful to say.

Successful enterprises will adapt to the new paradigm of business drivers; the customers and their time. What technology is providing, be it through the telephone, internet or skills-based routing, is giving people more time to have contact with the people that they want to have contact with, while eliminating non-important, frictional encounters. The message is clear. Do not waste your customers' time by not communicating meaningfully; you had better have something to say and do it quickly, reliably and knowledgeably and consistently.

Time can be demonstrated as becoming a critical issue in the medical care industry. It is very expensive for patients to go to doctor visits or, even worse, visits to the emergency room. Research has shown that, of those patients who use a telephone to contact a call center and talk with the nurse advisor, 50 to 60 percent choose self-care with no visits. Another 20 to 25 percent opt for a next day regular visit with their primary provider.

Further, the patient/customer satisfaction levels are high - which is important in attracting and retaining more patients/customers. Following the same phenomena described earlier in this chapter, it is also less expensive to retain and cultivate existing medical provider members than it is to recruit new ones, by a factor of three or four to one. And, if the use of nurse "triage" programs can decrease office visits by 15 percent, then it is true that more members can be served with no addition of staff.

Time has become the most precious resource in the customer's life. We are entering a millennial generation where customers, like patients, are increasingly exploiting the efficiencies of new technology. Missed connections (ringing, then a busy signal), broken transfers and improperly handled customer requirements can put reliability expectations seriously at risk and can certainly cost the enterprise much more to repair than having done it right the first time.

For speed to work to the enterprise's advantage, it is critical that the call center be able to recognize a caller's identity or needs before the call is passed on to the agent. The efficiencies created by the "screen-pop" (customer data appearing on an agent's screen before the call is answered) can be dramatic. The American Automobile Association found that screen popping lowered the incoming call answer speeds from 45 seconds to 17 seconds. They also discovered that abandoned calls fell from 5,800 to 542 during a six month period.

Al's, "Moment of Truth"

What makes call centers important in the overall scheme of things is that they are a precise point where customer service chain executives have proven their power to impact company business. Call centers are often the first, only and last point of contact, and this is where building important customer bonds starts immediately or is sustained.

Total customer service means that when a customer calls, at that point of contact his problem, situation or inquiry can be resolved. This doesn't necessarily mean that it is being resolved by the same media or the same agent, but it means that the resources reside within that point of contact, whether it is a sales issue, a service issue, a warranty issue or problem billing; any of these can be resolved in that single point of contact and moment.

To compete, enterprises are going to have to use their call centers to solve more than just the customer's problems; in fact, solving problems is fast becoming just a commodity these days. Executives demanding that CTI be used to pump more transaction efficiencies are missing the point that when you have a customer for four minutes and you have his mind share, sure, access is important and cost reduction is important, but what is more important is the quality of the contact, not the quantity of the content.

Marketing costs are skyrocketing. A company typically spends approximately 15 percent of its revenues acquiring new customers and communicating with existing customers. It is increasingly difficult to communicate with customers for many reasons; one is increasing media fragmentation (150 cable channels).

The inbound call, if it is measured by some speed of transaction metric, is likely just a "dumb" call, not an invaluable or important call, but a simple problem-solving transaction. Customer service has traditionally been a reactive function with a goal of transactional efficiency. For the most part, the typical customer interaction has always been and is a simple transaction.

Companies pay huge amounts of money for a thirty second commercial; what they care about is what is going to happen in that thirty seconds. How come people in call centers are not focused on the same thing?

The subtleties between a successful television commercial and a failure can be very simple. Why are not the same resources that determine whether or not that ad is a winner do not get invested in like that spent measuring the impact of an ad?

As marketing changes become more intimate, marketing's role will be the weeding out of the customer you do not want, actually paying them to go away. Another change has been the development of marketing campaigns based on specific customer events. There is a great argument to be made for where advertising dollars should really be spent. It is not the ad, but the impression that has an impact; a good ad has a tremendous amount of impact versus a bad ad. A good customer service call has the same parity in customer expectation.

Overnight parcel delivery companies are a particularly noticeable industry where call centers are being put in as a secret weapon for the future. They realize that the phone call itself, in contrast to the television commercial, is a four minute ad. The interaction event between the customer and the enterprise is not a transaction, it is a four-minute commercial that will leave an impression not less significant than a 30 second ad on the TV. These companies have learned to use this traditional transaction event as more powerful and impactful than any television ad.

The package delivery companies take tens of millions of telephone calls every year, each lasting a couple of minutes. Call centers are highly articulated environments capable of measuring the effects of subtle changes in people, application and technology. In fact, call centers are experts at measuring efficiencies, but how should a company measure the mind share of each one of those calls - each lasting several minutes or more? Particularly in comparison to the mind-share gained advertising on CNN, which on average has only 350,000 households watching at any one time.

As North America and the rest of the planet rapidly shifts to a digital storefront, it is the customer's service expectations that will have the greatest consequences on the call center.

Creating Relationship Expectations

"Mass advertising and marketing is an industry of alchemists who routinely use the sorcery of slogans and images to turn toothpaste into sexual lure, athletic shoes into totems of hipness, and gasoline into expressions of manliness. Yet in spite of its ability to transmute the base metal of human insecurity into gold on behalf of others, the advertising industry has been saddled with a decidedly poor image of its own and advertising executives were narrowly defeated for last place in terms of honesty and ethics by members of congress and used-car salesmen." (Unattributable.)

The point is that we just do not buy it any more.

In 1996, more than $300 billion was spent on consumer advertising and promotion. In 1998, the average consumer will see or hear 1 million marketing messages - this is almost three thousand per day. No human being can pay attention to this every day. It is an assault and we are turning it off in favor of things we are particularly interested in. "Winston tastes good . . . like a cigarette should." This commercial was aired thirty years ago. If you wanted to build a slogan like this, you would have to burn the message into people's brains and it would cost a huge amount of money. Do you know how much Nike spends on Just Doing It? Be like Mike, Obey Your Thirst. The most powerful force in the universe is denial.

The biggest problem with mass-market advertising, like Super Bowl television commercials, is that it fights for people's attention by interrupting them. Telemarketers interrupt dinner and a print ad interrupts the article you are reading; bingo cards fall out of the magazines you are already subscribed to. A thirty second spot interrupts "Seinfeld" and spots interrupt sports.

These interruptions steal our time. In fact, according to people like George Gilder, time is becoming our most precious commodity. We don't think of it, but one of the largest and most successful call centers of all time is Domino's Pizza. Domino's Pizza is entirely based, not on their pizzas, but on their ability to route and network phone calls. There are many other better pizzas than Domino's; there just are not many that are faster.

Disney is not only a global leader in theme parks, they are experts in customer service, as they have perfected the superb design techniques of persuading customers to wait in line, which has an interesting parallel to the call center experience. Keeping customer needs at the forefront of the contact experience is what Disney has learned. For example, telling those waiting in line what their expected wait time is at numerous points. They keep attractions available to distract customers from focusing on long lines and they also move the line back and forth to give the impression of movement and progress.

Customers don't buy into this stuff as readily any more. In fact, the average person today is tired of being assaulted and is noticeably beginning to demand that every engagement be speedy, accurate and consistent. The "bar" of expectations is no longer set by advertising slogans, but through the real experience of the emerging complexity of customer engagements (the internet has guaranteed that customers are more "knowledge-ified" than ever) and their increasing expectation for tiers of service - an expectation developed by airline frequent flier programs, for example.

Communication is more relevant to everybody when is it is initiated by the customer as opposed to when the enterprise decides to initiate it.

Call Centers and Customer Satisfaction

All customers are part of the shift from transactional efficiencies to technical intimacies. This is not the same as the shift to supreme technical proficiency. It is the quality of the contact, not the quantity of the content, that matters. There is a subtle, but sublime difference. We have failed miserably in understanding that customers have no way of knowing our expertise; but they do know the quality of the contact and that is what they increasingly compare our enterprise to. Call centers consistently confuse quantity of content with quality of contact. We now know empirically that the greater the quality of contact, the greater the retention. Mail order firms are providing better customer service than their retail competitors who face customers directly. Their agents (clerks) are better trained and friendlier.

Technical support operations often have a chain-like property of being no stronger than their weakest link. What differentiates support from service is the higher knowledge component required for support. These are predictable routine engagements. Support is more complicated; the customer is looking for answers, not information. When this link is broken, the customer's perception is that all aspects of the enterprise's customer support and service are broken. After getting nothing but busy signals on main support lines, attempts to access alternative support channels were met with long delays, inappropriate canned, pat answers or no response at all. Busy toll-free lines are expected and not surprising; what is surprising is the difficulty users have in finding solutions via other methods.

Competitive companies are extending improved customer engagements into life long customer relationships because it does not take much to realize that a satisfied customer is more likely to become a repeat customer. They know intuitively that small movements in customer retention can equate to large shifts in revenues. In fact, a small change in only a few data percentage points in customer retention can equal millions of dollars to the enterprise.

In a vertical market segment heavily dependant on call centers, direct marketers in particular have a myopic tendency to focus on prospecting for new customers at the expense of maintaining ties and maximizing relationships with existing customers. Besides, the downstream effect of a dissatisfied customer can be worse today than ever. Marketing's role evolves into intercepting the customer complaints before your competitors do.

Understanding your customers is the key to loyalty and retention. The importance and cost effectiveness of keeping the customers you already have is well documented. The average US corporation loses half of its customers each year. The cost of regaining a lost customer has been calculated at 12 times the cost of acquiring a new one, and finding a new one is five times as expensive as keeping an existing customer. It takes three to five satisfied customers to reach the same number of people as one unhappy customer. More than 90 percent of dissatisfied customers will not come back, regardless of the effort you make.

If customer satisfaction is ranked on a scale of one to five, from completely dissatisfied to completely satisfied, the fours, though satisfied, were six times as likely to defect from a company as the fives were. This was demonstrated in a study conducted by the Xerox Corporation. This contradicts what we are used to believing about customer satisfaction and loyalty being tightly related and linear.

Customer loyalty, we now know, rises little as satisfaction rises and customer loyalty only rises sharply at the highest levels of satisfaction (the fives). "If service is the key to customer loyalty and customer loyalty is the key to sales and profitability, then a crucial question for business is finding the best strategy for maintaining loyalty." Nadji Teharani, TCCS, 2/98, p. 24.

These "fives" are also called the Pareto customers, after the Italian economist who discovered the 80/20 rule (the rule that 20 percent of your customers account for 80 percent of your revenue or profits). If your Pareto customers are only two percent of your customer base, but they are responsible for 50 percent of your business, then the corollary applies that you can affect 50 percent of your business by working for those two percent.

Technology critical to satisfying customers has only relatively recently allowed the enterprise to track and analyze customer information. In call centers, the center of gravity is shifting from measuring the efficiencies of calls to the satisfying of customers. Customer expectations of consistency, effectiveness and efficiency of the customer interaction with the enterprise is increasingly being measured, not by the number of requests answered, but by the quality of the interactions. As a result, the enterprise's performance is being measured against more strategic measurements, such as customer retention, customer satisfaction, consistency in service level, application of best business practices and ultimately, revenue growth.

Many call centers have long been motivated by the reduction of costs, which leads to call avoidance. Inside the call center with all of the rigorous personnel and system performance measuring metrics and applications, it is much easier to measure the impact of saving a second or two from a call. Many call center managers still value transactional efficiencies over customer intimacies and they have not thought of using each "transaction" to pry a little deeper into what the customer may really believe about your products or service. This is an opportunity to query the customer about what they are thinking about your competition. Many enterprises would be surprised to discover who their real competitors are. Focusing on solving the customer's problems can still be accomplished on the call, but while they are on the phone why not do some other things?

The Technology and Data of Contact

". . . keeping up with the pace the blistering pace of a world open for business 24 hours a day."

It takes an awful lot of infrastructure to support the blistering pace of a world open for business 24 hours per day. Few people realize that the largest deposit of copper in the world used to be in Chile; in the last fifteen years it has shifted to New York City. There is now 43 million tons of it in North America, although we are lightening up to the rate of several thousand miles of fiber optics per day.

The universe may be expanding, but thanks to the microchip, our planet is definitely shrinking. Before we get into some detail, I want to point out that all of the marvelous technology affecting the technology-based delivery of customer service is brought to you by the increasing power of the incredible shrinking microchip.

I am certain that you have seen this in other presentations, but I still find that this figure keeps us in perspective. We are using big numbers today, numbers bigger than we have ever used in our entire history. We use numbers we never used before in just my lifetime: millions, billions and trillions. To give you an idea of the magnitude of these numbers: one million seconds is 11 days, one billion seconds is 31 years and one trillion seconds is 29,000 years before the birth of Christ.

Intel processors have gone from a thousand transistors (and one-quarter mile of wire) to a billion transistors and seven miles of wire! Each Pentium has three million transistors that can be operated in more different ways than there are particles in the universe. There are no fewer than 15 flavors of Pentium computer chip and this doesn't include the various flavors of Cyrix.

There is a direct, although distant, correlation between the rising expectations of service from customers and the dramatic falling costs of interaction and communication. Today, a single raw Pentium MMX chip is only $316.00! (Although the factories to make them cost more than a nuclear power plant to build.)

The performance of Moore's Law (processors double in power every eighteen months) has now held true for 35 years. For $200 today, you can buy 350 times as much PC hard disk as you could for the same price ten years ago.

On the power side of the curve, these same cheap chips are exponentially increasing in power. Intel scientists have recently built (at a cost of $55 million) a computer so powerful (9,200 Pentium Pro chips) that it has passed the tera flop barrier – more than one trillion calculations per second. This is two and one-half times faster than the nearest supercomputer. In a single second, this computer calculates as many calculations as the entire US population (220 million people) could do on hand calculators over a time span of 125 years! MIT recently unveiled a 26 giga flop machine and IBM has come out with a 4,099 processor supercomputer that can handle three trillion tera flops. IBM's new supercomputer runs 15,000 times faster and has 80,000 times more memory than an average desktop PC.

The change in the disk drive market is also equally astonishing. In the disk drive industry, the size of drives has consistently shrunk from 14 inches to 8, 5.25, 3.5, 2.5 and now 1.8 inches. In 1990, the common PC disk drive that could hold only ten thousand double spaced typewritten pages now can hold 1,450 average sized novels, or more than 725,000 double spaced typewritten pages (an 18 story stack) on a single square inch of disk! These disks will be commercially available in two to three years. IBM expects to reach the ten billion bit level by the end of the decade. This is important to the technologies of customer service because all of this disk space will be needed to store all of the customer information we will be collecting.

Not only are we able to process customer data faster and store more of it, but we can send it faster as well. Over the past decade the rate at which data can be transmitted over a telephone line has increased four fold. It is predicted that over the next decade it will increase 45 fold. The time it takes to transmit 100 kilobits of data fell by 75 percent between 1985 and 1995; by 2005 it will have fallen another 97 percent. In a span of six to eight years, the price per kilobit today of 0.31 cents per kilobit will plummet to 0.004 cents per kilobit by the year 2005 - a fall of 98 percent. (McKinsey Quarterly, 1997, Number 1, p. 11.)

Computing power will not be a bottleneck. Cellular, satellite, cable, and wireless technologies will expand the bandwidth available for communications. Processing power, memory, hard drive access and modem speeds will get faster, cheaper and more abundant.

These expectations of service are a direct result of the power of the computer; we now can keep track of every transaction, conversation and detail about our customers. Transactional data from sales and service "touch points" across an enterprise create an (often over-) abundance of information about the customer. This transactional and dialog detail enables an enterprise to execute strategies based on the concepts of mass customization or relationship marketing.

Based on the power of processing, a true knowledge-sharing company can now store, mine, and exchange any form of data including images, video, audio, graphics, animation and text. It can also access and exchange information over a variety of networks such as the internet or corporate or campus networks. Soon we will all have access to the ability to manipulate any kind of data you can imagine. Transactions, text, numbers, multimedia, web pages, geo-spatial maps, time series data and even data types that you create.

The Revolution of Contact

Technology's pervasive influence affects call centers in many ways, not just in the enabling of the media customers use, but in the demographics and geographics of who they are as well. Technology has defined the evolution of American cities and where we live.

In 1997, for the first time, more people moved out of cities than moved in. This is causing an instability we haven't seen since the change from the agrarian society to the industrial revolution because technology has reversed the need for centralization. Our customers are becoming more dispersed. This is an important relevance to the anticipation of the interfaces that they will use to engage the enterprise for service. When we consider a world where our customers are connected to the enterprise through vast fiber optic-based networks, the observation of customer demographics (where they live), says that the future won't be based on fiber-to-the curb, but fiber-to-the-farm. This is not likely to happen anytime soon.

Cities have always been shaped by the state-of-the-art transportation of the time. Donkeys, horses, wagons and Roman war chariots created Bethlehem; the automobile built Los Angeles; jets built Denver and Houston. PCs, TVs and the internet have become today's state-of-the-art transportation. We now move information without supporting the need for travel. The whole automobile industry was invigorated by the development of the interstate highway system. Alongside, literally, of the interstate system came an entire service station industry to service those autos. Remarkable parallels exist between the development of the interstate highway system and the emergence of the information super highway.

Both the PC industries and the automobile industries were started by hobbyists, pursued by fanatics and then embraced by the broad population. Sometime this year, IT will surpass the auto industry's share as a percentage of the US gross domestic product. In fact, Ford makes more profit from its information and data-intensive finance and leasing units, not from selling cars.

Techno-duped and Paving the Cow Path

When we look at the rush to incorporate new devices, media and the internet into the enterprise, we tend to underestimate the pragmatic nature of our culture and society in general. Trains, VCRs and computer keyboards are excellent examples of the persistence of legacy technology. You would think that after 120 years a telephone would have more than 26 keys to represent the alphabet. We, as a whole, do not change our interfaces quite so easily. In fact, accounting for the growth of the wireless phone, the telephone is still the fastest growing device in history - nearly 35,000 new subscribers per day are being signed on in North America alone.

The world is out to solve transactional problems with computers and they are not facing as much progress as they expected. It is often hard for people to switch to a new technology that is only slightly better than the old. A phenomena that can be described as path dependence has since become the basis for the tendency of high tech markets to encourage monopolies that may not necessarily offer the best technology (Microsoft, for example). The idea is called path dependence after the notion that once you are started down a certain path, it is hard to get off. Modern railroad gauges are an example. They have the archaic characteristic of being the same width as two Roman war chariot horse's butts. Often cited too, is the VHS recorder, where the VHS won out over the superior Beta format because of early market maneuvering, not better technology (all the good movies and all of the early adult content films came out on VHS). We don't even let go of our toys so easily either. The "Slinky" toy was invented in 1945 and by its 50th anniversary in 1995, there had been more than 250 million sold worldwide.

The telephone persists because of an institutionally embedded "use-to-it-ness." One of the criticisms, as well as strengths, of the traditional call center technology vendors is that they are influenced by executives who buy into the notion that free markets choose the best technologies. According to long held Ivy League economic theory, in free markets it should be impossible to have the persistence of inferior technologies.

Historical events have a large and unacknowledged influence in shaping economic choices, and we find ourselves today getting locked into inferior technologies and products because of distant and long forgotten events. The computer keyboard is the most used tool in the call center, perhaps as much as the telephone itself.

But let's look at the QWERTY keyboard, named for the first six letters on the top row of keys. The keyboard was designed in the 19th century to deliberately slow down typists because the earliest manual typewriters tended to jam at higher typing speeds. QWERTY solved this by placing frequently used letter pairs far apart. In the 1930's, a university professor named August Dvorak developed an alternative keyboard that was much easier to learn and type on, but nobody switched to it because the QWERTY keyboard had such a head start. In fact, estimates were that a company could recoup the cost of retraining a typist in as little as ten days but this retraining never took place because, in effect, the market had already settled on the "wrong" system.

The sensitivity here, and we recognize it, is the risk of losing the "human touch." For the past twenty years, delivering customer service over the phone has remained largely unchanged. While voice response technology has improved call centers by reducing live agent calls, its use has been limited to relatively simple transactions. The longer and more complex transactions influenced by ERM (Enterprise Relationship Management) and web knowledge-afied customers continue to require live agent assistance and the demand for agents (although different kinds of agents) will continue to increase.

In the last five years, there has been a lot of discussion and hype around CTI and many think that we are missing the boat on what the real focus is here. The focus should be on the actual interaction with the customer, for the three to five minutes that the customer is engaged in a conversation with the company; that is really the only time that the customer cares about. The enterprise is either going to make or break the event, whether that is selling them something or making them happy, in that three to five minute window.

The challenge with technology is that too much of it can turn customers off. Systems that offer functions that users don't really want and lack qualities they find important, can frustrate users. What the "advanced intelligent network" has delivered is CTI, telephone tag, voicemail jail, dropped connections and telemarketing invasions.

CTI is a small component of an overall solution. CTI gets more press than implementation and is a concept that is grossly misunderstood. CTI does provide some level of productivity, but the world needs to focus on the "moment of truth" and this is when the customer is engaged in the conversation with the enterprise. This isn't just for the phone conversation but also exists in other media as well, like web site or email.

Computer telephony applications will be to the 90's what LANs were to the 80's: high margins, great customer-pleasing solutions and customers happy to pay those high prices. For computer and network resellers, they are going to have to learn telephony, i.e., get trucks.

There is generally a lack of focus on the right issue with the call center. Harry Newton has done a great job of taking a component of a call center that happens to be sexy and making it a major event. So much so that this has emerged as the center point. Vendors are developing and delivering transaction-based systems because of the "cultural" belief that computers are for transactions; they did accounting for years and they should be used for transactions now and this is what most CTI data guys sell.

Take IVR as an example, where there are issues about the efficiencies of long menus versus the anger of customers stuck in them (or even worse, voice mail jail), generating a suspicion of evasive antagonism. The expectation of IVR to shorten calls on the front end has not proven to be true; IVR actually cuts time off of the back end of the call in reducing the number of calls handled by each agent.

We are starting to see all the way up to the enterprise's "C-level," an increasing demand to be able to bring telephony into the mainstream of business application development, treating the telephone as just another IO device in their business applications. This is partly influenced by the challenge that the internet has posed to companies. Information taken from already-written verbatim hard-copy documents and presented the same way to each customer.

The global emphasis on electronic commerce and the use of the internet as a delivery vehicle have sparked the development of new CTI applications that offer tremendous opportunities to call centers. Unfortunately, the sad fact of internet advertising is that most companies building a web site use "brochure-ware." Many corporate web sites have evolved from electronic versions of glossy brochures offering little more than a profile of the company to an emulation of the call center that offers an alternative delivery channel from which transactions can be conducted in a self service mode - without having to speak to a live agent. Now, increasingly, we are also seeing that in that same application, they want to be able to integrate the live voice of the call center agent, the recorded voice from a voice response unit and interaction from the web or from email in a single cohesive customer environment.

The Data Guys and the Telephony Guys

A vast array of forces - including pervasive competition, new legislation, new technologies and new customer demands - are causing the telecommunications industry to rethink every assumption it ever made, from mainframe central offices, to PBXs and vertical integration by telecom manufacturers; from closed systems to open systems.

There are several significant differences between the two industries, computing and telephony: telephony is government regulated, computing isn't. In telecom, marketing is an endeavor in asking the regulatory authorities for a rate hike without pissing off the public so that they notice. In computing, marketing is building a better mousetrap. The dichotomy is evident by observing that IBM lost a tremendous amount of money on telephones and AT&T lost a lot on computers.

Both the information (data) and telecommunications (voice) revolutions are converging toward the same objectives - a single network infrastructure that will carry voice, video and data traffic; but both have different visions of how it will be accomplished and how long it will take. Those from the voice world believe that melding the voice capabilities into the data network will take years; some even suggest that it will take decades. Many executives on the data side expect that the annexation of telephony into their networks could take as little as just a few years.

The telephony guys believe that the data world has drastically underestimated the effort and the expense of bringing latency-sensitive voice traffic to data networks based on the Internet protocol (IP), while at the same time maintaining the expected reliability and quality of the telecom network. "They don't even know what they don't know yet," said one telecom executive referring to the inexperience of the data world in the telecom world.

Where does this difference in beliefs come from? Their cultures. Time just moves a little slower in the quality over quantity voice world. New service rollouts in the telecom world come out at the speed of a glacier. It is not uncommon to find telecom switching gear, ACDs and PBXs that have been in use for ten to fifteen years. This mind set is the opposite of the data world side of the equation, where things move so fast that nothing is ever settled and investments obsolete themselves before implementations. The role of the router for example, has unarguably changed several times in the past several years. Traditional telephony devices such as PBXs, IVRs and ACDs are already being absorbed into the data networks.

There is no doubt that the data guys are pushing ahead faster into voice than vice versa. The data world appears to be rushing to see that the merger of the voice and data networks comes together before the telephony guys can complete their crash course on packet-based IP networking. Meanwhile, the telecommunications world is looking for the time to build up their data arsenal.

Largely left unsaid and un-media-cized, is the fact that the data world is dealing with substantial legacy issues of their own. In addition to their own legacy issues, there is still quite a bit of foot dragging when it comes to expectations of reliability and quality. In fact, based on the issues of reliability and quality alone, the strongest suit of the telecommunications industry is their deeply embedded techno-cultural delivery of reliability. Don't discount the voice world, any down time is an emergency. Don't write off the telecommunications industry as being the source for many of the innovations, applications and technologies that will provide the solutions of customer relationships in the information age.

Contrary to the perceptions generated by the popular media, the convergence of the data and the telecommunications worlds will see the significant, mostly unspoken, influence of telephony guys with laptops. Don't throw away those PBXs; they are the most reliable systems we have.

The Tensile Strength of Institutionalized Reliability

Because a commercial program of the complexity of the software used to run the space shuttle would have 5,000 errors in it compared to the 11 bugs found in the last 11 versions of the shuttle's programming code. But 99.999 percent isn't even good enough for the space shuttle. This software controls the space shuttle, a $4 billion (there's that billion again), the lives of a half dozen astronauts and the dreams of a nation. Even the smallest error in space can have enormous consequences; a bug of only two-thirds of a second while traveling at 17,500 mph puts the shuttle three miles off course in under thirty seconds.

The Denver airport couldn't open because of software, and the B2 bomber couldn't fly on its maiden flight because of software bugs. How many of you here don't think you have bugs in your computers? When the office LAN or voice mail goes down, we are inconvenienced, but we expect it to happen occasionally. No one expects his telephone to go out of service three or four times a year. We are not conditioned for web brownouts; AOL is in a lot of trouble right now over this.

Many IT professionals are saying that telecommunications are within the ken of IT; no way is down time an emergency.

Southwestern Bell is so proud of their reliability expectation that they even put an ad in the newspaper last month that reads: "Southwestern Bell Engineering has produced a network that's 99.999 percent reliable." When you don't get that dial tone, people notice. What kind of equipment do you think SW Bell uses to achieve this 99.999 percent level of confidence? By the way, SWB uses Lucent and Nortel-built switches in their central offices.

Unlike the space shuttle's software, it is a little harder to reboot a customer call. You want this kind of reliability in your call center, don't you? Networking and communications have matured, and so have our expectations. We live in a culture that has been conditioned to the reliability of the software used for dialing 911 for emergency assistance. We certainly don't think of dialing the Poison Control Center's emergency help on line forum on CompuServe or the local fire department's web page, if our child is choking. When we pick up the phone, we expect a dial tone not 99, but 100 percent of the time. Does your call center or company web page have that quality of service?

In computing, reliability is 23 hours a day; telecom reliability is less than six seconds of down time per year. You don't turn phones off for backups and upgrades.

Mixed Media, Mixed Results

Today's approach is piecemeal - setting up distinct operations to handle telephone inquiries and point-of-sale that are separate from web email teams, fax and other product and response groups within the enterprise. This approach makes for very inconsistent responses, fragments potential customer relationships and precludes the use of customer data across the enterprise units. Customers easily cross over between email and live contact without starting over, not to mention multiple business units within the enterprise. And the customer's account information shown on the internet may not, and frequently does not, match up to the VRU, agent's interface, branch office or point-of-sale.

The challenge of these technologies is to avoid serving customers inconsistently due to multiple highly independent departments and technologies in the enterprise. Customers want a consistent interface with an enterprise, regardless of the entry point.

While the web and the internet are similar to email, each has its own dimension with unique issues to consider. The web mail, "email us" button, is completely integrated as a part of the enterprise customer interaction system. That the internet-enabled interaction point is not established as separate customer stovepipes. And making it user friendly and creating browser echoing for agents so that the caller and the agent can be looking at the same information simultaneously.

Yes, there remain challenges in weaning current non-internet users off of traditional contact mediums such as the telephone and the fax and onto the exponentially diverse internet and email.

The internet can be used to strengthen current relationships and make them more efficient by lowering cycle times, order management costs and inventory levels by increasing the quantity and velocity of the information shared. There are drivers for the internet - other industries that have nothing to do with technology are being built on IP. Banking, gambling, travel planning, games, pornography and publishing are examples of the few successful applications of technology.

Virtually every computer is networked today and is a common mechanism for delivering information to people, whether the information is generated internally or outside the enterprise. On the face of it, electronic commerce's ability to reduce transmission and transaction costs makes it a natural for hard times. For the internet to work in this strategy, it must be scalable, be linked to business needs and deliver a real, sustainable advantage. The best markets are the most technically sophisticated. Putting a stake further out and guiding the acquisition of technology.

Call Centers and the Future of the Device

Many companies are considering ways to transform their enterprises into customer interaction centers capable of integrating all of the various emerging customer "touch points." Companies that are the most competitive are those that will take a consumer-centric approach by developing consistent points of entry for customer interaction that is consistent and personalized. For most enterprises, implementing customer caller applications where the "touch point" presents a unique opportunity to optimize the consumer request to service value and cost structure. This is the critical challenge for call center managers and executives responsible for service, sales and marketing.

The telephone is suitable for "once and done" transactions that require little or previous or subsequent transaction context. Often the goal is for each telephone call to be a single simple transaction. Complex transactions, by their nature, require the extensibility of multimedia interaction; when a multi-call transaction requires a significant amount of customer-owned information, it is emerging to be much more effective to collect this information via other media (email and fax, for example) than by telephone.

The endurance of the telephone comes from one source. One reason for the glacial pace of telephone innovation: if you own the infrastructure, you are not going to join the race to make it obsolete. The telephone number remains the most ubiquitous IP address on the planet and will be for some time. The biggest threat to the telecommunications world comes from the perception that packets are going to take over. When you consider the growth of wireless and the poor quality of telephony over the internet, this isn't likely to happen for some time.

70 percent of business today is still conducted over the telephone and this trend is expected to continue.

"The most common PC over the next decade will be the cellular phone," says George Gilder. This isn't so inconceivable when considering the continued growth of the phone as the medium for communications. Today there are roughly 54 million cell phones with 32,000 new subscribers added every day. By 2005, 47 percent of the North American population will have a cellular (PCS) phone, which is significantly greater than current PC penetration. 41 percent of North American households already use cordless phones.

All these phones mean more calls - not less and these people will be calling you. Voice as a dominant medium will not be going away for some time, which, by the way, supports the confidence that we have at Nortel that the communication solutions you use in your enterprises will continue to come from the Nortels and Lucents of the world - not the Ciscos.

No form of communication has the telecommunications industry as concerned as that of internet-based telephony. Have no fear, IP telephony is one of those internet applications that is getting far more attention than the market is supporting. In fact, the number of internet telephony servers with PBX/ACD systems in call center installations is still small, probably less than one hundred to date.

Internet-based telephony requires the use of a desktop PC or some other undetermined device. Eventually this process will be replaced by a device as common, easy and convenient as the telephone. The current telephone offers customers and users everything that the internet-based telephone does not.

We can say with some certainty that IP-based telephony will emerge as an important transport. Keep in mind that these are still calls and there will still need to be agents and call centers to take them. For now, there are some evolutionary factors that are driving the overestimated impact of internet-based telephony: 99 percent of the population does not have a static IP address; 99 percent does have a phone number.

Internet telephony, if it is to take off, will first have to become as easy to use, convenient, accessible and reliable as the telephone. There is no killer app for IP telephony identified yet. IP telephony is still complex, of questionable quality and does not save enough money. The current state of IP telephony is where the PSTN was in the early 70's before the advent of signaling systems that led to intelligent services, such as call forwarding and number portability. Circuit switches (such as PBXs) are one-tenth the price of IP telephony switches. The transmission cost of circuit-based phone calls (i.e., long distance) has become very cheap; two cents a minute for long distance when you strip away the tariffs and taxes surrounding those long distance calls.

To make desktop call control work requires PCs that are equipped for voice transmission; in a sense they have to be designed like the telephone. Although the PC should make a good telephone interface, the fact is that there is a certain comfort level users have come to expect in their experience when using the telephone.

Eventually the desktop phone in its current 12 button configuration will go away, but at least for the time being we can't force companies to reroute their voice traffic over their networks, because many companies are not ready for that next step.

When enterprises start looking at plans to come up with a PC-based phone, they get shot down pretty quickly because the reality is that management, much less than call center agents themselves, doesn't trust their computers. They don't trust their LANs, their servers still go down quite frequently and they can't get Microsoft's Outlook working right and so on. Everything that is dealt with in a corporate environment and the prospect of having the phone tied up like computing is scary.

The telephone is the cockroach of the computing world, though it is slowly being evolved into the PC. The fact of the matter is that you couldn't kill the telephone network with an atom bomb if you wanted to. But just because you can't kill the internet with an atom bomb doesn't mean that it won't be killed by the lunacy of major corporations. The world is now made up of a fifty year network of enormous complexity that presents a simple common interface to billions of users worldwide.

The Demographics of Contact

We rarely consider the influence of demographics on call centers. The impact is more profound than given credit. When we try to understand the loyalty of customers, it is (or will become) important to understand who they are, where they live, what kinds of resources they have and how they are changing over time.

If we could shrink the world's population to precisely 100 people, with all existing human ratios remaining the same, these one hundred people would look like this: there would be 57 Asians, 21 Europeans, 14 from the Western hemisphere, including North and South America, and eight from Africa. 51 would be female and 49 would be male. 70 would be non-white and 30 would be white. 66 would be non-Christian and 33 Christian. 80 would be living in substandard housing. 70 would be unable to read; half would suffer from malnutrition; one would be near death and one would be near birth. Only one would have a college education. One-half of this village's entire wealth would be in the hands of only six people and all six of those would be citizens of the US.

One of the most significant, underestimated influences on enterprise will be the age of our customers. When we start developing customer retention strategies based on the "lifetime" value of customers, knowing how long they are going to live becomes important. In 1960 there were 5,000 Americans who were 100 years old or older. Today, there are more than a million and there will be 5 million by the year 2010.

Not only do we have to understand who they are, where they are and how old they are, but we have to understand what kinds of devices and interfaces our customers will be using. Martha Rogers, the co-author of the best selling books, The One to One Future and Enterprise One to One, defines the importance of understanding what our customers use to talk to us with by expressing that if your customers live in the ghetto – where TV penetration is higher than telephone penetration – then you need to communicate with them through their televisions. (There are more TVs in the US than there are flush toilets!)

The telephone is a significant device, but not as pervasive as we would want to think. The stark fact remains that 50 percent of the world has never made a phone call. Many are often surprised to find that 30 percent of American and 35 percent of Canadian households are not able to use DTMF - dependant call processing. These callers are restricted to dialing in pulse because one or more components that make up the phone call – CO switches, CO lines and handsets – can't handle DTMF signals. Amazingly, 12 percent of the population is still rotary.

What is evolving here is the phone, in fact, roughly one-third of all PBXs are now shipped with ACD/MIS and account for almost all of the CTI shipments.

Toll free dialing has been around since 1967 and the 1-800 toll free service as we know it has been around since 1980. Americans dialed 20.6 billion calls in 1997; that was more than 56 million calls per day. It took twenty-nine years to exhaust the 7.7 million toll free 800 numbers. The rate at which companies are reserving the toll free 888 number is 62,500 per week; at this rate it will only take 2.5 years to exhaust the 888 prefix.

While electronic commerce gets all of the press, dependency on the PSTN is growing. We are adding an average of three new area codes every six weeks.

When it comes to the call center and its economic impact alone. Call centers are even bigger than the long distance services that fuel them. In North America, we currently make an average of 60 million calls each day to 800 numbers alone. Speaking of cultural pragmatism, despite the advent of electronic banking, we still write over 60 billion paper checks per year.

Telephone penetration is rising in all parts of the world regardless of income level, as the cost of installing telecommunications infrastructure drops dramatically. Lower income countries are registering double the growth rate of high income nations in newer wireless services as they attempt to leapfrog landline technologies.

A US Commerce study on computer and telecommunications sales found that from 1990 to 1996, sales grew 57 percent to $866 billion. Significant dollars are being spent on information technology. $54 billion market in the US for carbonated soft drink market. Average number of eight ounce servings that each American consumes a year. This is versus the internet revenues of around $1 billion in 1997. The world's revenue from telecommunications services is $600 billion, that's billion. The US is responsible for $179 billion of that.

Call Centers and the Internet

The internet is an unnatural phenomenon happening at quite a natural rate. When we talk about the internet and its effect on call centers, we have to look at it from the perspective of how the internet will displace the primary interface of the call center, the telephone. The Gartner Group predicts that within several years of the turn of the century, 35 percent of all transactions will be electronic (internet). This is certainly amazing growth, but it still leaves 65 percent something else (chiefly the telephone).

The growth of the internet and the migration of services and applications to it is consistent with earlier technology curves. We should not confuse explosive growth in traffic with a quickening of the cycles of technology. Likewise, we should not confuse a quickening in the number of software releases with the quickening of long term trends. The current trend of technology enabling customer interactions has a long history; we are just at the point where it is much more practical. We have been trying to make an interactive world for 35 years or more.

Up until now, and probably for a good time into the future, the internet has been a phenomenal waste of money. And here are four oxymorons that belong together: "soft rock," "military intelligence", "taped live" and "internet advertising". Some predict, and I agree, that by the year 2000 internet banner ads will be gone; they just don't work and they are pushed out of our periphery the same as roadside billboards are. Banner burnout. And sure, most of the growth in phone numbers is for fax and data modems but even the internet has its limits. Vinton Cerf, founder of the internet, predicts that the internet will run out of IP address by 2003.

Talk about internet usage rates. In California (a highly connected state) a typical ISP supports 15 end users per line. Generating on average a 3 percent usage basis per week, compared to 4.4 hours per day of television usage, web usage has a long way to go before people spend as much time on the net as they do in front of their televisions!

Even though there is still plenty of room for growth in telephony globally, the 80 million global web users is a small number compared to the world's 800 million phones and 6 billion people. Of those 80 million, 56.4 million of them are in the US, next is Japan with 8 million, the UK with 5.8 million, Canada with 4.3 million and Germany with 4.0 million. If these are not your customers, then the phone is still likely what they are using.

Even when we talk about a totally digitally wired world, The Gartner Group estimates that by the year 2002, 65 percent of "connected" users will still be using analog modems for their main access method. Most customers (as much as 70 percent) only have a single phone line in their homes. About a quarter of American households (which is less than 2 percent of the world's population) have computers with modems. 15 percent are expected to be ISDN based, 10 percent cable modem, 5 percent wireless satellite and 5 percent using Digital Subscriber Lines.

When we look at the end points of consumer technology, this is where we can find the pragmatic grip of the pace of technology. More than one-third of North American households do not own a PC and have no intention of buying one. Forrester research analyst Ken Clemmer is quoted as saying that "Generally these people are older; they are technology pessimists. Most just don't understand how a computer could make their lives any better. There is no killer application for their group." More than half of non-PC owners are over 65 and nearly 80 percent say they earn less than

$35,000 a year. 84 percent had no need for PCs, while only 6 percent cited cost as the main reason for not wanting one.

Referring earlier to the influence of demographics on the acceptance and use of technology, there is a tremendous inequity in the "balance of access." Knowing exactly who your customers are influences an understanding of how they will communicate with you.

The number of non-white households in the US without a computer and internet access speaks for itself. In fact, while the media glamorizes a fully wired world, looking at the dramatic and deplorable statistics of school connectivity in our ghettos and inner cities casts a pall on the digital future. Unlike the telephone, those that have access to the internet compared to those that do not demonstrates the existence of an increasing gulf between the information haves and the digital have-nots.

But, where there is money to be made, investment will lead. The amount that Americans spent on retail goods in 1997 was $2.5 trillion. Even if web-based retailing captures just 5 percent of all retailing revenue over the next ten years, this would be a steady growth of $125 billion a year. With over 20 percent of US households online, revenue from shopping on the internet exceeds a billion dollars a year and is growing rapidly.

The Future of the Internet

The Internet is important - after all it will be supporting one-third of all electronic commerce before long, according to The Gartner Group.

This new generation of contact centers can field customer inquiries via any communications medium and respond via the same or any other communications medium.

The economic benefit of using the internet for certain types of transactions is very compelling. In fact, in some applications internet transactions can cost approximately one-tenth the cost of live telephone transactions. Web support not only reduces the number and length of calls, but advanced internet integrated computer telephony applications provide sharper skills matching and call routing between callers and support personnel. Electronic support is all about empowering end users and customers to solve their own problems.

What we are starting to see, though, is a parallel between the evolution of functional web sites and the introduction of IVR (VRU) several years ago. As call centers began to realize the benefits of IVR, many call centers and enterprises began to deploy numerous self service applications in a stand alone role, but had to learn quickly to design applications that provided callers the option of "bailing out" and talking to a live agent or risk the accusation of being trapped in "voice mail jail". In the short history of the self service web application, this bailout is once again beginning to surface, becoming critical and creating the need to fully integrate the web with call centers via CTI technology to support this integration. Web-based self service will not address the need for live service, there will always be web users who will prefer to speak to live agents, just as with IVR.

It is more compelling than IVR was, but has the same kind of "burn-in."

The most important influence of the internet may not come from its ability to serve as a mixed media catalog (brochure ware), but in the influence of propagating email. One of the "killer applications" of the net is email and its importance is growing.

With all of the microchip muscle backing it up, email may actually be a cultural phenomenon of its own in contributing to the revival (survival) of the oldest of the office tools (writing). 50 years ago, people vociferously complained that because of telephones we were going to lose the art of writing. Email may actually be teaching us and preserving the art of expressing ideas using skills that we may not have used five years ago – although the annual shipments of stationery are running 15 percent less than a decade ago.

15 percent of the US population now has access to email and this will grow to 50 percent by 2001, with North Americans sending some 500 million messages annually - it's that blistering pace again. What's important is that the use of email for customer contact will grow from minimal today to 10 percent of all customer contacts by 2001. These email messages, because of the increase in delivery reliability (remember the AOL outages), are coming with a response expectation that is no different than customers' speed to answer expectation. Today, 95 percent of all messages delivered through the internet are received within five minutes, up from 81 percent in 1997.

In an age where employees, agents and customer service chain executives are squeezed for time and bombarded by information, email has its own advantages, disadvantages and pitfalls as well as its own unique idiosyncrasies. The subtleties of email are different than, and make it difficult to pick up on the subtleties of conversation, compared to the telephone, where an agent can hear the reactions of the other person and adapt the nuances of the conversation. With email, the sender's intentions are abstracted another step further.

Email adds a new media and twist to customer service politics. We have heard the complaint about voice mail jail and not being able to reach a live person so often now that we ignore it. Email can be worse. If the etiquette of email is emerging as being fine for quick messages, but not for condolences or most thank yous, then we should balance this against the use of email for sensitive customer issues.

It is still impressive to receive a thank you note in the mail from the companies we do business with. Because it is becoming more rare, from a customer enterprise relationship perspective, it is more unexpected and hence, more personal. Sending a written note should be part of the savvy enterprise's workflow process. The very nature of the ability for us to distinguish the quality between an email contact and a written note, should serve as notice that email, for the time being, cannot replace (type)written letters and communications.

With the exception of those transactions where speed is the quality criteria, not every customer who uses email wants better or instantaneous collaboration. Avoiding people is an excellent use of email. The customer has the power to make thoughtful, non-verbal choices about the communication, which more than anything, leads people to use email.

The Future of Everything Else Customer

What credible researchers are forecasting is that there will be a progression or transition of acceptance and usage of the various interfaces, mediums and devices influencing the call center. This progression started some time ago with mail. Today, for the most part, as a customer service tool, the mail is definitely gone – nobody writes the customer service center anymore. In the early 70's and 80's, you would just write a letter saying that you needed help and wait for their help. Next came the fax, a ubiquitous gift from the Japanese who have too many letters in their alphabet – kanji – to put all on a keyboard, so they designed a technology to take pictures.

Next came the 800 number, which we will see taper off by the year 2010, according to research by the University of Indiana.

What will be pervasive is internet-based fax and internet telephony. It is starting to take off now and will outgrow any other channel that we will see in the next ten to twenty years – this of course is the Web. IP telephony will emerge as the dominant voice carrier. The growth of reliability and quality will inevitably surpass these legitimate issues we have today. What this research says is that IP will have its greatest influence over the customer-to- business contact

All of the new emerging networks will be built on two basic logical building blocks, a core transport/switching layer and an access edge. At first, the core transport/switching infrastructure will be based on either IP or ATM core switches.

The future in consumer products is in the products that blend technologies (converged technologies) TVs and PCs, fax, scanners and copiers in one. It is estimated that by the year 2002, a quarter of US companies will adopt multimedia technology into their call centers, according to Datamonitor. Datamonitor forecasts that in 1998, web sites geared towards e-commerce will receive inquiries from 11 percent of their non-casual visitors. Corporate sites will get about a two percent email rate. Datamonitor, US multimedia Call Centers.

The popular media even influences call centers. One hundred percent buzz-word compliant.

We don't change our interfaces as quickly as people and the popular media would have us believe. If you count the growth of wireless phones (and why wouldn't you?), it is clear that the telephone, specifically audio as a form of communication, is not going to go away for some time (perhaps as many as twenty years or more).

While that 35 percent of the pie gets 98 percent of the media attention (how many telephony magazines can you find in the Borders or Barnes & Noble magazine rack?), it will remain the telephone (and your job) that will handle the bulk of customer interactions for some time to come.

When you stand at the Barnes and Noble magazine rack, you see that 95 percent of the magazines are about the internet and PCs; nothing is about telephony except for the stray Teleconnect or Call Center Magazine. Or a computer telephony. There is a disproportionate amount of attention spent on "other" media, not that this is not important. If one percent of your customers use these media, you have to provide it to them, in the customer loyalty model and the downstream effect.

Many believe that some sort of revolution will happen to get rid of all of the technology found in call centers and drive the enterprise back to just answering calls (or in the case of the information age, whatever media a "call" is). Back to a point when the call center agent was sitting at a desk and knew exactly what the problem was and could answer every question, in every satisfying way.

Conclusion

Call centers are, without question, not at the heart, but are the very heart-beat of today's customer focused enterprises. With the exception of a store-front counter, the enterprise's call center is about as close as the enterprise can get to its customers.

If Peter Drucker is right and most of the information (re)processed by the enterprise is internal, then call centers serve as one of the few sources of true and real time information that an enterprise has. This makes call centers the battery farms of the information age. Nobody wants to talk about batteries, they are just not as sexy as the internet, multi media and virtual reality. Nevertheless, thanks to the increasing pervasiveness of technology, customers want to get closer in many more ways than ever, meaning that there are many more "battery types" than ever, each with its own set of expectations and protocols.

Customer interactions with the call center and all of the other types of self help applications and mediums such as the internet, email and IVR now make a customer's entire impression of the enterprise. These impressions are less and less influenced by mass media marketing and more and more by the ability to recognize customers, their needs and preferences, and deliver real time solutions.

Call centers are where a customer's "moment of truth" happens with more clarity than with few, if any, other engagements with the enterprise. In that "moment", if your customer's needs are not met expeditiously and professionally, you stand to sacrifice quality in your relationship. One of the mistakes enterprises make today in the employment of technology to cultivate relationships is reducing points of human contact; unfortunately the enterprise sacrifices valuable opportunities to cultivate the very relationships they profess to value so much.

Those enterprises that have grasped the opportunities to exploit the cultivation of life long relationships with customers have taken advantage of the advances in the convergence between computers and telephony to move their call centers from the corporate backwater to the corporate backbone.

Wal-Mart, USAA, Nucor, Southwest Airlines and Home Depot are examples of companies that sell the same things as their competitors: supplies, tools and insurance. What makes them different is that Wal-Mart, USAA, Nucor, Southwest Airlines and Home Depot are also examples of companies that are able to prosper by satisfying customer needs that are being ignored by existing competitors who are mostly focused on beating each other up. It is the competitor that you can not see or hear, in the case of call centers, that will kill you.

We are also at a point in time where we have to give some pragmatic consideration and look at the true effect the application of technology has on customer service. Call centers are one of the few points where an enterprise has a human face, or at least a voice, anymore. Now at the confluence of critical commercial interactions between business, prospects and existing customers, call centers play three key roles: enhancing customer sales and retention, serving as a front line of support for internal and external customers and as the focal point for service operations.

Technology rarely is a good substitute for good business practices and never a very good substitute for superior customer service. Given the choice, most customers will choose superior customer service over things such as quality products.

What most customer service chain executives have been influenced by is the belief of expecting the call centers to be the magic bullet or total solution to a company's communication problems with its customers. In the relatively brief history of customer service technology, we know that an enterprise cannot just install an ACD, IVR or CTI and leave it at that. There are many large companies today that don't understand that the technical interface between the enterprise and the customer often simply replicates the poor ways of already doing things in the first place. "If we keep on doin' things we always done, we'll keep on gettin' what we always got" (Barbara Lyons).

Today we are so often focused on the technology that we often forget to ask if we are really serving our customers. There is still a sizable population of customer service executives enjoying satisfaction at the miscrably high failure rate of technology-based applications in call centers (mostly because technology is competing for their jobs). You would never get any of these executives to admit it, but it should be of no surprise.

When looking at the speed of technology's change over the past decade – the demographics, interfaces and devices customers used – it becomes evident that the movement from a phone-centric model of support to an electronic one will not happen at the speed we want it to, nor will it go in the direction we expect. In fact, the fallacy of picking one technology over another is just that what is actually happening will not be the emerging dominance or distinction of any particular technology, such as the internet, but less and less a distinction between emerging technologies.

The enterprises that are successful will create and market services with the same care and strategic analysis that they devote to their product offerings. When talking about the next generation call center, it is virtual, it's technology enabled, it's out-sourced integration, it's standards based and customer centric.

Leading edge call centers will have most, if not all, of these characteristics. Using technology basically as a competitive weapon against their competitors, call centers are taking advantage of the benefits of:

> The ability to lower cost without the lower quality or access
> Total customer satisfaction by any metric
> Member attraction and retention
> Revenue growth

Market differentiation
Higher fees for superior service
Decreased variation across the system
Increased customer expectations

The successful innovators will be those that develop the best understanding of the underlying change and act upon it. Success in the next ten years will depend on and require a deep understanding of the change in the power of interactive and communications capabilities in not just call centers and the enterprise, but in the global economy in general.

Service in the mixed media environment is not the same as in the phone-centric environment and to survive and remain competitive there are a lot of questions to ask. It's still early in the game; while promising products are coming into the market that offer new ways to communicate with voice, you are being cautious. Most agree that the tidal surge is still three years away, which isn't so far after all.

Establishing an interactive experience, regardless of media (including live agents), that is characterized by an obsession for reliability, speed and intimacy is the most significant way to effect and forge the relationships that will characterize the successful enterprise of the next century. The expectations of speed, reliability and intimacy are increasingly becoming the "expectation benchmarks" that your customers are using to measure the quality of the interaction with your enterprise. When we go look at the call center in the year 2000, the implementation of technology is used specifically to say that the enterprise can get above the bar much higher by using the web, email, fax or some other medium. These enabling technologies are the things, tools, processes and applications that allow us, in a very cost efficient way to exceed customer expectations, while at the same time internally maintaining a profit center that is meeting its goals as well.

Your enterprise must not only be experts, but futurists also. You are either right on, too early or too late. The transition of the call center from just a dumb interface to an point of intelligent collaboration. Call centers are the most visible opportunity for enterprises to meet competitive demands from customers for attention and service.

As the speed of the information age accelerates, the difference between finding a customer, growing a customer and keeping a customer is blurring. The call center of the immediate future will be charged with not only improving customer service value and cost of providing it, but also reducing the cost of attracting, retaining and securing customers – for life.

Chapter Three
A Paradigm Shift: New Call Center Strategies for Web Callers

Introduction

By the time you read this, you may already be familiar with the following kinds of statistics about the rapidly growing use of personal computers, the Internet, and the World Wide Web. What you won't necessarily know yet is how such activities should fit into your call center operations.

• According to the Spring 1998 Cyber Stats report from Mediamark Research Inc.:

- 35% more U.S. households own PCs than three years ago.

- Approximately 44 million U.S. adults - 23% of the adult population- currently use the Internet, a 260% increase in six years.

- The number of adults with access to the Internet represents 32% of the U.S. adult (age 18+) population, or some 62.3 million people.

- At-home usage now exceeds the workplace by 26%. Some 27.6 million people are estimated to have accessed the Internet from home versus 20.4 million from work.

• Based on a new FamilyPC reader survey, 83% of families polled were online in 1997 - up from 50% the previous year. The majority (59%)

connects to the Web roughly 35 times a month and spends an average of 16 hours online per week.

• "A poll commissioned by the Information Technology Association of America, a technology trade group, showed that more than one in ten Americans is purchasing goods and services online. The ITAA telephone poll of 1,000 U.S. adults, conducted by polling firm Wirthlin Worldwide for the trade group, found that 15 percent of those polled have made online purchases. And buyers tend to have comfortable incomes, with those earning $60,000 a year or more twice as likely to buy online, the survey found." - ZDNet News

• "Software is the No. 1 online seller, representing 38 percent of all E-commerce, with books following at 28 percent, and PC hardware at 20 percent, according to the results of a randomly conducted telephone survey of 500 U.S. internet users and 500 nonusers published in The Consumer Online Commerce Report by Organic ... Industries that saw a rise in their online sales during 1997 were general gifts at 18 percent, automotive at 15 percent, apparel at 14 percent, and food purchases at 4 percent...The number of online shoppers rose to 11.2 million in 1997, up from 6.6 million the previous year...Seventy-six percent of online shoppers made multiple purchases in 1997, totaling $3.3 billion in consumer spending...In 1998, this figure will grow to an expected 15.5 million purchasers spending a total of $6.2 billion... The diminishing fear of using credit cards online may be a contributing factor to the rising number of online sales...Two out of three online shoppers used their credit cards online to complete transactions and more than 7.3 million users made credit card purchases online in 1997." - News report from InfoWorld Electric

What are all these statistics supposed to prove? That the Internet and the World Wide Web are slowly but surely taking over many of the communication activities that the traditional telephone network serviced. Although we are not getting rid of the telephone and voice communications, the call center's role can no longer be confined to assisting traditional telephone callers. The consequences of that statement are not trivial!

Web Self-service: Greater Convenience, Lower Costs vs. Revenue Generation

The World Wide Web is exploding self-service, multimedia information dissemination, and electronic business (e-business), while the Internet's email facilities are changing public access, two-way, person-to-person messaging. The public data network (internet) is even usurping transport and switching of voice communications, with Voice over internet Protocol (VoIP) gateways that are becoming incorporated into traditional PSTN network switching platforms. This has already begun to impact call center technologies, as Web sites provide information and invite convenient direct communications contact from both new sales prospects and existing customers via this new method of access. In this chapter, we examine the implications of Web commerce and the new contact and response alternatives for the technology, staffing, and management of Web-enabled call centers.

Personal computers, "internet appliances", and Web access will provide a new form of customer interaction for many of the things the telephone network was traditionally exploited for, including both self-service e-business and customer services. According to a recent report published by the U.S. Department of Commerce, The Emerging Digital Economy, consumers find the convenience of self-service "as the number one reason for making a purchase online."

From the enterprise perspective, there is a huge amount of cost savings to be realized from any form of self service. The Department of Commerce report cites a Booz-Allen & Hamilton study showing telephone banking transaction costs potentially reduced as much as 98% with online (Web-based) self-services and insurance customer self-service over the Web having a cost advantage of 58-71% over telephone call centers. The report includes other case studies of e-business, showing significant enterprise cost savings from the deployment of Web-based self-service applications that would have required live assistance in a telephone call center.

Web-based self-service is also significantly changing the middle-person role in many kinds of traditionally local service businesses, including travel, real estate, insurance, and car buying. It is most certainly usurping the role of mail order businesses such as books, computer hardware and software, pharmaceuticals, and other commodity catalog sales.

However, completely automated self-service transactions and information access are not always adequate for every customer need, and human assistance will always be required for complex situations, particularly where problem resolution and decision-making are involved. Probably a more strategic consideration exists where the opportunity to have a realtime conversation with a customer is a valuable marketing opportunity for revenue generation that will often be more important than any cost reduction. In either case, that's where the next generation of Web-enabled call centers will fit into the future of e-business on the World Wide Web. Though traditional telephone and voice communications will remain essential elements of call center operations, there is already a slew of new operational requirements that will arise from Web-based access and internet-based person-to-person communications. It won't be a matter of choice, but competitive necessity that will drive businesses to bite the bullet of call center Web support.

Blending World Wide Web Self-service and Call Center Assistance

The ubiquitous telephone set made things simple for the call center, since all we needed to do was establish a voice connection between the caller and the call center staff. With IVR self-service applications, we needed to have the caller equipped with touch-tone telephones. Things become more complicated for Web-based callers, because of the variability in PC configurations that the caller may be using. Depending upon the availability of modem speeds, sound/video cards, adequate memory for multimedia client software, etc., there will be limitations on Web-based functions that the user can exploit, and, consequently, the interfaces with the call center. But even there, things are changing!

The growth of the Internet and the World Wide Web can be ascribed to the proliferation of PCs. However, the paradigm has shifted. Now that the power of the Web and the internet for information access and personal communications has been proven and accepted, "internet appliances" are being developed to exploit network usage with more simplified devices for the consumer public, rather than general-purpose and complicated "computers".

In a recent report, IDC projected the end of the PC's domination of end-user access as a terminal device. "The era of PC dominance may be nearing an end, as the explosive growth in users - and uses - of the Internet expands device requirements well beyond the design point of the general-purpose PC .... The growth of the internet is driving the development of a dizzying array of new user access devices, including TV set-top boxes, Web-enabled telephones, Web-enabled personal digital assistants (PDAs), and Web-enabled video game consoles. IDC forecasts that these non-PC devices will account for almost 50% of unit shipments by 2002, dramatically driving down the PC's share of the market."

The type of access devices employed for Web access will have an obvious impact on how users will be able to exploit self-service information retrieval, transactions, and communications. We have learned from our experience with IVR applications that live assistance is always required to handle telephone caller needs that can't be resolved efficiently or easily with "programmed" interactive applications. This means, then, that multi-access "Web callers" will place a new set of demands for live assistance on call center activities. Since we have only had experience with PC-based Web users, there is more learning to come, as these other, perhaps less flexible, Web-access devices enter the consumer market.

The Web site must be viewed as a principal means of public access to more efficient and flexible multimedia, self-service applications, and, like IVR telephone applications, to live assistance options as well. Call centers have evolved from the tradition of basic telephone answering and live voice assistance; these facilities will continue to be important even in the new era of the Web and the Internet. However, it is time to rethink the definition of multimedia live assistance and communication responsiveness that will evolve from both World Wide Web access and the rapidly growing availability of universal two-way email messaging. The blending of realtime Internet voice connections with messaging options is both a challenge and an opportunity for call center management to improve effectiveness of service performance and reduce costs. Most importantly, it will be a necessary, rather than optional step towards meeting the new needs and demands of the caller/customer in the next millenium.

Insight: When Charles Schwab reports that 50% of its trading activity is now done by online self-service from its Web site, you had better believe that it is the convenience and speed of such services that primarily attract their customers, not the need for call center assistance. Only when the Web caller runs into a problem, does call center assistance become necessary. The same incentive can apply to any sales and customer service support, when it becomes convenient and easier to "do it yourself."

What's A "Web Caller"?

For purposes of discussing the impact of the Internet and World Wide Web, we need to differentiate the caller/customer who accesses the enterprise through its public Web pages, instead of the telephone. Because such access will inherently enable new self-service capabilities that will change their support needs, Web callers cannot be treated simply like telephone callers; they will be also be more amenable to new response alternatives, such as two-way email messaging. It is therefore up to the call center to properly structure its response capabilities to conform to the various choices that the callers can exercise, within the context of available call center resources (staff).

Web callers are defined as people who contact and interact with enterprise call center staff through the Web page application procedures and facilities made available to them.

Insight: Although it's OK to handle a traditional telephone caller with a Web-enabled call center, it's not so OK to handle a Web caller with a support representative who doesn't have access to the same information the Web caller does!

The critical factor for Web callers is call center access via applications-controlled Web pages and structured input forms. Initial contacts with an enterprise workgroup will rely on a Web page as a starting point, even though subsequent communication interchanges may be freeform email messages or realtime connections. To highlight this emphasis on Web-based access, the term "Web caller" is more descriptive and it includes two-way messaging options to telephone calls as a form of call center communication activity. Needless to say, the same Web callers may also use traditional telephone access to the enterprise call center, so both forms of support must be available to an enterprise customer.

"Come Into My Web Page," Said the Spider to the Fly

Another new, but strategic, consideration about Web callers is that once they hit a Web page, that fact can be detected in real time, and can enable the Web server application software to dynamically react to the connection of the Web caller, even without knowing the purpose of the current access. This opens the door of opportunity for various proactive applications to be triggered, including the involvement of realtime interaction with call center staff.

Insight: The intelligence embedded in the Internet allows two-way accessibility whenever a Web caller logs on to the Internet. This is unlike the PSTN, which only lets the caller initiate a specific call destination. This new power can be used for overcoming the traditional outbound telephone problem of making contact with someone who is not accessible at a particular phone number, i.e., busy or no answer. It can also be abused by aggressive telemarketers and there will have to be safeguards for this new invasion of privacy.

Web-based interactions may include various forms of connectivity, ranging from realtime voice/chat multimedia connections and telephone callbacks, to message exchange via email and fax. Furthermore, since email offers multimedia options in terms of data attachments and Web links, email responses can also consist of text, voice, and even video information.

Finally, Web callers are not necessarily restricted to Web access, but can always revert to being traditional telephone callers, depending upon their particular needs and circumstances. However, the continuity and consistency of all forms of contact between the enterprise and the Web caller must be consolidated and preserved, regardless of the particular method used for a current contact. So, no matter what communications have taken place before, the results must all be taken into consideration for handling the present one. It's going to be a very dynamic "mix and match" world of communications media access!

Web Applications and Call Center Assistance

Call center assistance skills have always been based on upon the call-handling applications involved. Thus, the personality, verbal language skills, and subject expertise for customer service, sales, or collection applications, are the important qualifications for traditional inbound/outbound call assignment to call center staff. The differentiation of such call center applications becomes even more important for the strategic use of call center involvement with enterprise Web sites, since it not only affects skills-base routing (SBR) strategies, but also whether the Web application should initiate a realtime live voice connection (via internet telephony), a text chat connection, or callback/messaging communications.

It will make a big difference to the call center access strategy if the Web caller is a "surfer" (a first-time visitor), or a frequent visitor/customer at a sales Web page. It also will be a different story if the Web page is devoted to customer service support needs. Like using Dialed Number Information Service (DNIS) and deploying different 800 numbers for sales or service telephone access, the various application-oriented Web pages will trigger different user interfaces and different response options. Furthermore, like Automatic Number Identification (ANI) for inbound telephone call handling, Web "cookie" information stored on the Web caller's PC can also invoke personalized information displays (a caller's "screen pop"), and personalized response options.

How The Web Caller Will Impact the Call Center - The Top-Down View

The Web caller has to be viewed as different from the traditional telephone caller in some ways, while similar in other ways, but with new options for satisfying their needs. Such differences, however, mean that all the rules of the call center game have to be adjusted, from performance metrics to resource management tools and strategies, in order to accommodate Web callers effectively.

The best way to assess the impact of Web caller access to the call center is to look at the "users" and the human interfaces in the call center operation. I break down such "users" into three fundamental categories:

1. Callers /Web Callers - These will be customers or prospects who initiate contact to the call center from a traditional telephone, a Web page, or who may be contacted by call center staff on an outbound, callback basis.

2. Web Support Representatives (WSRs) - Often referred to as "agents" from the old days of reservation systems, CSRs (Customer Service Representatives), or Telephone Service Representatives (TSRs), the call center representative is anyone whose primary responsibility is to communicate directly with callers/customers by realtime voice connections (inbound/outbound) or by messaging. To highlight the new responsibilities, skills, and interfaces that will be required to handle the Web caller, it is more than fitting that we give call center staff that will support the Web caller a more descriptive label, such as "Web Service Representatives" (WSRs).

We may have to break down this classification even further, to accommodate the significant differences in message response support from realtime voice (telephone) interaction. This differentiation will help in the planning and management of staffing resources as Web caller activities become well-defined metrics.

3. Management - All areas of operational management will be affected in the ripple effect of handling the Web caller. This will mean keeping the old responsibilities for telephone callers, while adding new Web caller responsibilities as well. Such management responsibilities are primarily focused on the planning and control of both staffing resources and call center application technologies, processes, and procedures to cost effectively satisfy caller needs.

New call center technologies and the Internet are making call center capabilities much more flexible for both traditional callers and Web callers. It is important to understand and address what the callers will really need or want from call center support, both technology-wise and skill-wise from call-handling staffs.

The Web Caller's Perspective - Different From the Telephone Caller?

It is critical to start from the top with the Web caller, because it is this new breed of call center contact that must be fully understood in order to identify what must change in traditional call center operational functions. Even though experience with Web callers is still evolving in the footsteps of new technology deployment by leading-edge call centers, there is enough known about traditional telephone activities that can be logically extrapolated to the new Web caller and internet messaging environments.

How will the Web caller be different from the telephone caller? Here we must look at the subtle situational and psychological differences that can affect the caller's support needs. The expectations of the Web caller in terms of speed of response, information access, and technological preparedness, are all dimensions of interaction with the enterprise call center that must be evaluated carefully.

With the traditional telephone call center model, callers have instant dial tone before placing a phone call, expect no busy signals and a short number of rings before being connected, and then experience either an automated self-service application or a minimal wait for live assistance. The pain of waiting in a call center queue for assistance is exacerbated by the fact that telephone callers are truly being forced to waste their time waiting on hold. That's why speed of (live) answer has been a traditional metric for quality of service. The caller's alternatives to waiting in queue for live assistance include: abandoning the call (hang up), using a self-service option (that is often not too useful for the caller's real needs), or leaving a voice message for a callback (scheduled or ASAP).

Self-service for the telephone caller, using IVR applications, has always proven very effective for certain kinds of applications, such as simple (and short) information retrieval and limited data entry transactions. In fact, the Gartner Group estimates that self-service transaction costs are between 15-20% of the costs using a live agent. When 40-80% of the telephone callers can be completely serviced by the IVR application, the payoff is truly significant. However, for those applications that are too complex and cumbersome for sequential interactive menus or require textual data input, live assistance from call center staff is always necessary. Now the limitations of the telephone and voice can be bypassed and the potential of self-service expanded dramatically for Web callers and their screen-based PCs.

Self-service Applications, Not Dial Tone, Are the Starting Point for the Web Call

For the Web caller, the circumstances are somewhat different. The fact that the Web call originates from a screen-based Web page means that the Web caller is not navigating time-consuming (and often frustrating) audio application menus. Unlike complex interactive voice response interfaces, screen-based applications are inherently more efficient and manageable because of random and concurrent access to menus, help information, and other kinds of information that may be useful to the Web caller. It is not only faster, but facilitates efficient caller "multitasking" (doing several things at the same time). For this reason, call center self-service applications that used to rely on voice-only IVR technology, will find greater flexibility and effectiveness in the screen-based Web server environment, including access to live assistance.

Although today's Web caller uses a PC, the expansion of Web access through a variety of visually-oriented "internet appliances", including TV set-top devices and new, "smart" screenphones, will also bring practical advantages over the traditional audio-only telephone access to the enterprise call center.

Self-service applications associated with the call center must still be consistent for both voice or screen interaction by callers, whether accessed by telephone or Web. This is important for application design, implementation, maintenance, subsequent interaction with call center staff, and to minimize any confusion when callers switch from one mode of access to the other. This requirement has been recognized by the leading IVR software vendors, who have expanded their application development software tools ("application generators") to include both voice and screen interactive user interfaces for the support of common application call flow logic and infrastructure integrations (application database servers, operating systems). This means, that self-service applications can and should be designed for both telephone callers and Web callers, including access to live assistance and messaging options for both. However, there will always be differences between the two, in terms of caller options and interaction logic, because of the inherent nature of the voice and screen interfaces.

The Personalized Screen Interface for Web Callers

There's always been a lot of talk but little action for truly personalizing the caller's interface with a call center application. About the best that has been done within the limitations of ANI or an IVR caller identification input has been to activate the CSR's terminal "screen pop" for a particular application, along with database information about the caller. With self-service IVR applications, it is quite tedious to design and implement an interactive voice script that can be personalized, by using text-to-speech technologies for voicing the caller's name. With screen output, however, the personalized text is easily incorporated into the Web caller's interface, making Web-based applications more customizable, i.e., a "screen pop" for the Web caller's desktop. Screen output permits more information to be given to the Web caller than is practical for audio output to the telephone caller.

The more successful e-business companies have exploited such personalization quite effectively. For example, Amazon.com greets visiting customers by name, gives them access to their account information, and proactively notifies them by email of book availability (based on purchase history or specific requests). Given the past history of customer preferences, e-commerce Web site applications can automatically tailor the Web site information presentation and options to match customer preferences, or base them on currently outstanding transactions such as order status or billing problems.

Another aspect of personalization can involve enterprise support personnel that have specific responsibility for a customer's particular needs, like an account sales rep. Since Web caller intercommunication does not always have to be a realtime conversation, two-way email exchange with a call center workgroup (or an individual representative) can be a practical alternative to waiting in queue for a realtime connection. Customized person-to-person messaging, as discussed later in this chapter, will usually be more expensive to support than voice conversations, and should be reserved for high-priority situations in a call center environment.

The Web Caller and Online "Flow"

One of the phenomena experienced by people who access Web sites is a time warp called "flow," defined as a psychological state of high involvement. Donna Hoffman and Thomas Novak, marketing professors at Vanderbilt University, have been researching the behavior of Web surfers and its implications for e-business.

In an article in the Los Angeles Times, Hoffman and Novak describe flow as "what happens to you during network navigation. When you are completely focused on the activity...there is a loss of consciousness about what's happening in the external world. ...At the end of the experience, you have this sense of satisfaction..." According to Novak, "One of the most important components in our flow model is perceived control. The navigation has to be under the user's control and choice, has to be nonlinear and non-hierarchical."

The implications about flow may be subtle but important for e-business and its interaction with call center functions. On the one hand, according to Hoffman, "Flow may be important for encouraging repeat visits or repeat purchase behavior." On the other hand, what happens when the Web caller needs assistance and stops the flow by abdicating complete session control to a Web Support Representative in the call center? The transition can be disconcerting when the Web caller clicks on the "Call me" button for call center assistance.

The Web Caller's Options for Call Center Assistance

When the Web caller needs assistance beyond that provided by self-service informational or transactional Web applications, more selective options are available based upon the identity of the caller, the context of the call, and, most importantly, the caller's choice for accessing live assistance. Information about expected waiting time would be helpful to the caller in deciding whether to wait, leave a callback message, or indicate urgency. What is most important, however, is that intelligent decisions can now be made by both the caller and the call center routing software, rather than simply second-guessing what the Web caller will accept as "second prize" to an immediate live connection. The reason for this increased intelligence is very simple; the flexibility of the screen-based interface enables greater and more efficient information exchange and interactive negotiations for options between the call center system and the Web caller.

Of course, there are many situations where the option for live contact will be decided for the Web caller a priori. Telesales operations, for example, would want to have an aggressive salesperson take control of the call and engage a prospect immediately in a live conversation (voice or text chat). In such a situation, a browsing Web site visitor will be targeted for a Voice over Internet Telephony (VoIP) connection, which would enable the conversation to utilize the current, single Internet access connection. One can make the analogy here with outbound telemarketing activities, in that the Web surfer is relatively passive and the call center representative is initiating the conversation. The big difference is that the Web surfer already has a connection to the Web site and may have taken some explicit action to enable the call center connection.

Working While Waiting for Live Assistance

Waiting for assistance does not preclude productive activity on the part of the Web caller because of the multitasking capabilities of today's PC operating systems. There doesn't have to be any disconnection from the call center's Web page while the Web caller does other useful work, whether it be browsing other sites or performing some other PC application task. Then, too, Web callers are conditioned by slower Web response times, rather than immediate dial tone connections, so they will be more inclined to wait for a response than traditional phone callers. The bottom line here is that Web callers are already in an "online" information access mode that they control, and are not being forced to waste any time "holding" for assistance. So, even if they aren't immediately connected to a live person, they can essentially look at information or do email, while still maintaining their call center access connection.

Letting the Web Caller Decide!

With all the sophisticated weighting algorithms that may be employed in determining what kind of call center staffing skills will best satisfy the caller, "skills-based routing" (SBR) doesn't solve the problem of understaffing and tactical call assignments. In the simplest case, calls may be routed to anyone that is available within a certain skill group and it won't have to be a match made in heaven. However, once there is too much traffic for available resources to handle, it's going to be very difficult to make any accurate decision about assigning available resource skills. One of the benefits of having the screen interface is that it provides more options to the Web callers for assistance and support that will be acceptable for them.

Here's the way this can work: if the waiting time for the skill level that would normally be available becomes too high, rather than forcing such a wait, the Web caller can be queried for more information about the importance of their problem or about using other alternatives, including leaving a message or being directed to a FAQ knowledge database. If the Web caller just wants to discuss something with a warm body ("warmware"), or has a simple question that anyone can answer, that fact will make the call routing process a little more "intelligent." If the Web caller needs to talk to someone in charge, that is obviously a clue to upgrade the priority of the call, leave a message, or to warn of a longer wait for connection to assistance.

Insight: Just remember that waiting on the Internet doesn't bring with it the added penalty of paying for telephone charges that is becoming more commonplace for technical assistance.

Immediate Call Center Connections - "Callthrough" vs. "Callback"

It should be obvious from previous discussions that the power of call center assistance to a Web caller stems from the ability to share the same Web page informational content and for the Web Support Representative

(WSR) to consultatively guide or control the delivery of such information to the Web caller's PC screen. It is also important for the Web caller to have such dual connectivity in order to enable continued utilization of Internet facilities while waiting for assistance. This includes being accessible for realtime telephone calls, even while busy on the Web; Central Office telephone services will be offering "Internet call waiting" service options for this purpose.

The first attempts at providing call center access to Web callers required Web callers to have a second telephone line for voice callback, while retaining the first Internet connection for the Web page. Instead of a separate second line, a higher bandwidth ISDN connection would also work. However, internet telephony "gateway" technologies now allow a single Web caller phone line to be used concurrently for both the Web page and the internet telephony voice connections. This technology can be used for both an immediate connection with traditional call center system, or, with "Internet call waiting" service now available from telco Central Offices, for callbacks to Web callers with only a single telephone line. The call center's Web application server can detect the Web caller's PC hardware/software configuration and download appropriate client software or Java applets for establishing the Internet telephony voice connection. (Web callers will still need a fast modem, sound card, and speakers for using the PC as telephone!)

Insight: Even though computer telephony will move call control features to the desktop screen, the traditional telephone handset (or new screenphones) will probably remain the device of choice for Web callers, rather than headsets and microphones.

Web Caller Messaging - "Web Mail"

If Web callers decide not to wait for immediate live assistance, organized messaging is an option they can exploit for a scheduled return telephone call or a message response. The kind of Web caller messaging we are talking about will be structured, i.e., Web forms, and contain the necessary context information that can facilitate automated message distribution and response processing. Because Web callers will implicitly have personal email mailboxes, two-way messaging is now a more viable alternative to live telephone connections. Not only is there public access to the Web caller's personal mailbox, but multimedia informational attachments that might normally be mailed or faxed can also be immediately emailed digitally in response.

Once a messaging transaction has been initiated between a Web caller and the call center, when a request has been processed and a messaging response delivered to the Web caller's mailbox, there is no guarantee that further communication with the Web caller will not be required. This presents a complication to Web mail processing that is analogous to a caller having to make more than one call to resolve an issue, and there is now an existing context that must be included for efficient follow-up contacts. In such cases, the Web caller may want to talk to someone immediately, or reply to the call (Web) center's response message by normal (freeform) email. A message transaction tracking number ("trouble ticket") will be important for all such follow-on correspondence from the Web caller. However, because such messages will involve freeform email, Webmail processing technology products must include scanning through such messages as well, to insure proper content identification, accountability tracking, and response routing.

Sending and Receiving a Chunk of Information (Documents/Data)

There are frequent call center situations when the caller will need to receive or submit non-verbal information, such as documents, forms, reports, or product literature. (We are not talking about small data items, like an account balance number.) In the past, "snailmail," and, more recently, fax, have been the most practical means of document transmittal, and usually as a post-call session task initiated by the call center representative. Self-service IVR applications have also included options for information fax response where appropriate. Such responses could either be standard information common to all callers, or database information extracted into a customized report for transmission to a fax number.

Both forms of information are now more accessible to Web callers from their screen-based terminals, primarily for immediate receipt from a call center system via self-service Web applications, or manually delivered ("pushed") as a Web information page by a WSR action. Right there, Web callers get the benefit of immediate call center responsiveness that is better than previous technology offerings. However, what makes it even more practical is that when the WSR is actively connected during this process, the loop is closed for extremely efficient consultative interaction with the Web caller to bring closure to the caller contact. (Some folks like to call this "collaborative" interaction, but the customer relationship is based on assistance, not collaboration!)

How about the reverse, when it is the caller that needs to provide some type of digitized document (scanned, faxed, or emailed) or data files? Sending such information as attachments to Web mail from a self-service Web site application keeps the information together with the context of the Web caller's other information, making it much more efficient for response processing by call center staff. It helps eliminate the problems of delays or big mistakes that can result from the lack of supporting information associated with a Web caller's request, simply because they are transmitted separately. Here we see one of the major benefits of multimedia messaging, where messages and information objects are kept together during transmission and subsequent retrieval.

"Different Strokes For Different Folks!" - Not All Web Callers Are Configured Equally

With the traditional telephone caller, there was only one variable that had to be considered for providing self-service application functions, and that was touch-tone vs. rotary pulse dialing capability. Lately, Automatic Speech Recognition (ASR) capabilities have improved enough to enable voice input instead of just touch-tone. Once a voice connection was made to a CSR, there was absolutely no difference for the call center as to the type of telephone instrument the caller used.

Web callers, however, will be using different PC configurations that will indeed impact their options for call center assistance. In particular, the availability of a single telephone line vs. two phone lines or an ISDN connection, or low-speed modems, can make a big difference on the level of call center assistance that can be provided. Such variances will spell the difference between enabling a voice connection during a Web session or using "chat"- realtime text message exchange - instead. Voice conversation, however, is clearly much more time efficient and natural than chat, for both the WSR and the Web caller, but when the quality of internet telephony or the Web caller's PC configuration cannot support voice, chat communication may be a practical alternative.

The consequence of Web callers having different levels of communication capability means that the call center has to be prepared to serve them all. Call center technology providers are scrambling to develop "Web enabling" or "Webifying" capabilities, but the current products come in many flavors, with both subtle and significant differences between them that will impact both Web callers and WSRs. Such differences must be taken into consideration when planning call center capabilities to support Web-based activities.

The Three Web Caller Response Modes

If you read every call center vendor's so-called white papers, you will find them all plugging their ways for Web callers to reach call center support. What makes things confusing, however, are the various assumptions they make about what the Web callers' PC and phone line configurations are, and how they will "integrate" and "blend" Web call handling assignments with current call center ACD activities. Everyone has implementation strategies for accommodating Web caller support functions, which boil down (so far) to three basic forms of manual support and two forms of automated self-service. The former are extensions of traditional call center responsibilities for telephone access and text chat, as well as non-realtime email responses to Webmail. The self-service functions encompass both screen-based interactive (immediate) Web applications, as well as automated message responses to specific Webmail requests.

Insight: The call center response to Webmail message requests is interesting in that Web callers will not necessarily know whether their messages will be handled by a person or an automated application process. This could make a difference if that were known!

The need to be responsive to Web callers in immediate or deferred modes has attracted the attention of traditional call center operations to support such capabilities. However, doing so will have significant impact on the call handling staff, in terms of workstation software, skill requirements, blending of task assignments, and measures of performance.

Live call center responsiveness can logically include:

1. Immediate interactive response
   - Immediate callback telephone connection
   - Callthrough voice and data connection
   - Chat (Instant text message exchange)
2. Deferred or Scheduled Contact
   - Call center outbound telephone (voice) connection
   - Attempted connection next time Web caller is detected on the internet
3. Message response
   - Manual control text message response
   - Voice message attachment to email response

Depending on the various implementation strategies of the technology product providers, there will be different implications for both the Web callers and the WSRs.

Immediate Response

Technically speaking, callback strategies can be used by call centers for immediate or scheduled return calls from the call center. However, immediate response means providing live call center support (voice/video) at the time that the Web caller activates a request for assistance and while s/he is still connected to the internet and the Web site context. Maintaining the Internet connection is essential to obtaining the benefits of multimedia consultative interactions for both sales and customer service situations.

For an immediate voice connection, a couple of alternatives can be provided by available technology products. All start with the Web caller clicking on a call connection icon. The first approach, based on having separate telephone access to the Web caller, will trigger an outbound (callback) telephone call from the call center to the specified telephone number. However, this outbound call approach is the most expensive one for the call center, since it must pay for the calls without the benefit of toll-free or 900 access numbers. Straight telephone callbacks will certainly be costly in the global e-business marketplace, when international callers need assistance, unless some form of Internet telephony bypass is utilized. Finally, and most importantly, such outbound activity relies on the Web caller having a second telephone line.

A better methodology, callthrough, exploits Voice over Internet Telephony (VoIP) protocol, using H.323 standard "IP phone" software on the Web caller's PC. Client software that is efficiently downloaded (if necessary) as JAVA applets to the Web caller's browser, essentially enables IP telephony in conjunction with a gateway server. The most important benefit is that the Web caller doesn't require a second telephone line. The IP gateway server integrates with the call center's ACD, making it practical to direct such incoming voice connections to telephone call handling staff. This approach makes it perfect for accommodating callers coming in from anywhere on the World Wide Web. However, public internet traffic doesn't insure reliable voice quality, and other implementation strategies, such as switching the Web caller's PC connection from the internet to a dedicated "Intranet" access number, are available to insure a reliable and adequate path for voice conversations.

This gateway technology is also applicable to immediate callback situations as well, where new "Internet call waiting" services from local telcos can be exploited. Such technology enables the Web caller to accept an incoming telephone call via the local telco Central Office, while working on the Web and connected (on a single telephone line) to the Internet. However, bandwidth requirements for multimedia consultative connections, using today's common 28.8 KBPS modems, has left much to be desired for help desk technical support applications, as opposed to sales support interactions. The implementation of the T.120 document transmission standards will help improve this situation.

Interactive "Chat" and Web Site Visitors

Because Web callers are typically in desktop typing mode, it would seem practical to exploit chat text exchange for their interaction with call center staff. This might also be appropriate where the Web caller's PC is not configured to support Internet telephony and voice, such as a slow 14.4 KBPS modem. However, the relative inefficiency of half-duplex text exchange, compared to full duplex voice, makes this strategy highly questionable for maximizing call center staff productivity. Text exchange is a slower and less convenient means of communication expression for both parties than a voice conversation.

One application of text chat that is being promoted by chat technology and service providers is a Web site equivalent of outbound telemarketing activities. That is, based upon Web site visitor's actions, a call center representative can be assigned to initiate a text chat conversation with the Web caller. Monitoring Web site visitor actions is definitely a practical marketing strategy, but it doesn't necessarily mean that a text chat interchange is automatically called for. First, the detection of visitor activity should be done as a basic Web site application server function. Second, enabling the Web caller to initiate or allow any immediate, realtime contact is definitely part of the Web site self-service application, not a chat function. Finally, recognize that one of the perceived benefits that Web callers expect from the using the Web is the ability to be in full control and maintain maximum privacy over their activities. Any invasive response to their Web site experience will probably backfire, unless it is effectively qualified and presented properly.

Insight: Think about it! When would YOU rather use text chat to communicate with a stranger for e-business purposes, if there can be voice conversation alternatives? Furthermore, do you want highly skilled, expensive call center staff spending their time "cold messaging" with unqualified prospects? Preliminary estimates of comparisons of using text chat vs. a voice telephone conversation show that, on average, the text chat sessions are twice as long as the voice sessions.

Deferred Scheduled/Unscheduled Callbacks

The Web caller may want live assistance, but may not be able to get it during this Internet session. This will be particularly true if the caller is not configured for a voice connection, if there is going to be any significant wait (in queue), or there is a need to supply information for preparation on the part of call center staff. In such situations, rather than simply abandon the connection attempt, the Web caller can be offered the option to schedule a callback by telephone at a particular telephone number and time that would be most convenient. This information, typed into a Web form, can be submitted into a call center scheduling process, such as a traditional outbound dialer application, along with any context data (Web page information) that should be included in the "screen pop" for the call center representative.

Scheduled callbacks can not only be traditional telephone calls, but may also be "meet me" Internet appointments. Using software like NetMeeting and "Instant Messaging" connections to make contact on the internet, call center scheduling software will assign the outbound task to an available WSR, who will make contact with the customer. The connection will be an Internet data connection, with voice and data exchange ("white board") capabilities.

What will be even more practical is the unscheduled Internet callback. Rather than guess when the Web caller will be connected to the internet at a specified time, the "appointment" doesn't even have to be scheduled, but can be based simply on whenever the customer is next detected on the internet. Using internet service facilities like the "Buddy system" and "Instant Messaging", the call center's Web site application can be notified the next time the Web caller accesses the internet and it can reconfirm his/her need and availability for immediate call center assistance.

Telephone Callback in Response to Webmail

Before the internet promoted email for the masses, voice mail or IVR voice messaging was always a practical means for telephone callers to request a telephone callback response rather than wait in an ACD queue. That was in the days before public access, two-way messaging was available, and the telephone was the only rapid alternative to snail mail. Now, however, the response alternatives can be selected by the Web caller or the call center WSR. Either web callers, who send in a Web form or an email message, may receive a telephone call or an email message response, depending upon the nature of the request and the contact information provided. However, it should be noted that making a successful outbound telephone callback is still an iffy proposition, because, unless a specific callback appointment is scheduled, the callback attempt will end up with dialer retries. The messaging response alternative offers practical payoffs when dealing with Web callers for most applications.

Insight: It's not the speed of response that typically will require the telephone callback, but rather the complexity of the subject matter that requires a time-efficient discussion to gain understanding or negotiate agreement.

It's All Up to the Web Site Applications and the Web Caller!

The enterprise can inherently exercise control over the method and conditions of call center access by Web callers, just as publishing an 800 number for sales or customer service invites telephone caller access. However, it would be dumb to open a Web site for the marketplace and not have the proper means of supporting the expected Web callers' needs. Therefore, it is strategically necessary to thoroughly understand and prepare for the call center staffing issues that are associated with creating a Web site and supporting Web-based self-service applications. Depending on the needs and preferences of your enterprise callers, your plans for supporting Web callers will have to keep pace with their demands for the conveniences and payoffs of Web access.

Insight: Just remember, it's NOT the Web master who is running your business! Call center management must be responsible for all customer application interfaces that lead to live assistance, with both realtime voice connections and messaging responses. Unless there is are significant benefits for Web callers, in terms of convenience, saving time, or saving money, to access your Web site, they will still use the telephone, if they come at all!

Summary

There is no question that the Internet and the World Wide Web have created a revolution that will impact how customers and businesses will communicate. As one seasoned call center technology executive commented to me, e-business and having a Web site for sales and customer service is going to be "table stakes for staying in business." The telephone and voice communications will not disappear by any means, but person-to-person voice calls will become subservient to the greater flexibility of digital information exchange.

Web callers will be generating increasing amounts of call center traffic, and, rather than simply emulating telephone callers, they will also be exploiting both the informational self-service facilities of Web application servers, as well as the features and benefits of two-way messaging and multimedia information exchange. The challenge for today's call centers is to understand how this trend will affect their current operations and start planning for such changes. With Y2K issues hanging like a sword of Damocles over all computer-based systems, there will have to be a slow evolution from legacy technologies to the post-year 2000 future.

Chapter Four
The Call Center Meets "Webmail":
Get Ready to Deal With Email Processing

The headlines and the statistics say it all! The world is moving swiftly into two-way digital messaging, which includes both personal email and enterprise "Webmail."

• Email has replaced traditional letter-writing and expensive long-distance telephone calls for many families, according to the Washington Post.

• Forrester Research projects that the number of email users will grow to 130 million in 2001 and to 170 million users in the year 2005. Such users will also be exploiting electronic commerce on the Web, and the use of "Webmail" for two-way customer messaging.

• Industry research indicates only 30 percent of Fortune 500 companies respond to questions directed to the Web site's Webmaster, which means a large number of customers aren't getting the response they expect.

• A recent study of a group of 258 companies with call centers that support email shows that those companies receive approximately 300,000 email messages per year, with 55 percent of the messages going straight to the call centers. The study indicated that these businesses expect to receive approximately 2 million messages per year by 2000. The study also showed that the current mean response time for handling email (the response being in the form of email or fax) was 17 hours, the mean cost of handling email was $17.85 per message, and that 54 percent of the cost is directly related to labor cost!

So, what does that all mean for the enterprise and its future call center operations? If it hasn't happened yet, it will happen soon. That is the day that your Web site manager will come to you with a problem. They want to find a cost-effective way to deal with customers who will make contact via the Web site, instead of the traditional telephone call. Why are they coming to you? Because you know all about communication traffic and managing the staffing to handle the influx responsively, and they want to know how your call center facilities can help manage the processing of email traffic from customers.

Of course, you will have to tell them that your legacy ACD switch system was never designed to control and manage this kind of message traffic, and new technology must be added to make email response processing cost-efficient. This is especially true when the Web site application can't always be "self-service" and completely automated.

"Web Mail" - Why Would Web Users Message an Enterprise?

The alternative to establishing a realtime connection with call center staff assistance, is through two-way messaging, except that the interaction is not person-to-person, but between enterprise workgroups and the Web caller. The workgroup can include not only people, but self-service applications as well, such as typically associated with "help desk" support.

There are many practical reasons why Web callers will choose to send a message instead of establishing a realtime voice connection with call center staff, including the following:

• They can't or don't want to wait for someone to assist them.

• They will use the context of web page information for the basis of their message inquiry or transaction.

• They need the convenience of 24x7 messaging access.

• They don't necessarily need to "discuss" anything about the information they want or the transaction requested.

• They may want to send information and data attachments first, before any interactive discussion is engaged in.

• They want a well-documented audit trail of the two-way messaging interchange.

• They want to eliminate the time, errors, and effort involved with transcribing detailed information during a live conversation

• They don't have a required second telephone line for an immediate live callback while still connected to the Web.

• They want to direct their communication to a very specific group or individual that may not be readily accessible realtime.

• It's just more convenient and cheaper than a live connection.

Messaging is a call center communication access option that Web callers can exploit to either request an informational message response or a scheduled telephone callback. Because Web callers will implicitly have their own personal email mailboxes, two-way messaging exchange is now a more viable alternative to live telephone connections. Not only is there public access to the Web caller's personal mailbox, but multimedia informational attachments, that might normally be mailed or faxed, can also be immediately emailed in response.

Implications for Call Center Activities

First, there is no question that enterprise "callers" will include a healthy percentage of "Web callers," who will connect through the enterprise Web site, for either immediate call center assistance, or a deferred response (telephone callback/message).

Second, processing email messages is not cost-efficient, unless a high degree of automated intelligence is used to minimize expensive labor.

Third, messaging responses to Web callers, while not necessarily as pressing as picking up a telephone call, must still be handled within a reasonable time frame. Replies should reasonably be expected to range from less than an hour to a "next day" response.

Fourth, both realtime voice connections and email messaging correspondence will remain logical alternatives for supporting customer contacts originating from the World Wide Web, and must therefore be managed as related responsibilities.

Finally, just as traditional call center staffing activities must be properly managed, from recruiting, training, scheduling, to performance monitoring, so too must message processing activities also be organized and managed in similar fashion. This is an area that call center people know a lot about, but must now apply differently to email messaging communications.

Call Centers and Message Processing

There has been a growing exploitation of (two-way) email messaging from Web site visitors, but it was not done within the context of traditional telephone call centers. Until recently, such email activity has been relatively unorganized and often supported outside of the traditional call center's operational domain, typically as part of the IT department's email or Web site responsibilities. However, call center managers and "application managers" are starting to realize that the objectives of Webmail processing are identical to those of traditional telephone call centers, and it is now important to understand the differences in the operational strategies involved in order to merge them with current call center facilities.

From a practical implementation perspective, it would be foolhardy to assume that providing message-based Web caller support is just the same as servicing regular telephone callers. For this reason, it will be wiser to approach Web message response services separately from the traditional telephone call handling tasks, so that such capabilities can evolve effectively at its own pace. While this means that the tasks that involve direct communication interfaces should kept separate initially, i.e., the "front ends", response resources, and procedures, basic call center infrastructures, however, such as knowledge bases, application processes, and caller database information, must be integrated from the get go.

Insight: Not only do you have learn what your Web callers need to supplement self-service application functions, but you also have to find out what the message traffic will be like, and how to plan for the WSR skills that will be needed for message handling.

Email vs. "Webmail"

New technology gets into trouble with potential users of the technology by misusing terminology, and it is important to differentiate traditional, person-to-person email messaging, from enterprise correspondence. Webmail is email that originates from a Web caller via an enterprise Web page, and is not addressed to any particular individual or personal mailbox. Although Webmail includes freeform text messages, it will be critical for efficient message response processing to structure such communications as much as possible with Web forms. Since Web callers will usually gain messaging access to the enterprise call center though a Web page, the structured format for messaging communications can be easily enforced. So, although freeform email messages will also be part of Webmail, particularly for follow-on messaging replies, structured Web forms will remain key to cost-efficient Webmail processing.

Where a single message response to a request is not adequate, "two-way messaging" (Reply) or a conversational call will be required to complete the interchange between the Web caller and the call center. Continuity with the Web caller's self-service activities, call conversations, and messaging transactions must be preserved, no matter who within the call center becomes involved with that caller, through the use of tracking numbers and identifiers (e.g., Web caller or company names), activity logs, and multimedia transaction folders.

Webmail Processing

Just as ANI, DNIS, and IVR facilities help identify and route callers to self-service or human-assisted call center applications, so too will a combination of message-oriented processes intelligently expedite the routing and disposition of incoming Webmail. These message-processing facilities can effectively work with your existing email network operations or with Internet email access.

1. Message Content Scanning and Routing - Automatic text analysis provided by content mining software is useful for both structured and freeform message analysis, and can even be applied to language translation for global Web callers. Advanced artificial intelligence (AI) software using knowledge databases, and case-based reasoning, can analyze the full content of a message for disposition routing to fully automated response generators or staff-assisted processing. The use of such natural language processing can eliminate or minimize a very labor-intensive step and allows practical context-based priorities to be exercised before any message routing (e.g., skills based routing) is performed. Natural language context scanning will be particularly useful for follow-on freeform message interchanges, after an initial response to a more structured Web form.

2. Webmail Accountability - Proper tracking and accountability are the hallmarks of efficient AMD and Webmail management. Since messaging is traditionally fraught with sender insecurities and practical methods of determining accountability, Webmail management software must "intelligently" confirm message receipt to the sender, indicate a realistic response time, and provide a practical method for tracking the individual messages associated with a Web caller transaction for future reference.

In addition to scanning the information about the sender and the nature of the message, it is also important to check for other requests from the same originator, even when a tracking number is not included. This may uncover changes from a prior request, additional information for a prior request, or cancellation of the prior request. Repeated requests may indicate the urgency of the problem, and trigger special treatment, but should not blindly generate redundant responses.

When we use the term "message" for Web mail processing, it is not just the raw message itself, but the results of any automated pre-processing used to scan the contents and route the message to an appropriate WSR. Such pre-processing can include an abstraction of the message content, suggested "canned" response components from a knowledge base, and any other "intelligent" suggestions for efficiently completing the response process. In many cases, it may a final manual review for quality control of an automated response.

The AMD software will track message processing assignments, turnaround times, and the follow-on email activity that results from an initial Webmail response, etc., for purposes of evaluating the adequacy of response information content and WSR activity. The critical objective here is being able to continually expand the scope and quality of automated message processing.

3. Message Processing Assignment Queues - Traditional call centers are well known for their call assignment queues, where incoming callers wait for the "next available operator" with the prerequisite call handling skills. Incoming messages are treated in similar fashion, but with a different perspective of priority. Just as priorities escalate over time for telephone calls waiting in queue, so too will that apply to email messages being managed by an "Automatic Message Distribution" (AMD) software package that can interact with your existing email facilities. The AMD software will track assignments, turnaround times, and the follow-on email activity that results from an initial Webmail response, etc., for purposes of evaluating the adequacy of response information content and WSR activity. The critical objective here is being able to continually expand the scope and quality of automated message processing.

Several message assignment approaches can be taken. First, message "routing" distribution can be made to specific WSR mailboxes, and then it will be up to the individual WSR to process the message in a timely manner. A second alternative is to keep the messages in a shared, common queue displayed to a group of WSRs, letting them choose their next message assignment. (A "pull" approach.) For maximum management and control, however, the AMD software keeps all messages in queue, just like an ACD system, and delivers individual messages, one at a time, whenever a WSR indicates availability for a new task assignment (a "push" approach). Even after assignment, the messages are still controlled through the AMD software, and can be reassigned, if necessary, if not processed promptly. This insures that messages are not forgotten about, and their inherent priorities dynamically maintained. New, sophisticated AMD software products provide such centralized message management for applications that must process large message volumes "responsively."

4. Message Response Processing - Because the labor costs of dealing with reading and writing text messages can be so much higher than talking on the telephone, there is a driving need to automate as many aspects of Webmail message processing as possible. This will not only minimize staffing requirements, but will reduce the need for additional skills training.

The text-scanning technology employed to analyze email content for message routing is also used for selecting response information and generating the responses automatically, or presenting such information for manual review and approval by a WSR. Although Automatic Speech Recognition (ASR) technology has been applied in similar fashion for voice messages, it is a lot more efficient to deal with the textual information of email and Web forms. The "worst case" situation, however, is to have WSRs read Webmail (or listen to voice messages) and manually type a complete email response.

Fortunately, many frequent Webmail requests can be fully automated (like FAQ) or, while still requiring some customization by a WSR, can also be quickly disposed of with standard message templates and cut-and-paste knowledge base response information.

Realistically, however, Webmail processing requirements can encompass a spectrum of routing and response procedures, depending upon the Web caller's needs. These can include:

• Automated acknowledgement of message receipt ("mailbots"). These do not do anything with a Web caller's message, but send a canned response to every message received.

• Automated text content scanning and analysis, with fully automated email (or Fax) responses. The latter can still be "personalized", based upon database information. Given the many advantages of email (data attachments, privacy, security), fax responses to a standalone fax machine, or even to a mailbox, will be of questionable value.

• Automated text content scanning, with automated, skills-based assignment to an appropriate, available WSR.

• Automated routing to an available WSR, with manual content review and processing

• Response message templates, with "cut & paste" information from a knowledge database.

• Webmail can be quickly and painlessly transferred to more expert staff, complete with all necessary context information.

• Manual customized email response created by the WSR.

• Return telephone calls (callback), rather than an email response, based on complexity, need for discussion, and urgency of situation.

• "Instant Messaging" or "chat" connections can be activated if the Web Caller is logged on to the Internet; however, text messaging is not necessarily the most efficient way for call center staff to communicate with Web callers in real time.

• Where customized responses are always necessary, new "cross-media" messaging techniques can be applied, since it is faster and easier to create a voice message response (sent as an email attachment), which avoids the problems of spelling and typographical errors, and increases personalization of the response.

Mix and Match - Using Email for Immediate Call Center Assistance

One of the benefits of Internet-based email, is that URL access can be provided within the text message content. So, when the Web caller receives a call center email response, and live assistance is desired, immediate call center access can be initiated by the recipient from the email message, just like from a Web page. This approach also has the advantage of establishing the voice connection in conjunction with being on the Internet, and enabling multimedia consultative interaction.

Insight: Think about self-service IVR applications that let the telephone caller "escape" from the automated application to get immediate live voice assistance. This is also an "escape" from the messaging mode of Internet communications to immediate multimedia assistance.

The Importance of Contact Management and Message Logging Information

Customer contact information has always been important information available to telephone call handling staff, in order to maintain continuity of customer activity between contacts. The new wrinkle with email messaging is that it documents the exchange between the Web caller and the call center, not just for the call center, but also for the Web caller. Thus, the customer has a record of what was communicated, and it will be essential that the WSR have that same information at hand for any discussions that refer to past communication content.

Because Web callers can easily switch between email communications and realtime voice connections, it will be necessary to track all such activities in order to stay in synch with the most current status of the Web caller's communications. For example, what happens when Webmail is sent, but when the Web caller finds no response in their mailbox, they immediately get on the telephone, or go to the Web site and request live assistance, or send another Webmail missive. Clearly, the operational software has to recognize this set of circumstances, apply suitable routing logic, and provide the WSR with appropriate information to handle the situation effectively and efficiently.

WSR Message Processing Skill Requirements

As indicated earlier, Web caller text message processing must be as automated as possible in order to be cost efficient timewise, as compared to voice call handling. This is particularly necessary to support the following kinds of skills necessary for message handling:

• Email message management - Sending, retrieving, addressing, routing/ forwarding, replying, archiving, data attachment handling, etc.

• Written language skills - Reading and screening Web caller text content, grammatically correct writing, selective use of technical terminology, properly employing customer-sensitive verbiage, etc. For global E-business, multilingual language skills, as well as being able to understand poor English text, will be an important consideration.

• Typing proficiency - Speed and error-free typing to minimize the time to create a text message response. Accurate name spelling and data entry will be extremely critical, as usual. This includes accuracy in procedural keyboard entries for email messaging and data file management.

• PC usage literacy

• Internet/Web site navigation skills

• Web caller applications procedures and information

• Understanding Web caller perspectives, mindsets, and psychology

Text message processing is still going to be more time consuming than voice, even with the use of skilled personnel, and, because such personnel will be now be more expensive to recruit and retain, their time has to be used much more selectively on an exception basis. That is why the real solution is to be much more organized and automated for email response processing.

We should also make note of the fact that the skill requirements mentioned above are also necessary, and perhaps even more demanding, to support interactive "chat" sessions with a Web caller. Because the WSR must rely primarily on their own writing and typing skills in real time, there is clearly a higher performance requirement, less manageability, and more questionable benefits for WSR staffing, when compared with a voice interchange.

Keeping the Voice of the WSR in Email

The new text messaging processing and management software described earlier will be extremely useful in providing and managing automated solutions for the messaging activities of Web callers. In particular, standard problems and questions can be dealt with packaged responses. It will be the "exceptions" that require the personal attention of a WSR, whether because of the level of authority or special expertise that is required for a response, the need to "personalize" the response, or because the Web caller's needs are simply something new that doesn't yet have a "canned" response. Although the numbers may vary from application to application, the need for WSR involvement with email responses may typically be reduced to below 20% of the total email traffic. ????

But, what about that remaining 20% or those applications where the human touch is always needed? The predicted increase in email traffic will be so big, and the demand for highly qualified "gold-collar" workers so great, that any strategy for increasing their productivity and making their tasks easier should be vigorously pursued by call center management. One simple alternative, the continued use of voice for personalized messaging responses, should help provide those kinds of benefits for WSRs.

Insight: It's the message response customized content that can be time-consuming because of the writing, spelling, and typing skills required for email response efficiency. The voice skills of telephone call handling, however, are easier to find and train, and are ultimately more time-efficient to use operationally. From the recipient's perspective, voice messages will be acceptable and have more "personality" than cold text.

By the time this is published, I wouldn't be surprised to see call center product announcements that enable call center staff to respond to email messages by simply recording their responses (as .WAV attachments to the response message). For those Web callers who need it, "player" plug-ins can accompany the message to the recipient's mailbox. So, what's the deal? Simple! The WSR can review the Web callers needs, record the voice response more quickly than by typing it, AND, if necessary, still attach data files, documents, etc. to the response message. The bottom line is that we have made it easier for WSRs to communicate with natural voice, including multilingual situations, rather than having them get a college degree just for the writing skills that would be necessary.

What about the audit trail provided by text messages? If this is indeed needed, the "new and improved" Automatic Speech Recognition (ASR) software can be put to good use here, especially since it doesn't even have to be so speaker-independent. (After all, call centers will be using regular employees to support their critical operations.)

The IVR Connection: Web Forms vs. Voice Input

There is a similarity between application-structured Web forms for capturing caller request information and the use of Interactive Voice Response (IVR) voice scripts for capturing similar information as recorded voice or DTMF data for call center applications. The latter may be numeric data or menu item selections.

The limitations of the voice interface include:

• Information selection limited to short lists, in order to simplify user interface

• Information collection time-limited to insure acceptable user interface

• All information input must generally be included in pre-programmed scripts

• Freeform information is recorded voice input, which must then be manually transcribed

Although speech technologies like Text-to-Speech (TTS) and Automatic Speech Recognition (ASR) can alleviate some of the above constraints for traditional telephone callers, the Web Caller will already be in screen mode, rather than in voice mode. Interactive Web forms provide advantages over freeform email messages by enforcing required information input and providing interactive error checking of selected entry fields. Input guidance, help information, and comprehensive menu displays all make screen-based input much more time-efficient for the Web caller.

The screen user interface lends itself more easily to self-service applications, Interactive Voice Response (IVR) technology has expanded to accommodate Web callers, by also becoming the development tool for creating and processing the user interface for Web forms that integrate with traditional call center functions. Since there needs to be consistency in content given to telephone callers and Web callers, a common call center application can now be used to drive both the voice and screen caller interfaces in a similar, but not identical manner.

Where Does "Unified Messaging" Fit Into the Call Center?

It's unfortunate that the fast pace of digital information and communications access has created so much confusion. The concept of "unified messaging" pertains primarily to the need for consolidation of personal email, voicemail, and fax message management, either via a common message store (mailbox), integration and message "synchronization" between message servers, or by coordination through the user interface client software.

However, "call center messages" are not personal, cannot be controlled entirely by the individual WSRs, and may well have different priorities and routing rules for processing, depending upon the form of access involved. For example, an incoming fax message, which is a form of "one-way" messaging, will not be as demanding as a Web caller waiting for a voice connection, but may be considered more pressing than an email message. It will be the routing "queues", rather than a unified mailbox, where message management logic will be applied for voice/fax/email messages that come to the call center separately. However, because Web callers will receive and may send multimedia email messages, such messages must be managed as email (with attachments) for call center routing, retrieval, and archiving. Although the IS department would view Web voice calls and message management as simplistic "groupware" or "workflow" applications, realistic call center management will want realtime facilities to monitor and assign WSR resources for both message processing and voice call handling traffic.

Insight: The telecommunication industry is still struggling with the definition of "unified messaging," in terms of what it means to the end user vs. how it can be implemented. The call center's focus will be on multimedia message exchange at the user desktop, which email technology already supports.

Managing Webmail Processing

Typical call center management responsibilities will apply to staffing for Web mail processing. These include recruiting, training, work force scheduling, and performance monitoring. In addition, management must also take responsibility for specifying the rules that will be applied to message routing and disposition, based upon content analysis and elapsed time priorities.

Call center management has already developed most of the tools necessary for managing voice call handling, and some of these may be adapted to email message processing. However, new management performance criteria and metrics will be involved, and software facilities are coming from the call center industry to support such added requirements.

Web Application and WSR Performance Monitoring and Evaluation - Just as call centers must monitor and evaluate the performance of their traditional telephone call-handling activities and "applications", i.e., IVR call flows/information content, CSR scripts, and individual CSR performance, so, too, must there be auditing facilities for regularly evaluating the activities associated with Web callers. From the Web caller's perspective, there may be Web page applications (self-service), and both voice connections and email correspondence to be evaluated. In other words, a total transaction has to be taken into consideration, in order to properly evaluate the impact on a Web caller. This will require collecting data from each of these activity areas into a unified picture of all events in a completed Web caller transaction.

Insight: Just when we thought we were getting "end-to-end" telephone call activity consolidated with better, "open" call center technology, now we have new functions that have to be included in the call center activity stew.

Call monitoring technology products allow the selective recording and collection of voice conversations, along with associated desktop screen actions performed by call handling staff. Such capability should take care of real time Web caller connections handled by WSRs. What must be added in are the Web callers activities on the Web page, which is already being collected for proper call handling purposes, and the activity data associated with email response processing.

For the moment, these will not be quickly "integrated" into any consolidated reports, just as the industry had to wait for IVR activity to be tied into live call handling reports. However, with "open systems" and network access being de rigeur for the future of all call centers, it is only going to be a matter of time.

Adding Webmail Processing to Your Call Center

The technology to manage Webmail processing is becoming available from various sources, including traditional call center and ACD system providers. Two approaches are being touted; one that separates Webmail message processing from realtime call processing for Web callers, the other attempts to "blend" message processing assignments with live calls (normal telephone call traffic and/or Web Caller outbound "callbacks" or inbound "callthroughs").

There are several practical reasons to go slowly in merging voice call processing with Web mail processing in the call center.

1. There will be much to learn about Webmail processing, traffic, staffing, and skill requirements, for your applications. Until they are fully understood, the traditional call center operations should not be exposed to any perturbations from these new activities.

2. The critical application-based automated processes are going to be very difficult to design and implement, even with the best software tools that are starting to become available. Its not a matter of programming, but rather an issue of heavy-duty analysis of Web caller needs, both past and future, and insightful understanding of effective solutions. This responsibility belongs in the bailiwick of the "application manager," who must fully understand where Web callers are coming from. If you have never done this kind of thing before, you better get help from those who have!

3. Realtime connections ("callback," "callthrough") should also be cautiously implemented in order to learn how best to handle the "immediate" needs of your Web callers. Because there will be more of an impact from this activity on staffing and system resources, depending upon the applications involved, i.e., sales, customer service, Webmail processing may be a more practical starting point.

4. Even though these different caller interfaces should be implemented individually, the "back end" information databases must be consolidated and shared in a consistent way. Thus, all customer information, activity logs, and even past messages, must be accessible and strategically utilized for all self-service applications and CSR-assisted tasks.

Once all Web Caller support activities have been successfully implemented as separate operational functions, it will be appropriate to evaluate the ways in which they can be consolidated and "blended" from the perspective of shared staffing and relative assignment/routing priorities. Even though call center personnel can handle different types of task assignments separately, it may be more complicated and ineffective to intermix them sequentially or multitask them.

Initial Email Traffic Statistics

Web eBusiness is still in the transition stage and evolving towards a more steady state of multimedia communication activity. This will only happen after the technology shift has been completed, both from the callers' side as well as at the call center end. The following early data reported cannot be considered conclusive, but may be interesting to track for the future:

• There does not appear to be a correlation at this time between the amount of incoming voice traffic and email traffic. This may mean simply that email traffic is a new source of additional communication contact by Web callers, that has no significant impact (yet) on traditional telephone traffic. Some call center operations report 20-25% of all incoming traffic is email. However, for pure web-based activities, the call center statistics shift in favor of email; one such operation reports 88% email, 8% chat, and 4% live calls. This distribution may reflect the requirement for the Web caller to have two phone lines in order to effect a voice contact, while remaining connected to the Internet.

• Although the numbers will vary with individual applications, typical fully automated email responses constitute 20% of the responses, while 80% involve human effort. Simple queries for information retrieval, not requiring judgement or decision-making, are the primary targets for such fully automated responses. Of course, some of this kind of information may also be provided directly on-line by an enterprise web server application.

• Email processing times range from 30 seconds for inquiries requiring nothing more than a "canned" response to 10 minutes for messages requiring research of multiple "back office" databases for customer information, etc. At this stage of initial implementation, there is less concern with processing time than meeting response time service levels.

• The need for a "follow-up" email exchange after the initial email response is not known, and most operations attempt to avoid such situations. One industry provider estimates this happening perhaps with about 10% of the responses.

• Typical email response times today (using email processing technologies and WSR staff) aim for a "next-day" objective, but actually range anywhere between one hour and two days. However, a same day response objective is a current target for agent-assisted responses, and fully automated responses being immediate.

• Various measures of email processing performance are being utilized, although often in relatively simple ways. Such measures include overall service level attainment, number of messages processed, average time per message, quality of response message content, etc. The technology for making this task easier is still evolving.

Summary

The World Wide Web and Internet email will require that the power of two-way messaging be added to the repertoire of call center. Using two-way messaging technology expands upon the sophistication traditionally found in "help desk" environments, and makes such technology useful for almost any call center application. This will ultimately prove to be a major benefit to the call center's most important operational problem, staffing and labor costs. It will offload call center operations away from the staffing pressures of the telephone traffic "busy hour", towards more manageable and cost-effective support activities.

However, because of the increased skill requirements for processing text messaging, new technology tools and the use of email-based voice messaging will be an absolute necessity. Such capabilities can be added to supplement traditional telephone call centers, with either legacy ACD systems or the newer, network-based "all-in-one" communication servers.

Chapter Five
Technical Intimacy and
the Art of Customer Loyalty

Introduction

The "call center" or "contact center" or "transaction center" is the point of engagement where your company's network meets the great wide-open public network. It is where your enterprise's nervous system interfaces with your customer's touch-point. These touch-points and the customers that use them are increasingly exploiting the power and convenience of digital communications for information and personal contact; supporting the blistering schedule of a world that is open for business 24 hours a day. The call center will be the focal point - the front lines of frustration where customers are defined and dealt with.

The fundamental premise throughout this chapter is that the only way to adapt to the accelerating pace of change is by overcoming the natural resistance to such change and by discarding obsolete concepts and processes. Provocative and practical operational insights on the strategic role of new call center technologies are introduced that will undoubtedly generate controversy in the industry.

As this chapter was going to print, I discovered a report developed and written by PW Coopers consulting firm. The firm studied a number

91

of North American companies and came to the conclusion that all companies could be stratified into three groups, or "stages of evolution."

The Stages of Customer Evolution

The PW Coopers "IDEAS" study found three stages in their model of the "Stages of Customer Evolution:"

Stage One - Customer Acquisition 35%. 35 percent of North American Companies are in Stage One. Stage One companies can be characterized as "hunters." They are focused entirely on customer acquisition; hunters swoop in on the opportunity kill with little or no thought to their next meal, margin or customer.

Stage Two - Customer Relationship Management 59%. Stage Two companies are considered "ranchers." Ranchers cultivate their customer margins for margin slaughter later. Many more companies are in this category and do not want to realize it.

Stage Three - Customer Asset Management 6%. Stage Three enterprises cultivate customers using sustained yield management practices. This paper outlines some of the defining characteristics of an enterprise that is practicing true sustained yield management.

While this PW Coopers definition of the stages of customer evolution may be simplistic (and even if it is off by even a few percentage points), it is an eye-popping effective model in its demonstration of how 50 percent of companies believe that they are actually in the top 6 percent class of companies!

These three stages also reflect the evolutionary shift from measuring day-to-day transactional efficiencies to gaining lifetime customer intimacies. The difference between these strategies is why a Home Depot can know more about you than your dentist does. Interestingly, these 6% companies that are implementing progressive customer intimacy strategies more effectively than others are also doing much more outsourcing of their non-core competencies.

Expectations

Call centers are, without question, at the heart of today's consumer-focused enterprise. The three or five minutes that a customer is engaged with your enterprise represents a "moment of truth;" the moment that, if your customer's needs are not met expeditiously and professionally, your company stands to sacrifice quality in the customer relationship.

Rising expectations from callers and customers are being created by falling interaction and communication costs. The "bar" of expectations is being raised through the emerging complexity of customer engagements (the internet has guaranteed that customers are more "knowledge-ified" than ever) and their increasing expectation for tiers of service - an expectation developed by airline frequent flyer programs, for example.

These expectations of service are a direct result of the power of the computer because we now can keep track of every transaction, conversation and detail about our customers. This transactional and dialog detail enables an enterprise to execute strategies based on the concepts of mass customization or relationship marketing. Establishing an interactive experience that is characterized by an obsession for reliability, speed and intimacy is the most significant way to effect and forge the relationships that will characterize the successful enterprise of the next century. These expectations of speed, reliability and intimacy are also increasingly becoming the benchmark that your customers are using to measure the quality of the interaction with your enterprise.

Make It Consistent - No Time For Downtime

It is amazing how many call center managers and directors "check" their real-world experiences at the door of their enterprises when they come to work. Most call center managers may recognize themselves for just that - managers, but as consumers with their own hectic, confused daily routines, they tend to forget that they too live in a world steeped in their own customer interactions.

Although this is a small space for a long subject, many managers miss the point that caller expectations are not set by your industry-specific competitors; they are set by other call centers. What we often fail to realize is that we now compete with better service from places we never suspected. A common mistake made when benchmarking call center services is peer comparison; if you are a bank, you tend to compare yourself to other banks; if you are a utility company you tend to compare yourself to other utilities; insurance, retail, and help desks are all apt to compare themselves to their respective rivals. Why? Your customers don't. Your competition is no longer from the usual competitors. You now compete with Citibank, Disney, Fox, Brand X, Microsoft, USAA, the electric company, my bank and VISA, who comprise some of your "expectation" competitors, not your same-industry rivals. Consistency is not measured from transaction to transaction, it is now measured from company to company.

The relationship line between the customer and the company is moving, blurring and changing in different directions at once. Increasingly, you must look further and further outside your own business segments to discover where expectations about service are being created. When Home Depot knows more about your customer than you do, it is a sign that a fundamental shift in the power of expectations is happening. A key consumer shift caused by technology is that every customer now has the ability to survey the market place and make optimal purchases - a knowledge-ified power over the market.

Customers and enterprises alike have developed an appreciation of the potential of technology - we know when we want to use it (account balance retrieval, for example) and when it is poorly designed (long IVR menus). Expectations about www.com are now the same as those of an 800 number. The expectation problem emerges when managers refuse change or ignore what happens when technology is misused. Missed connections (ringing, then a busy signal), broken transfers and improperly handled customer requirements can put reliability expectations seriously at risk and can certainly cost the enterprise much more to repair, if even possible, than having done it right the first time.

Make It Quick - A Rebate In Freed Up Time

Time has become the most precious resource in the customer's life. "The entire economy is riddled with time-wasting routines and regimes that squander much of the time of the average customer. Suffice it to say that the concept of the customer's average life-span as a crucially scarce resource, indeed the most precious resource of the information economy, has not penetrated to many enterprises." (Gilder, Forbes ASAP 4/6/98, p.76). Higher clock speeds are giving consumers a rebate in freed-up time, and the need for speed is an expectation that comes from the time-wasting routines we have in our daily lives. So much so that consumers today will pay a premium for speed whenever they can buy it in airline e-tickets, microwave ovens, computers with modems, on-line banking, wireless toll collectors, and credit card swipes at gas stations. The customer who exploits the speed of new consumer technology is no longer willing to put up with slow lines or queues, filling out complicated forms, or telling tele-marketers whether they have had a nice day or not. As Gilder says, "Are you a life-span extender or a life-spam vendor?"

Customers are looking for business relationships that give them a rebate in time. At least this is my justification to my wife paying for lawn service, when I really just hate mowing the damn thing. Too many enterprises today waste our time; they make us drive to the bank, grocery store, bookstore, post office, telephone company, software vendor and schools. All make us line up in a queues, literally.

The fact is, if you keep your customers waiting, you won't keep your customers. However, be leery of the misnomer of "speed." If you do it fast but you don't do it right, you have sped up nothing. Focusing on transactional efficiencies over customer intimacies is the slippery slope of substituting activity for achievement. If you know much about your customers but are slow getting it, then it is useless to you. The slowest thing customers hate is not being able to reach you at all.

Make it Accurate

Customers have become so accustomed to the technology that they are now impatient if an enterprise does not know everything about their histories and transactions as soon as their agent answers the phone. Consumers do not want to waste time communicating unnecessarily - so you had better have something meaningful to say. The convenience of doing so is reflected in the service you provide. Done correctly and remembering the dialog you had with a customer the last time you talked, you can create a "barrier of inconvenience" - the reason for your customer to never want to deal with your competitor again.

As Harry Newton (we explain him later) wrote before he exited the computer telephony industry stage left; "So stop asking me, your loyal customer, who I am or how I plan to pay. You already know this; just connect your phone line to your database and you will get me off of the line faster and I will call back sooner." Make it consistent, make it quick and make it accurate. Never require the customer to tell you the same thing twice. Customers do not want noise, they want the news.

The Complaint

Customer satisfaction is at an all time low.

Harvard Business Review contends, in a recent series of articles and studies, that customer satisfaction is at an all time low. "Relationships between companies and customers are troubled at best." People are getting fed up. Complaints, boycotts and other expressions on consumer discontent are on the rise. Cell phone hell; voice mail jail; call center limbo are easily recognized examples. Customers believe that companies are disorganized, unresponsive and uncaring - even if they make reasonably good products. This is a reality few executives are willing to admit.

The slowest moving target of all is a competitor's unhappy customer and many smart companies are turning to call centers, web sites, and interactive software applications to bond with their competitors slow-moving, unhappy customer. We are increasingly hearing about confusing, insensitive and manipulative companies which trap and victimize their customers through mazes of technology. Which works, because from a consumer perspective, consumers are even less sophisticated than ever. Cheap PCs create more illiterate users, unfortunately.

Customers Want to Complain

My father, a respected and retired military person himself, verified that the generals and admirals at the Pentagon may just be right when speculating that the absence of a global enemy has made Americans turn on themselves. Because the economy is good, one of our focuses is on service. Customer want to complain and you should make it easy for them. In the one-to-one model if you get this wrong, you are shut out of a dialogue with customers that could teach you about how their tastes and preferences are evolving over time.

The Most Damaging Competitive Tool is the Service or Product Forum

Want to know what the most damaging competitive tool going nowadays is? It's the product or service forum: sometimes it's ad hoc and sometimes it could even be created and threaded along by your rival. Customers want to complain and the internet-based service or product forum is one of the easiest ways to listen to them.

Customer service has always been a double-edged sword, and technology makes this even more pointed. Jeff Bezos, president of Amazon.com said, "If you create an unhappy customer on the Internet, they don't tell six friends, they tell 6,000." News travels fast these days and knowing that they are not alone with their problems empowers customers even more. A single grudge page can hurt a company in ways that far exceed the value of what is being done.

While electronic communities may contain a good amount of flaming and complaining, they can also contain powerful and articulate insights and observations that would otherwise be impossible to come by in the course of traditional customer interactions.

Mining the electronic communities for terrific and significant ideas could benefit your enterprise and customers greatly. An enterprise's marketing strategy, indeed its mission, should be achieving a "feedback loop" where customers perceive that they are known, remembered, listened to and catered to. Customer satisfaction can be garnered by sending a signal that your enterprise is in a constant state of improvement - a signal that you are busy doing what you don't know how to do in order to learn how to do it.

Insistence Isn't Resistance

A minor but annoying characteristic of technology and product managers is to view negative feedback from customers as a temporary resistance to change. Don't fall into this trap because customer trust is hard to win and even easier to lose. Customers will cope and tolerate companies soliciting them for information, if management really acts on it. A real-world example of this phenomena is with Microsoft's Windows 98. How many of us really want Windows 98?

Seeking The Pareto Complainer

The whole genre of one-to-one marketing was created by Dr. Martha Rogers and Don Peppers on the philosophical ideas of a 19th century Italian economist and sociologist named Vilfredo Pareto (1848-1923). Mr. Pareto discovered the 80/20 rule that essentially says that 20 percent of your customers account for 80 percent of your revenues or profits. Every industry today has "Pareto" trends. The "Pareto Customer" is the customer in a significantly more valuable class of customer than most others. The "Pareto Complainer," is the customer who generates a lot of value but also does not have a problem telling you what you could be doing to do what you do better.

British Airways knows that 35 percent of their customers account for more than 60 percent of their sales. 20 to 25 percent of cellular customers account for 60 to 80 percent of revenues; retailers find that 20 to 35 percent of their customers generate 70 to 80 percent of their profits. A recent study by Mercer Management Consulting showed that banks do not make any money on 40 to 50 percent of their retail customers. Credit card companies, clothing retailers and stock brokerages all have distinct segments of Pareto and unprofitable customers. Call AT&T with a question about your long distance service and the company will route you to any one of several different call centers. Based on your usage history, if your bills are high you will get what AT&T calls "hot-towel" service - a live, human operator. Spend less than three dollars per month and you get the automated routine.

Since building relationships is not a cost-free proposition, customers with the highest potential to perform should receive the most attention. Marketing becomes important to not bringing in the loser in the first place. One time customers or those that are identified as churners represent losing investments. Companies like AT&T have gotten much smarter about separating the "cream", the Pareto customers from those they don't want.

Competitive companies are extending quality customer engagements into life-long customer relationships, because it does not take much to realize that a satisfied customer is more likely to become a repeat customer. We in the call center industry have been inundated over the past several years with the one-to-one customer intimacy marketing message. It is a message steeped in the observation of how expensive it is today to find new customers and how much more efficient it is to keep existing customers. Propagated in the mainstream business strategy circles as the Loyalty Effect and the Peppers and Rogers phenomena, one-to-one marketing includes the intimate tracking of customer histories, mining databases and proactively anticipating customer needs.

A Few Percentage Points in Retention Equals $M's in Revenues

The change of just a few percentage points of customer retention can equal millions or more of dollars to the enterprise. Customer acquisition is 5 times more costly than retention and the average company loses 25 percent of its customers per year. The more products that you have to hook your customer with, the more loyal they will stay. A GTE study found that customer churn for customers with one product was 50 percent per year. For those customers that had two products churn dropped to 25 percent per year. Customers with three or more products had dramatic churn rates of below 5 percent! There are plenty of books out there that have all of the Harvard Business School level math, but the math has been done and acquisition vs. retention is a very proven and stable business equation from revenue and profitability standpoint.

The biggest challenge of one-to-one is putting the squeeze on losers and not offending your Pareto customers. Where marketing becomes important is in avoiding bad customers in the first place, then trying to find ways to get rid of them. So, when companies focus more on creating deeper relationships with existing customers than on attracting new ones, marketing will become a less visible engagement. It will develop into a private, intimate affair between the customer and the enterprises that they buy from.

The Pareto Customer - One-to-One Too Much

Enterprise Relationship Management (ERM) projects, an enterprise's MBA term for one-to-one marketing - are hard to do, take a long time to implement, are very expensive, require strong executive support and require considerable downstream administration. The construct of customer intimacy and one-to-one marketing is a valid idea. However, at the end of a seminar or conference, the managers of call centers will go back to deal with the operational issues of transactional efficiencies and one-to-one marketing strategies will have little influence on the decisions they make next week. It is neat stuff, but conference attendees don't do, instigate or manage the type of ERM projects that one-to-one requires to be successful.

Not to be ignored, though, in this 1:1 model is the mistake of underestimating that a customer may be a valuable source of new ideas, as a reference, or as someone who spreads a positive message about the enterprise through word of mouth. Communication Week won't give me, a technology writer with thousands of readers, a free subscription to their magazine because I am not the CEO, CIO or buyer of technology in a company with more than 500 employees and $30 million in technology purchases.

Proactive dialing is one of the underestimated technologies of customer intimacy. The DoubleTree Hotel in Austin uses a predictive dialer to call me regularly and ask me when I will be back in town and if there was anything they could do for me. Hotels are one of the better indicator industries to observe the pace of relationship marketing because hotels are most interested in determining their "acquisition-versus-retention" expenditures. They want to know exactly how much they should spend to grow their customer base.

The Theory of Intimacy

Loyalty is different than no choice; utilities and phone companies are examples. The theory of intimacy says that switching to another provider of anything should get harder and harder for the customer as they arc increasingly offered service tailored to their specific needs. After building a relationship with a customer and learning all there is to know about them, there is little chance that they will leave for a competitor even if offered a better price. The enterprise must weave a web that is hard to break and as services become individualized, lines of comparison will become blurred making it harder for the customer to compare apples to apples.

The new span and power of technology makes it possible for every enterprise to remember each customer as readily as the customer can remember an enterprise – like the proverbial old corner grocer could. The logic is that by having as much knowledge about its customers as possible, an enterprise can more effectively serve and interact with its customers, improving customer retention and enterprise profitability.

Loyal Customers are the Most Unsatisfied

"It is startling how wrong we've been about what it takes to cultivate intimate relationships with customers." says the Harvard Business

Review in January, 1998. A study by the University of North Carolina at Greensboro found that your enterprise's best customers are also more difficult to please. Roughly five percent of a large US bank's customer service calls are from its best, most profitable customers and, while these customers typically receive special services, they abandon their calls at more than twice the rate of the average customer. The most loyal customers were actually the least satisfied. These most loyal customers may expect more, perhaps because of better knowledge of your enterprise's products and services or because of what they have experienced in the past. The point is clear: when talking to your customers, it certainly helps to know how loyal they are . It will help you interpret their messages.

Relationship marketing is powerful in theory but troubled in practice. Misguided manipulation of sensitive information has sparked a consumers backlash that endangers the very credibility and reputation of relationship marketing. Enterprises are consistently underestimating the new ethical challenges the use of data warehousing introduces in the enterprise/customer relationship.

Data-Mining: Information is Now More Valuable Than the Real Estate or Technology It Sits In

The value of the information surrounding a transaction may now be worth more than the goods or services being transacted. In 1996 Chase Bank discovered that the value of the technology in Manhattan was worth more than the real estate that it sat on. Not too long afterwards, they discovered that value of their information may be worth more that the technology it resides in. It is no longer a battle for the corner office, it is a battle for the corner server - the one with all of the data.

Data mining helps an enterprise understand who its customers are, what they are doing or not doing, and if the enterprise is delivering against the customers' expectations. Data mining is used to produce high- quality business intelligence, such as association, classification and regression analysis to determine these customers that have a higher propensity to spend money with you. It was the mining of data that did overturn the conventional wisdom that the customers of banks who had multiple accounts were the bank's best customers; in fact, they are actually unprofitable. The enterprise that formalizes the way it sorts, analyzes and applies its data will have the competitive advantage. In the end, he who has the biggest database and, knows how to use it effectively, shall win.

Information Exhaust, Thousands of Attributes

Companies that are looking to turn data into new products have to begin by sifting through the enormous quantities of "information exhaust." From the vast numbers and combinations, very fine opportunity segments can be identified. One consumer credit card company has almost 1,000 attributes, or data-points per customer. One insurer tracks 150 variables with 40 to 50 parameters on some 6 million customers. A single mortgage application can have some 300 data-points per application. The software of data-mining can evaluate millions of records with hundreds of variables. Wal-Mart leads the trend for deeper thoughts on using raw customer data to identify and exploit very fine opportunity segments.

Wal-Mart analyzes each of its 90 million transactions per week and manipulates a year's worth of cash-register transactions, right down to each shopping cart to see how purchases of different items are related. The computers Wal-Mart uses are able to analyze up to 700 million possible, price, store and item combinations. Wal-Mart spends more money on their on information technology, more than $500 million, than the GNP of many countries. They have recently tripled the size of their data warehouse to 24 terabytes and now have the largest commercial database in the world, second only in size to the US government.

Wal-Mart knows that the customer who buys Barbie - which it sells one of every three seconds, has a 60% likelihood of buying one of three types of candy bars. Wal-Mart is looking to identify products that sell well together so the company can display them next to each other. If someone wants to buy toothpaste, it is on the shelves. But, if they don't want to buy it all of the time, Wal-Mart does not want to have any more on the shelves than needed because it costs money for the inventory. Which leads me to wonder about the seasonal variations in the use of toothpaste and mouthwash. Which seasons and what parts of the country is what I would like to know!?

Big Guys, Little Guys; Technology Levels the Playing Field

What makes data warehousing uniquely relevant to call centers is this convergence (rather more like an intersection) of low cost storage, very fast processors and parallel processing applications that make it possible for data mining to ask new questions about more data. Moore's Law (Moore's law is about the doubling of processing horsepower every eighteen months) allows the little guys to increasingly do what only the big guys, like a Wal-Mart, could do.

Now it is possible to keep in a database the kind of information the old corner grocer used to keep in his head such as recognizing and doing favors for his customers. Although I have not been alive long enough to know what a corner grocer was, apparently we have gone a full circle and found ourselves now doing, because technology now allows us to keep track of customer dialogues and interactions, what the old corner grocer did mentally. Enterprises today have tens of thousands of customers, yet for the most part, these companies do not have a clue as to what makes their customers tick.

Panty Hose and Jelly Donuts

L'eggs pantyhose reviewed some of the customer comments left in their forum section of their web page and they discovered the popularity of pantyhose among men. They were surprised to learn that a select group of men like the warmth and comfort of these traditionally female-only products. Mining their information exhaust they discovered three distinct opportunity segments; law enforcement officers, hunters in the north east and serious outdoor athletes. Maybe L'eggs should consider a camouflaged king-sized brand. Until relatively recently, it would have been difficult for enterprises that practice customer intimacy to have discovered this new market segment.

Take the GM television commercial for Saturn cars where the jelly donut junkie has a history of complaining to the dealership about all sorts of imagined car ailments. The Saturn dealer, scanning his customer database discovers that what this customer really wants is the jelly donuts in the customer lobby. This brings up an interesting question about GM's use of customer data, because I'm not sure that customers would want GM mining their extensive data base for obnoxious jelly donut scammers.

The question that Michael Schrage brought up in a recent column was what happens when your records become annotated by customer service agents with comments like obnoxious, complainer, whiney or manipulative? This is the antithetical treatment that we are giving when we empower the agent taking the call with a subjective power like this. How does a company use databases to defend against abuse of service guarantees, like jelly donuts?

It is through the call center or point of customer contact that this friction will occur. What if it is the agent that is having a bad day?

Privacy: The Key Consumer-Protection Issue of the Information Age

Privacy is the key consumer-protection issue of the information age. Privacy is more important an issue than many think in the relationship marketing revolution. Privacy and intimacy are closely related and the problem is that businesses today don't tell consumers what they are doing with personal information and consumers have no idea what is happening to that information.

Not even our laws can keep up with technology and, in fact, if you do business in Europe or want to do business there beginning October 25, 1998, you must adhere to a global privacy code regulating the international transfer of information: no privacy, no trade. No personal information can be sent to countries that do not adhere to this code - including the US. American Airlines is required to delete health and medical information on flying passengers such as dietary needs, disability access and other medical conditions.

Data-mining leaves us with a number of information paradoxes. Your videotape rental history has much better privacy protection than your social security number. There is no federal law forbidding the disclosure of Social Security numbers. But a video-rental privacy law was enacted after a Supreme Court nominee was embarrassed by the publication of a video list that included adult titles. Do I really want anybody tracking my movements through the Melrose Place web page, or the L'eggs pantyhose forum or Victoria's Secret's on-line catalog?

The Fear of Digitized Discrimination Runs Deep

New technologies may facilitate information collection and dissemination, but they also can enable behavior that violates many consumer's sense of privacy. As technology permits us to quietly accumulate knowledge and information about customers, chances increase that we will unwittingly or intentionally violate a customer's expectations of privacy and misuse their information.

Consumer anxiety about the mishandling of personal data is a significant barrier to online usage and electronic commerce. The internet is an environment where there is absolutely no trust. By now most of us know that the internet was designed to survive a nuclear blast that would knock out a large portion of the network, so robustness and survivability, not credit card security, was the most important design criteria. In *The Net,* a 1995 cyber thriller starring Sandra Bullock, she gripes that each one of us has an "electronic shadow, just sitting there, waiting for somebody to screw with it."

Information abuse has serious consequences. For example, a farmer in upstate New York has placed tiny transponders (internet "cookies") around the necks of his 800 dairy cows to enable weighing meters to measure and track how much milk each cow produces. They can identify which cows are making money and which ones are not. The result seriously affects the cow - automatic gates send some back to the pasture, some to the veterinarian, some to the breeder and some to the slaughter-house.

There is the potential for serious abuses and we have become cultur-alized to it through movies like *The Net*. There is a deep-seated anxiety by society that database marketing of the one-to-one sort will lead to new forms of customer discrimination as offensive as racial discrimination of the past; a form of customer segregation by personality. How about being branded as a jelly-donut abuser, an obnoxious complainer, or even worse for failing a medical screening? Are we willing to give up this kind of personal information? Do we have choice? Do we think that this will really change?

New technologies may facilitate data collection and dissemination, but they also enable behavior that violates many consumer's sense of privacy. Many consumers are refusing to shop and avoid requests for or are falsifying personal information, thereby corrupting whatever data is collected.

Violate Trust and Destroy Relationship

The fastest way to destroy a relationship is to violate customer trust. Enterprises must respect the privacy and understand the sensitivities of their customers because trust is hard to win and easy to lose. What one person views as an exciting application of technology, another may view as an invasion of privacy. There may also be times when information use violates rules of etiquette without necessarily violating privacy - like Amex's Caller ID folly.

American Express briefly used Automatic Number Identification (ANI) to answer the phones by their customer caller's names, "Hello Mr. Anderson." Call handling times shot up in response to the customer service agents having to explain to callers exactly how they knew their names. The issue was not only creepiness, but a violation of etiquette. This goes to point out that it is at the call center or point of customer contact that this friction will occur.

Companies that offer sales discounts or other perks to "elite" Pareto customers fall victim to a new type of phantom customer who, increasingly, gives fake names and fake information because they feel, in spite of what you want to believe, that taking a few cents off of the price of the product is too low a price to pay for a window on their private life. Ask any data warehouse manager how much information they are hoarding about fake people and fake addresses with fake buying habits. How many of us fill out technical and trade subscriptions with the title of CEO just so we won't get booted off of a free mailing list. In our customer intimacy one-to-one model, many would claim that this is a fair trade; that personal information for personalized service is worth it.

Anyway, It's Not Invasion of Privacy; It's Invasion of Time

This not so much about an invasion of privacy as it is about an invasion of time. George Gilder wrote, "In general the threat to your privacy and the menace of intrusion on your life does not come from true information." (ASAP p. 82, 4/6/98).

An example of an invasion of privacy and invasion of time is the dinner-time tele-marketer who calls to sell me siding because they do not know that I had just built an all-brick home. Invasions of privacy can reflect an inadequate knowledge, not excessive knowledge. Gilder points out that in a sense, telemarketers and other advertisers fail to invade our privacy enough. Many customers are surprised by calls for products they want, i.e. the credit card company that calls to verify the funds being spent. Someone whose certificate of deposit matures at Citicorp's bank, now may get a call from a Smith Barney broker pitching a mutual fund investment. Or selling pharmacy customer's medical information to marketing companies that send coupons related to their disorders.

The call center will be the focal point of this exposure, as they are the locus where undesirable customers are defined and dealt with (a la AT&T automated routing for bills less than three dollars). Interesting abuses and embarrassing stories will emerge: "I am sorry sir, I can't help you today, you were rude the last time you called." Never mind that it was the agent that was having the bad day.

Humanware: The Gold Collar Worker

Since we know from practical experience that greater than 60 percent of the cost of running a customer service entity is in the cost of people and call center staff. There is a discernable shift happening among technology vendors to become more sensitive to the customer service representative (CSR) end of the call center equation. Seeing that the switching technology vendors slowly shift their focus to the application of technology to CSR work quality issues and not entirely on just improving transactional efficiencies has been noticed. The market is very interested in any business message that talks about fairness in agent utilization and reduced turn over in agent positions.

It is too broad of a topic to be discussed in depth here, however a driver of the increasing numbers of applications in the market focused on "agent fairness." Creating "agent burnout" is awareness that powerful Automatic Call Distribution (ACD) technologies foster the potential to turn clusters of gold-collar workers into white-collar sweatshops. Certifications and professional organizations built around the emerging professional breed of super-agents, gold collar workers whose skills and knowledge will require enterprises to pay them possibly more than they pay their managers.

Agents are Where the Next Envelope will be Pushed

The next step in the intimacy evolution does not stop at gaining lifetime-long customer intimacy, the next great gains will come from the agent; the humanware side of the technical intimacy equation. Subtley, but increasingly, the observation is being made that we are burning agents up, exhausting their supply to call centers. It is no secret that turnover, ranging anywhere from 15 to 300 percent per year, is a major problem in call centers. Now agents are smarter, they are needed to be smarter, they are organized and they are professionals. It is with the agents - the new generation of the gold-collar worker, that the next productivity envelope will be pushed.

Best Agent, Best Customer; Flash Point of Productivity

Bringing your best customers together with your best agents can create a "flash-point" of productivity far greater than what traditional customer service technology has offered. In time, we may see productivity improvements of greater than 25:1 or as much as 50:1 when the Pareto customer is matched with the best agent. The point needs to be made here that the "best agent" is not the same thing as the "same agent."

This isn't exactly skills-based routing, which itself has enough longevity to prove that, as a function if implemented incorrectly, actually costs you more in "agent burnout" than it creates customer satisfaction. In today's call center service world, if I have an agent that takes on more skills, I penalize them by burning them up because they are utilized more then someone with fewer skills. With skills-based routing in the long term, the agent is essentially penalized for becoming more valuable.

You Cannot Script Intimacy

It is the agent and the new subjective, decision-making skill-sets they will have that are the most critical piece in the whole one-to-one equation. Think about the Saturn Dealership's service manager and the jelly donut scammer from the context of an agent and caller. Customer intimacy requires alert, sensitive dialogue, but scripting can dumb down an engagement. You can not script intimacy very well, because the agent, as a gold-collar worker, has evolved to the point where they can no longer be considered an just an interface; they're a decision maker now. In fact we approach a point where the data from touch-points becomes quite subjective. Don't tell them how to do it, tell them what you want them to do, then reward them for doing it successfully.

One to One Management-ware

Part of the humanware evolution, is obviously a management-ware evolution. One analyst at Advanstar's Call Center 98 show in Dallas, Texas estimated to me that by the year 2000, 25% of today's call center managers will be gone. They will be replaced because of their lack of adaptability to meet the technology challenges of the next century. There was a clear message to this population of managers: re-skill or perish. Many of these attendees had their antennae up higher than ever, since they realize that they must learn, adapt, re-skill or lose their jobs to - God forbid - a data guy.

Because of the "whack-a-mole" perception of technology "popping" up all over the call center, it takes a different kind of constitution to complete a CTI based intimacy system and applications. The increasing telephony-grade robustness of networked and voice enabled PC platforms is emerging as a real threat to the traditional telephony skill sets managing the ACD platform.

The defining characteristics of most customer service managers are that they operate within the limitations of one-year budget cycles, they are graded on transactional efficiencies and their predominant day-to-day issue is not technology, but human resources. Since call center managers do not, for the most part, operate in time frames of greater than one year, they are looking for incremental and tactical "proof of concept" implementation of applications and technology. The vendors with successful "booth hits" were the ones that could demonstrate proof of a product or application concept in less than a single year's budget cycle.

Being efficiently incubated in the wings of the call center and customer service industry is the Call Center Advisory Council industry certification initiative. Many of us, vendor and end-user alike, recognize the benefits of having a standard industry professional certification, both for managers and agents. Many of us agree that this would go a long way to transforming what we do from being just a job to being a profession. Information and progress reports can be found at www.callcenteru.com. The Call Center Networking Group is another executive resource that could have impactful use in the day to day operation of the customer service center. They can be reached at www.ccng.com.

For the most part, all of this is a moot point because, except for those few call center managers, executives and directors with executive-suite aspirations on their minds, and most call center and customer service focused executives are - at the end of the day, going to return to their call centers and get back to dealing with transactional efficiency issues.

Improving Your "Like-Ability" Quotient

If you want to change your company, change how it relates to its customers. You need to build a communications pipeline that forces to the surface the bad and the good stories from your customer base. Increasingly "like-ability" means insuring that people inside the company are attuned to what people are saying on the outside.

Creating a corporate culture that truly supports customers is perhaps the most difficult thing to do. According to the PW Coopers report mentioned at the beginning of this chapter, perhaps this is a contributing factor to why only 6 percent of companies accomplish sustained yield management status. Management change is tough sometimes, and sometimes it is just not worth changing at all.

Initiatives to improve your enterprise's "like-ability" quotient start in the call center because, even though the call center still suffers the stigma of not being as "sexy" as other parts of the enterprise, the call center represents one of the last great opportunities to differentiate yourself and set new levels of service expectations. If you have a hard time convincing executive management of the value of your call center; consider this: it cost the United Parcel Service, UPS, some $1.2 million for a 30-second television commercial during the 1998 Super Bowl. At the same time, UPS received approximately 70 million customer telephone calls last year, each lasting an average of four minutes. Where do you think UPS's better media buy is? With 70 million four-minute opportunities or a single thirty second Super Bowl commercial?

Be leery of the often fatal results of seeking the Pareto customer. The lure of a few percentage point change in customer retention can result in millions of dollars loss to the enterprise. As with all computer telephony integration implementation projects, leave ample room for heroic failure. Return on investment and information stories like UPS's, combined with the narcotic effect of Newtonization, is one of the reasons for the dismal failure rate of CTI applications. These projects are often rushed into with little or no strategic planning or scheduling demanded of any large technology integration project.

The Petty Tyrant and Champion Sputter

A call center essentially performs a huge, virtual middleware job. This requires the connectivity to new sources of data and information throughout the enterprise. The vital information of customers is most often found accumulated in silos, legacy systems and private tyrannical departments. Mentioned earlier was the fact that the value of information about customer transactions is now more valuable than the technology it resides in has not been passsed up by a new breed of executive - the data baron. Data barons no longer fight for the prized real estate of the corner office, their turf is the information on the server in that corner office. Just going out to fetch some information from a petty tyrants database to populate an agents screen is not as easy as it would appear.

The silver lining to the problem of every call center's petty tyrant is the fact that, because of customer issues like privacy and convenience, much of the petty tyrant's data is corrupt, inaccurate, incomplete or stored on incompatible media or formats anyway.

Lasting and impactful information technology revolutions have always occurred from the top down. Champion sputter is when a project's sponsoring executives start ducking out of "on-track" meetings. Reality looms, interest wanes and the entire project sputters to a slow, grinding halt.

In the absence of leadership, the best advice for call centers is to "just do it" with selected types of technologies, not everything that is in the arsenal. When implementing applications, the call center must focus on the real needs of its callers with practical conciseness and consistency, not simply showcase every possible technology available. Using voice recognition as an example, an enterprise instructs callers to either press "one" or "speak one" ("one" as in a menu selection), but it should specifically offer one way or the other, not both interface options.

Camels and Caravans

Enterprise customer relationships can not change when "the camels at the back of the caravan get the beatings while the one's at the front hold everything up." (Ethiopian Proverb). The core competency of call centers has shifted and call center executive management can no longer value transactional efficiencies over customer intimacies. Those that survive into the next century will be the ones that hone their skill of connecting the dots between the tactics of transactional efficiencies and the strategies of enhancing customer relationships.

If you do not take ownership and start buying into these new solutions, applications and technologies (such as proactive outbound calling, callback messaging, predictive dialing, webmail processing, self-service web and telephone applications, and IP telephony), someone else in the enterprise will. Unfortunately, as your traditional telephony-based vendors rapidly gain data world experience, they will increasingly circumvent you and sell directly to the enterprise CIO/MIS department because they are the ones that "get it."

Newtonization: The Provocative Glamorization of Technology

Newtonization is the glib, topical and provocative glamorization of computer-telephony technology that is far too sophisticated and complex for the users that put it in; when plug and play is in fact plug and pray.

You don't have to know who he is, but Harry Newton is the classic proof in modern day mass media of how you can create an industry on marketing hype and magazines alone (note: Harry Newton recently reported that he sold his CTExpo tradeshow, *Teleconnect, Computer-Telephony, Call Center* and *Imaging Magazine* empire for an eye-popping $130M and split it among several partners). Miller-Freeman's (who bought out Mr. Newton) huge shrine to the incestuousness of the computer and telephony industry has proven to be just fun and entertaining replete with stylish exhibitor "booth bait" and "show goodies."

The problem with these magazines is that they editorially portrayed CTI as an easy "application kill," but in reality many of the implementations of CTI applications were dismal failures. Statistics about CTI implementations demonstrate a nearly 90 percent failure rate of those that are put in without a vendor, a systems integrator or a consultant. I would consider one of the traits of the very evolved 6 percent of PW Cooper's survey from the beginning of this chapter, was that they probably used a consultant, systems integrator or the equipment vendor. Newtonization is about the over-simplification of customer service technology and communication and the de-evolutionary influence on the entire customer service and CTI food chain. Enterprises now have been "Newton-ized" enough to know from experience that, if they can not keep up with the blistering pace of announcements of new platforms, applications and services, then they had better find somebody that can.

Big boats turn slow, but even the largest of the traditional vendors are showing major evolutionary shifts. A new generation of thought leaders is emerging that is beginning to gain deeper understanding and appreciation of the day-to-day functional realities of the call center. Look for these issues and concerns to increasingly have a greater reflection in the vendor's services, applications and solutions. While it's good to see new product developments and application innovations, the typical customer would like to see less "PowerPoint" and more practical. In either case, neat graphics, screen shots and persuasive presentations belied the fact that few of these companies had actual implementations of their showcased products and even fewer were overtly oriented toward practically addressing the technical requirements of one-to-one marketing. This is the same challenge that exists in the consultant community.

While the consultant community may have plenty of great ideas, if they cannot also specify how to make them work they are not very likely to garner support from the nuts-and-bolts transaction manager in a call center. Like the vendor community to a certain degree, there is a consistent tendency for consultants, particularly if they deal on the strategic level with enterprise executives, to disregard and neglect the practical nature (and implementation requirements) of call center managers.

This technical intimacy stuff is hard to do. With the proliferation of technology and applications, the need for competent guidance - "whack-a-mole" experts - just to pull it all together is becoming more important, if not critical.

It's Holes, Not Drill Bits

It is harder than you would expect to pin down the right number, but the Industrial Machine Tool Distributors Association says that there are tens of millions of drill bits manufactured every year. In the middle of trying to find out the exact number, I read a brief editorial that pointed out that people really don't care how many drill bits that are made, what they want are the holes. Computer Telephony Integration, as an entire technology industry, has been duped - "Newtonized," by the drill bit. Customers want solutions, not drill bits.

One of the opportunities many of the vendors are missing is doing a better job of relating their particular product strategies to messages of one-to-one marketing. And, while the application of one-to-one marketing in call centers has its challenges to the end-user community, the vendors could all do a better job of synchronizing their messages with how this one-to-one stuff is actually being done.

You can give away all of the drill bits you want, but don't forget that what customers really want are holes. Too much technology can turn off customers. Systems and interfaces that offer functions users don't want and lack qualities they find important can generate resistance and frustrate users. IVR is a good example of a technology which often generates a suspicion of evasive antagonism.

Legacy Hesitation

The current vice president of the United States, Al Gore, is a champion of the Information Superhighway's bridge to the 21st Century. Now here is a man that has probably not driven his own car in years. So, from the comfort of his air-conditioned Vice-Presidential Suburban, he has optimistically forgotten to calculate in the condition and effect of bridge fright. Bridge fright is the phenomena that many of those who regularly drive on crowded city-highways recognize as when everybody instinctively slows down as they approach a bridge or freeway overpass. Since they can not see to the other side, they, the herd, instinctively slows. It is the same thing with technology.

While Vice President Gore may be able to see clearly over that bridge into the 21st century, the rest of us are driving at pavement level, and we are not about to cross over so fast. Since we can not see over and beyond that bridge to the 21st century, we remain pragmatic as a culture and we will continue to cling to our legacy technologies and interfaces. We just don't change our user interfaces as quickly as the mass media would have us believe.

Don't underestimate legacy hesitation's influence. User interfaces, operating systems, the telephone, wireless, Windows 95 and UNIX are examples of players with underestimated longevity. Martha Rogers tells people that in ghettos, television penetration is greater than telephone penetration. "If these are your customers, maybe you should learn to talk to them through their televisions," she asks.

Telephony Guys With Laptops or Data Guys With Trucks?

The company's wide area network (WAN) or your cable TV may go out for hours at a time, but when the telephone network goes out, as during the dramatic 26-hour AT&T failure in the spring of 1998, we bolt upright and take notice. The inconvenience caused by no phone service is apparent. No time for downtime is the greatest of the customer expectations and the company that provides this has a tremendous competitive advantage over the ones that don't. From a customers perspective, there is no such thing as service that goes down for regularly scheduled repairs.

On the rubber chicken road-show tour, a frequent question that is discussed is who are you going to buy this customer service technology stuff from? From telephony guys with laptops or data guys with trucks?

Meeting the dial-tone grade expectation of reliability is one of the issues that will keep the "data guys" from taking over the call center anytime soon. As far as reliability is concerned, they have not yet caught on to the call center axiom that "downtime is an emergency." Because of the 100 years of institutionally embedded experience with zero-tolerance to downtime (allowing seconds per year at most), I suspect that it will be from the telephony guys with laptops that the technology of service expert will emerge.

The Peripheral Edge: Columbus Wasn't That Brave of a Guy

History is obviously a little more complex than this, but essentially all Christopher Columbus did was observe the masts disappearing over the horizons. It was obvious that Columbus wasn't a genius, he just could see what was coming over the horizon. This was the simplified version of how he figured out the world was round but, like Al Gore too, the predictive observation of technology is fairly straightforward and it does not take much (well, perhaps a lot of study) to triangulate in on the obvious.

There are several indicator trends and technologies that are more important than others on the horizon. For example, every customer call to Federal Express costs FedEx between $2 and $3 - in fact FedEx loses money on the package. But, when you go to their web site and track the package yourself, they make some money. Another trend example is from a company called Digital Worldwide Services which provides technical support for 14,000 products from 1,300 companies and handles 5 million service request calls a year. DWS resolves three-quarters of their customer orders and queries within one hour.

Look at What the "Net Dragged In" - In a "Net-Shell"

There are plenty of more credible resources available on the internet than here, so I will be limited in my constructive observations and let the reader infer their own conclusions by only pointing out the following statistics.

Business on the internet is growing twice as fast as the rest of the economy and doubles every 100 days and $300 billion in business will be transacted over it by the year 2020.

35 percent of all commerce by 2005 will be over the internet; that still leaves 65 percent to something else, and that is the telephone. Not to mention wireless is growing at 35,000 new subscribers per day. America's public telephone network still carries 40 times more traffic than the global internet.

At any one time, 15 to 35 percent of internet traffic is from adult content sites. In case you are wondering how this could be possible, consider that this book may have somewhere around 10 million bits to it. A video transmission over the internet consumes about 10 million bits in four seconds. So while your company may be sending thousands of emails, it is no match to the bandwidth demands of a few good seconds of video.

Data may be growing faster, but people are still talking. And, in general the end game will be about the touch points, not data points - It's the interface, the touch-point that we should most observant of.

Conclusions

In today's hyper-competitive world, one in which enterprises engage with their customers through a variety of media, keeping customers loyal will demand heightened attention and greater focus from operational management on new strategic business rules rather than old, traditional efficiency measurements. The future of the competitive, successful enterprise is not in the struggle for obtaining and exploiting information, it will be in the cultivation of life-long customer relationships. But let's be pragmatic here and not forget that we, the call center managers and executives, are still captivated by the goal of providing the best possible experience at the least expense to the enterprise.

Reliability, speed and intimacy are increasingly being measured, not by the number of calls answered, but by the quality of the interactions. As a result, many call centers are beginning to see their performance measured against more strategic metrics, such as customer retention, customer satisfaction, consistency in service level, application of best business practices and ultimately, revenue growth. The border between getting a customer, keeping a customer and growing a customer is blurring.

Seeing who represents the greatest profit potential, most likely a customer we can call the "Pareto Complainer," can only be achieved by considering the cost and revenues of customers throughout their life cycles. Customers who, by the way, are getting older and living longer. Calculate that customer behavior will change over time as well.

The cost of winning back customers gets higher every day. Better customer service leads to better customer retention. Successful enterprises will adapt to the new paradigm of business drivers; the customer and their time. What technology is providing, be it through the telephone, internet or skills based routing, is giving people more time to have contact with the people that they want to have contact with, while eliminating non-important, merely frictional encounters. Your enterprise's customers wouldn't tell you this if it was a problem, because they are probably long gone by the time you get the message. The message is clear. Do not waste your customers' time by not communicating meaningfully; you had better have something to say and do it quickly, reliably and knowledgeably. Be intelligent, understanding, and, most important, responsive!

The skills required to manage the Pareto complainer are not trivial skills. Accomplishing technical intimacy is much more challenging than most of us ever expected. The blistering pace of technology innovation isn't just happening "out there" but in call centers as well. If you intend to be a call center manager into the 21st century, then there needs to be less avoidance and more ownership - which is job security. It is easy to be intimidated by non-telephony technology, but the call center is the appropriate place to take ownership of these new media and applications because the call center is the appropriate place to apply the expectations of service levels (downtime is an emergency). The call center will be the focal point - the front lines of frustration where customers are defined and dealt with.

Technology now can provide a foolproof memory of customer interactions, needs and preferences. Once you have been mined, you have been branded for life. Some of the evidence is found like the type of studies by PW Coopers mentioned at the beginning of this chapter. The evolution from farmer to rancher to sustained yield manager coincides nicely with the observation that the most successful enterprises are making the shift from transactional efficiencies to customer intimacies. To adopt these new technologies and the customer expectations they create requires substantially more vision than seeing beyond the time frame of a one-year budget cycle. Take ownership of the Pareto complainer before the wrong department does. In conclusion, management need more strategic vision or they will lose their jobs while the traditional telephony-oriented vendors need less "PowerPoint" and more tactical solutions ,or they will all lose their customers to others that are faster and nimbler.

Chapter Six
Call Center Humanware: White Collar Slave or Gold Collar Worker?

The following was a question asked of Marilyn Vos Savant - who claims to be the world's smartest woman - in Parade magazine, published Sunday, November 6, 1998:

Q: Why do big businesses keep buying phone systems instead of using real people? I am positive they do not save money. All I can guess is that the phone companies have the best sales people in the world. - Jerry Sobotta, Hermiston, Ore.

A: There are lots of good reasons, but I think the best one of them is automated phone systems can free those real people to do something far more productive than repeat computer generated information like your check account balance, flight arrival times or theater show-times. This is how automation helps society progress. We lose a little, but we gain a lot.

Do we? Do we really gain a lot? At what expense?

There is a sublime fear expressed in this exchange that most likely only a few customer service chain executives and managers will recognize. In spite of the fact that an overwhelming majority of the expense of providing customer service is with the humans that provide it, it is the technology we use that dominates our attention.

There is an extraordinary amount of focus in the call center on the "plumbing." Many enterprises do not realize that they (and the "plumbing" that supports them) may be setting themselves up to be branded, chastised, accused or ostracized in the global business environment of dangerously exacerbating the problems of industrialized mass production in the white collar field. We can even find recent written parallels of the "Orwellian" potential of the "perfect prison" described in the Panopticon. (Is it any wonder that, in fact, some of the more successful call centers are staffed by incarcerated inmates of our federal and state prison systems?)

The overwhelming tendency for enlightened customer service chain executives today is to believe that call centers are the battery farms of the information age. They envision and realize that their call centers are a pure source of the digital fuel of the information age - the digitized dialogs that describe and define how customer's needs and preferences are evolving over time.

But, are call centers really battery farms or just factory farms? Are call centers the new sweatshops of the information age? Call centers are emerging to be the most remarkable employment opportunity of the information age. Likewise, there is growing controversy over the quality of jobs at call centers. We can not escape the growing comparison between the high pressure work of call centers and the production pressures of factory farms that make soccer balls, shoes and clothes. The call center phenomenon dramatically demonstrates that changes in technology do not always produce the predicated or intended effect. Better telecommunications was supposed to release thousands to work from home. Instead, we have developed the huge telecommunications factories called call centers.

Technology, in many instances, has redefined the workplace environment from sweatshops to robotics. Computer Telephony Integration (CTI) is the robotics of customer service. However, enterprises cannot script the intimacies required of the one-to-one relationship revolution. You cannot script or flow chart customer intimacy. To the very human customers of an enterprise, the call center, the telephone conversation is the technology. Somewhere in the accelerated spin of Moore's Law (the doubling of computer processor power every 18 months), the demand for service from real, live humans takes a vigorous turn off-track.

Customer service chain executives consistently make the mistake of assuming that the insistence for human contact by customers is a resistance to technology. How much productivity and business has been lost to an enterprise by people who refuse to leave voice mail messages? Our culture has even coined a sufficiently popular truism called "voice mail jail" to support this experience.

Today, many customer service chain executives fail to account for the value of a proven, efficiently working call center. Unfortunately, the next evolutionary leap will have to come in convincing them of the underestimated value of proven, efficient and highly productive humans, the agents that work in them. Agents seem to have become a forgotten lot, not only from a quality of life perspective, but from the position that they are the ambassadors of their organization; they are the company. Making sure that they always have a fair and efficient environment is important and this is not always the case.

The glitz and hype of technology today has created a misdirected focus that is missing the human agent component and how that agent is applied against the goals and strategies of the enterprise itself.

Today, even the venerable management consultants and business seers, Dr. Hammer and James Champy (who co-wrote the book Reengineering the Corporation: A Manifesto for Business Revolution) readily admit that they forget about the people part of the reengineering process that has guided business change for the past decade. Reflecting their influence from an engineering perspective, they agree today that they "were not sufficiently appreciative of the critical, human demand" of the enterprise.

Today, not only does the enterprise need to track and react to the needs and preferences of its customers, but it needs to do the same with its agents. The new labor resources of call centers will quickly emerge as having far different needs and preferences than any generation before it. We are seeing the emergence of the fast-finger-twitch Nitendo generation of worker who has a completely different outlook on work, challenges and expression. The challenges of dealing with Generation X-ers, who have no problems changing jobs as careers and opportunities present themselves, dealing with single parenthood, increasing child care expense, elder care issues, loyalties and leisure are certainly unique, but they are not insurmountable and they can certainly be exploited to achieve the goals of the enterprise.

One of the real dangers of call centers in the information age is that enterprises compromise their relationships with their agents in pursuit of their relationships with customers. Companies can identify customers, but only people can identify with customers. The most powerful computers in the world are no substitute for the power of an intelligent conversation between an agent and customer. What's most powerful about computers are their human parts.

The definition of the new generation of call center agents will be one that can turn an incoming call from a confused, upset or disgruntled customer into a rich stream of impressions, ideas and data. "Deliver a mediocre presentation and you risk the chance of being toned out, deleted or ignored as the consumer searches his or her voice mail, email, or mail for more interesting items." (Angela Karr, Teleprofessional, Oct. 1998, p.8.) In a dialogue-based relationship, the result is a permanent conversation about quality, performance and standards. The successful enterprise will need to have the most talented people at the right place and at the right time. The service agent is the critical component for managing the customer "touch point." Most customer interactions with the enterprise have a human component that remains largely unaffected by technological innovation.

A good example of this is found in saying that a "lowly" call center agent certainly does not know more about a product than the engineer who built it does. But that agent most certainly knows more about the customer than the engineer does. However, too often it is the engineer that drives the product or service issues of the company and not the other way around. This is particularly acute in technology companies with help desks and it may be more important than anything else. The evolution that we are seeing is defined by the shift in awareness that agents and the communicative functions they provide may be more important than developers and marketers of the products they support.

More and more enterprises have reached the same conclusion that customers have become so important that they don't just want people talking to them, they want their very best agents in the world talking to them. Computer companies, for example, should adopt the philosophy that they don't just make high performance computers, they make high performance customers.

For most people, interacting with a person is a more fulfilling experience. A human "hello" is promised by an Allstate Insurance Company office in Sedona, AZ which runs ads in the local paper that assure callers of "an actual, real live hello no matter what time you call us." After normal business hours the calls are transferred to a call center in

Nebraska.

Human beings, in the end, execute the work and, as a result, they are at the intersection of the demand for service and the expense of providing it. While we know that the expense of call center agents ranges from 60 percent to 70 percent of the cost of operating a call center, they are more than 90 percent responsible for its success. There is an effective threshold to be balanced between wasting money on overstaffing (the inefficiencies of idleness) and when the availability of too few (or even too many poorly trained) agents exists, customers become dissatisfied, lower their expectations and perhaps never call back. Where is the greater expense to the enterprise?

Many companies say they are obsessed with customers and many companies promise to delight customers - but companies do not help customers, people do. The quality of customer service can not, by default, exceed the quality of the people who provide it. It is with the agents of call centers that the customer service chain strategy must start. The challenge will be maintaining and preserving humanistic functions, actions and the fundamentals of good customer care such as open communication, positive attitude, courtesy and understanding. Today, we face the challenge of infusing and extending all of these humanistic attributes into the electronic realm as well.

In the past, the call center agent was viewed as a low paid, clerical person that primarily just answered the telephone. Today the call center agent is evolving to someone quite different. Increasingly, we are seeing in the enterprise fewer and fewer subordinates - even in low paying job functions. Ideally, call center agents are empowered, incented, motivated, and positioned in learning environments dedicated to meeting customer expectations and the business objectives of the organization.

An increasingly popular description of the new information worker is "knowledge worker." A distinguishing characteristic and the very nature of a knowledge worker today is that he knows more about his job than his boss does - or else what good is he?

Who Should Take That Call?

The concept of the "universal agent" is the Holy Grail of the call center; an agent who can respond to all of the caller's questions and requests as well as proactively recommend new goods and services. Contrast this to the majority of call centers, which are small (under 25 agents) and support small companies. In small companies the customer is always first - not that this is not true for the largest companies, but how often in large companies is the enterprise infrastructure architected to support enabling the lowest clerk to the CEO as a potential call center agent?

This means that at some point in time or for a particular customer, in the right setting, every employee, including the CEO may be called upon to respond and answer the phone (or communication). For example, if there is a big business deal being developed and the potential partner calls the enterprise and the partner is identified by his account number, IVR identification or ANI, and he was calling for the senior VP of sales, the question is, "Do you want that call to go to voice mail or to their assistant?" If neither is available, wouldn't you really want that call to go up to the CEO? And imagine a CEO that responds by saying, "I am so delighted you called, how can I help you?" At that point in time, the CEO has become a call center agent.

We can broaden the definition of "informal agents" when we consider employees outside of the enterprise's mainstream call center as described above. Everybody in the company, even though there may be a formal call center whose main function it is to take calls from customers, is an informal agent. To a customer seeking a conversation, there is little difference (other than perhaps the immediate result) between the shipping clerk at three o'clock in the morning taking a call and the CEO.

Reconciling With the Emerging Demands of Satisfaction

A 1996 Harvard Business Review article pointed out that U.S. companies lose one-half of their customers every five years. Customer dissatisfaction is at an all time low, running at an unacceptable level, with more than one call in ten leaving the customer feeling irritated, anxious, frustrated or furious, particularly in the media, insurance and utilities industries. As e-commerce is driving new levels of richness in shopping online, however, personal service is continuing a slow downward slide globally. These statistics are most likely quite related.

Only 32 percent - less than one-third - of customers with complaints were completely satisfied with agent responsiveness in a recent survey conducted by Hepworth & Company, Ltd. This is an important metric because customers who are partially satisfied are far less likely to make repeat purchases from the company.

So why don't companies recognize the dismal levels of service customers believe they are getting? There are two reasons. The first is institutional denial (not covered here). The second is that only 30 percent of call centers actually measure customer satisfaction (not covered here either).

One emerging strategy for limiting these defections is to reduce customer hassles by making it easier for customers to deal with your company. Customers want to complain; you should make it easy for them. Since call centers represent by far the largest customer touch-point, improving access to agents, information and support services to enable the customer complaint and its resolution.

The challenge is that the bar keeps getting raised in customer service by companies and enterprises that in the past would never have had an influence on your business. Disney is one of the best queue managers in the world. These are not the queues found in their call centers, but the queues for the rides found in their theme parks. In a direct or indirect fashion, the same intrinsic expectation for efficient queuing is applied to the call your customer makes to your call center. People do not compare you to other software, payroll, manufacturing or any type of company. They compare you to where they last got best-class service from such companies as FedEx, Fidelity, USAA, or Disney.

Customer expectations today are such that they want resolution the same day, not sometime. You can no longer tell people that you will look into it and get back to them in three or four days. Customers would laugh at you today for this type of perceived inefficiency. The customer and his time is emerging as the most significant criteria as to whether a customer does business with you or not.

For the past twenty years, delivering customer service by telephone has remained largely unchanged. While voice response technology has improved call centers by reducing live agent calls, its use has been limited to relatively simple transactions. In fact, call volumes are increasing and transactions handled by call center agents are becoming more complex because of the increased information that is available to callers through mediums such as the web and fax back. Longer and more complex transactions continue to require live agent assistance and the demand for live agents has continued to increase - which is different than the number of calls.

The average representative handled 45 fewer calls per week in 1997 than in 1996 (305 vs. 350), but the average call was more than a minute longer (6.26 vs. 5.14), said a poll by the Consumer Support Group. The percentage of calls resolved in the first contact remained at 76 percent and the percent of calls resolved on follow-up dropped one percentage point to 17 percent.

According to The Gartner Group prognostications, shortly after the year 2000, 35 percent of all commerce will be electronic. The ignored irony to this trumpeted expectation is that this still leaves 65 percent something else. For many, and for more time to come, the telephone, either through IVR or with an agent, will remain the more significant and the more preferred approach.

If you look at a typical customer service chain blueprint, there is an area that surrounds the call center customer service applications called the "customer access interface." Basically what the blueprint defines is that regardless of how the customer engages an application, be it an agent, the internet, IVR, telephone, fax or email, the result should be the same - but the result is rarely the same.

The reason that the verbal phone conversation will not go away any time soon is because the customer speaks volumes in every verbal way. The call center environment will remain the most cost effective way to gain insights about the customer's behaviors, emotions, motivations and how his needs and preferences are evolving over time. An IVR or a web page simply cannot accomplish this. When talking to an agent, what determines a customer's satisfaction level or excitement level of that call? The quality of the interaction can be, and often is, very subtle. There are just not many tools that can make a bad agent into a great agent. If you can drive agents up a couple of notches with the proper interaction systems and support systems, it is amazing how much impact you can have on the productivity of the call center and rate of customer satisfaction.

For this reason, moving customer knowledge closer to the customer - such as in the call center, through the use of scripts, cues, and prompts to help agents immediately recognize and then engage more profitable customers. This enables them to communicate more relevant messages and offers while they are on the phone. Effective communication will require accent-free speech patterns, a clear voice and a sense of enthusiasm. Customers are most satisfied by conversing with an agent who is able to carry on an intelligent conversation. Agents that are reticent, easily embarrassed or self conscious do not work very well. A technical support desk agent whose job it is to provide the soothing voice that gently leads confused troubled callers back to digital bliss of bits and bytes.

However, the pragmatic fact is that accomplishing customer intimacy is more difficult than it sounds. A singular problem is that, despite sophisticated database systems, few agents are adequately trained or motivated to make effective use of them, both in the retrieving and inputting. We are simply not capable, for a variety of reasons (that will eventually evolve away), of making other than a superficial use of the information and the raw data from agents' conversations with customers.

In one respect, our increasing dependence on technology for service, while beneficial in certain cases (i.e., bank account balance retrieval through an IVR), is contributing to the fact that agents have become the weakest link in delivering customer service and collecting customer data. They need to be the strongest.

Technology Agents and Influence

There is a Dutch call center - and they consider themselves a call center - that does nothing but answer email for their clients. Like the convoluted interpretation of the term "call center" (similar to "dialing" a telephone), today one can even ask, what is an agent?

Is an agent a live agent or is it a VRU port, or web application? Agents are lots of things today: video agents, software agents, voice response agents and so on. The availability of a variety of media today means that the enterprise has to deal with not only live agent queuing, but queuing with other media as well. There are various philosophies you can apply to queuing multimedia calls in a fashion similar to the queuing of voice calls. Unquestionably, the call center is really the environment that we have grown up with around deterministic rules governing voice calls (average speed to answer, average hold time, etc.). Increasingly, we will have to consider influencing any type of media with (or without) the same set of deterministic rules.

Bring in email, transfers from voice response, video kiosk calls, web transfers and voice calls as well - all now must follow similar deterministic rules. However, the conditioning factor here is economics.

Say a call center is paying $50k a year for an agent and that agent is conducting an internet style transaction. If I can move the customer onto an internet platform, that employee expense can be reduced. Without question, the internet transaction is cheaper than the voice model of transaction. Federal Express has discovered that it costs them $7 - $8 per telephone transaction, but only $2 per internet transaction. Not only do the numbers speak for themselves, but there is also a growing wealth of experience being garnered by consumers from their internet based service experiences. Compare trying to do a stock quote by IVR versus the internet. If an enterprise can move their business onto the internet then they can satisfy their customers with fewer precious resources. This is why many consider the internet as a "third paradigm."

"CTI will have an impact on the most valuable asset in any call center

- the agent. Today's technology is changing the way call centers are managed by providing a positive human impact to create a good first impression with customers." (Communication News, 1/95).

In a complete technology-based transaction environment, and assuming that things go right (the item is in stock), ideally a customer service person would rarely need to intervene. Guaranteed information accessibility is what technology provides, it is with the agents where personalization best occurs. The logical preference is to devote that agent's time to up-selling, dialoging and keeping customers than on performing speedy transactions, which is a data entry function at its core.

Technology based self service offers many benefits to both the enterprise and the customer. Technology has provided call centers with two different self-service tools. However, while the internet has several powerful advantages, not everyone has access to the internet. For a majority of the U.S. population, telephone based communications, including the rapidly growing segment of wireless and satellite mobile phones (multiplying to the tune of 35,000 new subscribers per day) is driving voice as the principle communicative medium for some time to come.

Today, unfortunately, helpful technology is running ahead of the ability of most people to use it. Customer service chain executives to this point have in fact acted somewhat irresponsibly in relying on technology to solve deeper problems. For decades companies have been devoting half of their capital to information technology - what do they really have to show for it? The design of call centers has been influenced by the failure of the simplistic assumption that improved information results in increased productivity. Worldwide, companies spend hundreds of millions of dollars annually on technology upgrades to existing systems, new electronic hardware and software, sales and lead tracking applications and various other technologies peripheral to the call center, but do we ask often enough how much is spent on the human resource side of the equation?

Electronic support offers no relief from the mandate of being sensitive to customer's needs. If you remove the option of live time support, you need to state response expectations up front. Here it means that you are proactive as opposed to being reactive and it means providing world class, best-of-breed type of service. It means that your enterprise is becoming totally customer centric.

Front-line service people are taking more calls as a result of technology and a single "point-of-service" contact person may need to access as many as 40 or more separate systems or applications. The biggest problem addressed by the emerging legions of front-office software is that the very legacy nature of incompatible data systems has prevented the enterprise from presenting a unified face to the customers. Software systems in particular can not talk to each other, so many enterprises see no way of commonly identifying a customer across different systems. It is with data-telephony or Computer Telephony Integration (CTI) that enterprises are striving to harmoniously consolidate all of their available disparate technologies. But it isn't happening as quickly as we would want to believe.

Dataquest found that, outside of IVR, less than ten percent of call centers have any CTI functionality installed - blaming the lack of integration on poor systems integration and support expertise by many vendors. Another statistic provided by Datamonitor indicated that, of the 60,000 to 90,000 call centers in the US, only 5 percent (3,000 to 4,500) actually use CTI applications other than a screen pop.

The unfortunate result is that the call center application and technology market has been growing at such a rapid rate that even crummy companies can survive. In the emerging age of customer centricism, the demand from the technology-based customer is masking the quality of the available technology to enable it. At some point, enterprises will have to reclaim dialogues with their customers, stop listening to market hype and hold vendors' feet to the fire. The fact is that most enterprises generally use technology in low-risk applications first because enterprises, unequivocally, have a significant tendency to avoid experimenting with their customers.

Successful information systems must focus more on customer relationships and interaction than on the information itself. Enterprises are catching on to the fact that it takes more than a slick router and a sensational server. If you think about what CTI does at its base level, it enables everything around a customer interaction up to and after (and sometimes in between, in terms of transferring), but ultimately it only enables a conversation to begin or happen. From that point on the customer cares little about what happens.

To enable the customer relationship side of the business equation, work-flow process applications are increasingly seeping into the call center environment. However, for now, companies are using these new applications for simple transaction tasks such as tracking customer interactions, and will adapt them later for tactical purposes, like measuring the results of different promotional campaigns or incentive structures. One of the keys here is how well your agent, whether it is a live agent or an automated one, can access the infrastructure of the enterprise to be able to intelligently deal with the customer.

After decades of investing in personal computers and software tools designed to maximize individual productivity, we are now turning to maximizing group or enterprise productivity. Front-office applications can be considered "top-line generators," meaning that they actually increase revenues by increasing agents' closure rates, improving customer retention and creating new sales opportunities.

The Measurements of Sweatshops

Though the danger of the accusation will increasingly become more acute, of enterprises course will deny that they run sweatshops; the agents in call centers fear that the measurement and metric function software found in call centers will evolve into total control made easy. Some of these monitoring tactics may seem to promote "big brother-ish" mentality from the perspective of the call center workforce. Graphical user interface, integrated forecasting, scheduling, daily management, long-term staff planning, team, agent analysis and database administration are all applications that envelope the agent's role.

Measuring in call centers will change. When you deal in the lifetime value of a customer, measurements of efficiencies in increments of seconds don't size up for the task. You can run reports and provide quantitative data, but the way something is said - what a customer emphasizes - can be more important.

As an example of the implementation of the "big-brother" technology, as call centers identify the traits and characteristics of a successful agent, enterprises will increasingly turn to high-tech evaluation and profiling prior to employment. In a fashion, a flight simulator for call center agents will emerge as a powerful tool. These tests evaluate the prospect and his ability to handle a healthy level of tension while learning to navigate difficult situations and avoid mistakes. The underlying theory is that if the prospective agent cannot handle the simulated call center environment he more than likely won't handle the real call center environment. This can help predict those agents most likely to be successful.

Designed to screen prospective call center agents against an existing "successful agent" standard, benchmarks have been developed by examining the qualities of proven and successful call center agents. These new applications send to an agent prospect several hours of carefully scripted computer-generated inbound telephone calls and as the simulated caller talks to the agent, the applicant responds. Each call is scored and compared to a statistical database profile of successful agents. The measurements include typing skills, listening ability and problem solving logic.

Another emerging "big-brother" call center tool is the use of workforce management. This is the ability to track agent adherence to an assigned schedule, historically or in real time. We are now precisely alerted when agents sign in late for their shifts, take unscheduled breaks, lengthen their breaks or spend too much time in after-call wrap up. Workforce management application's intention is to alert to deviations from schedule adherence and to resolve conflicts quickly.

But, while workforce management endeavors to keep customer calls from becoming backlogged and service from suffering, it may be measuring the wrong thing. It is easy to set impersonal service standards such as average speed of answer and average talk time. What will emerge to matter more may be the intangible and un-measurable human elements such as attitude, energy, enthusiasm and intelligence. Customers want to deal with people who are bright, perceptive and sympathetic and they care little if an agent is on time, took too long of a break or takes too long for an after-call wrap up.

This is not to say that workforce management software, applications and companies will go away, it's just that they (most appropriately) will evolve into being the most capable of creating the new measurements required in call centers to track the full extent of the customer's related work being performed, not just the number of telephone calls handled. New metrics of the information age will include, for example, the speed of writing, the emotional satisfaction of the customer or the speed of a response to an entire transaction. When new mediums for customer communication emerge such as video, equally unique and new metrics will arise as well, such as degree of tele-genics.

Not Just Techno-Stress for Management, But Agents as Well

While the advantages of enabling every agent with unlimited access to the entire corporate database (an embellished concept, granted) are attractive, its implementation leaves ample room for heroic failure. It is cliché, but technology and the information it enables are a double-edged sword. And, as much as this sword swings to one side as productivity, efficiency and enablement, it swings as clearly to the other of burnout, information glut and the trap of substituting activity for achievement.

Give agents a browser and they will browse. One of the consumptions of workload productivity of agents as they go "offline" to address these requests is costly and quality levels are difficult to monitor. The most difficult and time consuming issues are locating the customer information file, having to "hand-craft" individual replies and determining the optimal medium for service. Today people have to sift through massive amounts of data to find what's useful and meaningful to them. Never mind that much of the information is downright useless, peripheral or inaccurate.

The average American now receives 3,000 advertising message a day, up six-fold since the 1970's. Office workers today spend 60 percent of their time processing documents. A typical call center manager now reads one million words a week. Don't be misled by the notion that techno-stress results from the call center environment provided for call center agents. They are bringing this stress to work with them. The average agents today are not necessarily barraged by technology at work, they are barraged by technology outside of work.

There is a growing concern that the call center environments that we are proposing, enabling or may already have are contributing to already high levels of "techno-stress." Techno-stress is a very real condition that researchers define as the negative effect of technology on people's thoughts, attitudes and behavior of bodies. Techno-stress affects everyone to some extent because we all come into contact with televisions, ATMs, cellular phones, computers, internet, pagers, email and VCRs.

The danger of turning employees into information junkies is that one out of two people actually crave information and they experience a huge gratification when they find the information they seek. There are voice messages and fax messages but the internet has a true addiction to it, particularly on-line news feeds feeding America's fast-food mentality toward information. It is instantaneous gratification and it entices you to use it more often.

Information addiction clogs data pipes, slows down legitimate business access and works against call center and enterprise productivity. Data-holics. Information overload can reduce your attention span, disrupt your family life and impair judgement. Info-glut leads to boredom, stress, loss of sleep and loss of productivity. As call centers become a central indicator of the differences between the environments of gold-collar workers and white-collar slaves, one distinguishing characteristic will be increasing the availability advice for dataholics of cleansing data fasts and data naps - regular breaks away from exposure to information.

Who is this New Agent?

The Nintendo generation is entering the workforce, and they are coming to work in your enterprise's call center. This next generation of worker will transform the nature of the enterprise and the way that wealth is created as they create the new culture of work. The new generation has a level of technical savvy-ness and a thorough set of expectations and values that are quite a bit different than the traditional corporate and call center culture.

The call center and its derivatives, increasingly ill defined by the nomenclature today, represents one of several enterprise functions where we see the significant emergence of the gold-collar worker. What exactly is the "gold-collar" worker? (The term gold-collar worker was first advanced in 1985 in a book titled the same by Robert E. Kelly.) The gold-collar worker is fundamentally a new class of call center agent whose skills and knowledge will require enterprises, eventually, to pay them more than they pay their managers.

What will drive the emergence of the gold-collar worker is the fundamental tenet of economics; the availability or scarcity of resources. Increasingly we will see the intrinsic demands of agents becoming a strong bargaining point because of the demand for these skill sets. Combine the demand for skills (this is why skills-based routing was developed) with the ease of changing employers and the cost of replacing agents and you have a formula tilted to the agent's favor. Unhappy employees can switch companies more easily when the economy is doing well and replacing an agent costs one to one-and-a-half times the departed agent's annual salary.

An increasing number of skills will be required by agents, many related to the internet medium, and finding experienced, trained agents will become more difficult. The more complex the transactions, increasingly found in today's world where customers are increasingly knowledge-ified, the skill sets of agents are not so easily homogenized. In fact, the enterprise must be careful that they do not hire computer geeks with the right skills but the wrong disposition.

They have an ease with technology; digital tools spell trouble with the traditional enterprise and the traditional manager. This generation will create huge pressures for radical changes in existing companies.

The pool from which we will increasingly be pulling our agent resources from is from the so-called "Generation X-ers.

Generation X is considered to be those born between 1965 and 1976.

They are the first generation to have grown up with the technologies of information and they have learned to communicate far differently from any preceding generation. Generation X is the first generation, as author Don Tapscott says, "bathed in bits" and that "for the first time ever children are the authority on an issue of importance to society - technology."

Effective management of the gold-collar agents will rely on subtleties, adeptness and deftness to a degree never employed before. Understanding these agents' important issues is the key to avoiding the stinging brand of "white-collar sweatshop."

The decade of downsizing and right-sizing has definitely seen a drop in employee loyalty from where the company came first. Now it is the family; my own personal desires are all taking much more influential positions that say that the employee no longer thinks of himself as a company man as in the past. It is the changing fundamental economics of business that are changing the employee's desire for a higher quality of lifestyle, because this is a higher priority than it has been in the past.

Talented Generation X-ers want no part of companies that deliver conformity, rank and overly controlling practices requiring dress, travel, hours and office recreation, but promise an exciting career with plenty of educational opportunities.

They have a very strong sense of social responsibility and they care about the collective, but they have a strong sense of entrepreneurial risk. Many recent generations of workers have a very deep social sense; their causes include support of education, environmental issues and a belief that technology can solve many human problems. They will demand time for private projects and renewal.

This generation is exceptionally curious, self-reliant, contrarian, smart, focused, able to adapt, high in self esteem, and posseses a global orientation. They are more technically literate but with shorter attention spans. Generation X-ers prefer information that is concrete, concise and to the point.

There is a clear connection between the attitude of it reps, the quality of their performance and the amount of information they gather. Forty to fifty percent of the success of the call center is in the attitude of the agents. The skills needed are not just creative brilliance or intelligence, but also require a certain attitude. An increasing characteristic of success-ful call center managers and customer service chain executives will be a trait (again framed by Watts Wacker) of intelligent disobedience. Intelligent disobedience is what seeing eye dogs are taught, essentially that they are to obey unless they have a better idea. The act of intelligent disobedience allowing the agents greater decisions making discretion's. Disruptive people are an asset.

There is great value in agents that rely on their seat-of-the-pants impressions of customers (just like the old corner grocer used to) with no hard data to back up their intuition. As the actual dialogues and the preference and needs nuggets they reveal become increasingly important, accurate subjective observations with customers become a critical skill (How else can an enterprise identify and measure a mean customer, for example?).

Today, call center agents are employed based on their verbal talents for customer service and subject matter experience. Increasingly we can expect agents to have internet skills, writing skills, navigating web-sites and experience with computer supported environments.

One of the surprising results of the information age is the momentum that has turned back to the written word. Demand for agent's skills and competencies will continue to evolve, especially writing skills. Writing will become increasingly important, specifically with customer communication. Finding agents that perform well on the telephone and can perform well electronically means that basic skills cannot be taken for granted. In electronic environments, writing skills are much more necessary than talking and articulation. The fact is that good talkers may not be able to develop the succinct summaries and concise statements required when building net-based knowledge bases and customer relationships.

There is real advantage in being able to craft precise written communication. Technology may enable an agent (or his manager) to write and distribute an email very quickly, but it doesn't help much in what to write or how to say it. The problem with the too technical person is with how they communicate. A agent's skill may well be in overusing technical or clinical terms such as, "dollars-per-kilobit-per-second" or "average speed per answer" as opposed to revenue, competitive advantage and lifetime value terms more familiar to his peers. In the technical support environments in particular, agents may be one-hundred percent buzz-word compliant, but need a greater characteristic of not needing to demonstrate it.

I can attest to the conversation with a retail catalog agent who, at the conclusion of my call, asked me if the "n" in Anderson was "n" as in knife! A call center manager colleague of mine also related a story, still used for training purposes, about an agent who asked a customer if, "that's 'q' as in cucumber". Basic writing skills are critical.

Finding the Right Agent in the First Place

One of the meta-trends of the information age that will have a significant impact on call centers is the decentralization of location. Agents, in a few short years, will be engaging customers from the mountains, beaches or even in space. Companies now are beginning to understand that they have to broaden their reach to these virtual resources because the people are out in the countryside now. Technology isn't just making for virtual customers' it's creating virtual employees as well.

In the enterprise we should define virtual as being two things, one being the non-living agent application (not discussed here) and the other virtual implies that there is an organic being located somewhere other than a centralized call center (or highly networked for that matter). One form of virtual is an agent working from home. The next generation won't be bounded by brick and mortar, it will be virtual. The agents can be working from home, they can be telecommuting and they can be working from anywhere.

Also, agent turnover is at an eight year high and the cost of replacing a good employee ranges from one-half to several times a year's pay, depending on the job. Some suggest that high turnover in the industry is skewed by the high concentration of call centers (Omaha, Phoenix, San Antonio) because they poach each other's staff. But handing out raises is costly and works less and less with today's increasingly diverse, life-style conscious work force.

High turnover, wage competition and guarding against natural disasters and network failures are just a few of many influences causing companies to scatter call centers all over the country. But significant also are employee desires for remote connectivity. The Nintendo generation is beginning to realize that they don't have to go to the company, the company will come to them.

The fact is that, although the labor pool and the cost of living may be terrific in Sioux Falls Idaho, there is just not the type of, for example, Java windows NT resources an enterprise may need. The fact is that these very same enterprises can't afford these same resources when they live in a Silicon Valley or the Massachusetts Route 128 high tech belt. In the technical support area particularly there are areas that have the resources available like may have to draw on to serve your customers you have to find those people and contract them where ever they are. Agents do not want to move and they do not want to change an established quality of life where they are, so the enterprise has got to figure out how to secure that resource without having that resource on site, in a chair or desk at its location.

In the old industrial age model, if you wanted a job you had to move to Pittsburgh because that was where the steel plant was. Today, in the information age, we have built interstates and superhighways and the tables have turned. Now enterprises must go to you to have you as the resource. The company needs these employees now, more than ever. This explains why regions in Texas, Oregon and Wisconsin are fast becoming growth Meccas. Employees are finding that they do not want to compromise the quality of life available there and this is what these resources are looking for. They know that they can become telecommuters and they can still find work and be productive employees, making a good living by living somewhere that is very comfortable for them.

Striving to boost productivity, companies have spent billions of dollars on information technology, but as the asset base of many companies shifts from factories to talent, attracting, motivating and retaining quality employees at every level becomes not just a vague slogan but now a matter of survival. But for now, many of these new high tech tools are often left idle by a very old fashioned labor shortage.

In fact, there is a growing, not declining, dangerous shortage of talented people who can fulfill the enterprise's mission. For the immediate future, agents who know your business and can handle customers appropriately will be harder and harder to find. Labor resources will increasingly become scarcer. This critical trend intersecting the critical shortage of information technology workers is entering a new phase. This labor shortage is no longer just an inconvenience for businesses anymore. The shortage is having an obvious bottom line effect on companies particularly in technology businesses.

One of the emerging challenges for call centers will be in finding labor markets that can support the call center. The number one criteria for site selection today is labor demographics (followed by space availability, telecommunications, infrastructure and tax climate). Other factors such as weather conditions and economic development incentives also weigh in on the formula.

Enterprises are finding that they are having to move their operations to more resource available areas, particularly companies that have traditionally been based in the downtown areas of major cities.

Increasingly, these companies are concluding that they are not in the train business, or the people moving business. They are moving to where taxes are cheap, there are incentives to develop in other areas and these central locations do not have to support a large labor force.

Ultimately the call center labor supply will catch up with demand. The nurses' shortage of the 1980's, for example, has turned into a glut.

From a management perspective, one of the unspoken threats to the efficiency of call centers will arise, slowly and unsuspecting at first, of organized agent unions. Losing political weight in the realm of industry, organization activity of the information workers will increase under the aegis of guarding against the exploitation of "workers" in the white-collar sweatshops.

To preempt this trend, one of the best propositions emerging from the call center industry in the past years was the idea of an industry certification initiative. Many of us, vendor and end user alike, recognize the benefits of having a standard industry professional certification, both for managers and agents. Many of us agree that this would go a long way to transforming what we do from being just a job, to being a profession. In this initiative would be the type of evolutionary protections against the fears of call centers becoming, or being identified as the poster environments of information factories.

To Train

Many methods have been devised to minimize turnover in call centers, ensure that the workforce is happy, motivated and has plenty of incentives. One of the prevailing characteristics of the Generation X-ers is their desire to learn (although you may not be able to tell it from their school grades). Continual education will be one of the most significant incentives for attracting and retaining the knowledge workers of the information age. The new agents of today need to be trained because that is what they want. Improve workforce skills by investing in training agents on how to make the best use of the technologies at their disposal.

One effective training trend of enterprise is to "cross-functionalize" their employees from one department to another. In the telecommunications business, for example, one of the reasons that service from the RBOCs is so poor is because their agents often don't understand their own business. In these environments (where customer loyalty is different than no choice), all agents know is how to follow scripts.

The definition of "knowledge worker" must expand to include agents that clearly understand their own business and that they can answer more questions about their business and give the customers a better feel for the competencies, services and products in the enterprises. To accomplish this, for example, it will become entirely appropriate to have those working in accounting participate regularly in customer calls. For that matter, perhaps we should encourage the CEO and other executive officers to participate as well. Let them take a call from a customer and see how difficult it is to collect a payable or resolve a technical issue.

For "cross-functionalization" to be effective, call center management must constantly find ways to expose agents to the rest of the organization – and the rest of the enterprise to the agents. There are effective benefits to be gained from interaction through boards, groups, committees and teams where the call center is represented. Referring to the educational desires of Generation X above, the desire for education extends to the benefit of working with other smart peers, teams and leaders. To this end, one of the emerging roles of call center managers will be the ability to create highly collaborative environments.

Beware, like substituting activity for achievement and paving the cow path, teamwork isn't always good. The danger in cross-enterprise fertilization is that it often spares the feelings of those who make peace with shoddiness and imperfection. The last place that an enterprise wants institutionalized poor quality is with the enterprise's relationships with customers. If an agent has learned that it is acceptable to stonewall an enterprise's vendor on an account receivable, then the influence may extend to not aggressively resolve a customer's problem.

Related to this is the overwhelming simplicity of believing, in error, that an enterprise can throw hardware and software (workforce management and schedule adherence being two) at call center problems. The management of call centers will require a more holistic approach. If human resources, product development and IS are not involved in the day to day operations of the call center, somebody ought to lose their job.

Turnover in call centers is high. It's tough being nice day in and day out for weeks, months and quarters at a time. (Teach that to the CEO.) What if they are treated poorly by supervisors or looked down on for doing "phone work"? The most significant hit to morale is when the agent realizes that there is no true career path at the company.

In pursuit of good agents, most enterprises paint positive, glowing pictures of the jobs they are seeking to fill. Many agents start off with high expectations about their opportunities with the enterprise such as expectations of, "you will double your salary in six months, you'll move up to supervisor and you will rarely have to work weekends." Ohio State University Psychologist John Wanous has discovered that enterprises can actually reduce turnover by lowering the expectations of new employees.

He found that using realism can reduce turnover by as much as ten percent. In his studies he discovered that after one year of employment, fully one-third (33 percent) of employees who had been optimistic about their opportunities had moved on to other jobs. This is compared to the one-sixth (16 percent) of those who got cold-water treatment before or right after their employment, that had left their jobs.

Knowledge Managers or Slave Tenders

Although the provacativness of characterizing call center agents as "white-collar slaves" is an intentional embellishment, this unsettling possibility can only be enabled by the future managers of call centers. It is the characterizations of these managers that attention will now be turned to.

If, and when, the call center gains the recognition as the only source of raw, pure and true information regarding how customers' needs and preferences are evolving over time, the role of the customer service chain executive will change significantly. Forward thinking organizations will reconsider and rethink the call center manager role in the context of being "knowledge officers," which has a far broader scope than the view of the traditional ACD, human resource and network manager prevalent today.

Broadening your skill sets and technology application experience will be the only way to insure job stability. The model of the next generation call center executive includes fundamental proficiency with new media all day long to communicate internally and externally to the company. If you and your agents need to know how to write, consider the demands executives will face.

The new customer service chain executives and managers will build their enterprises based heavily on internetworking; striving to create a real time company from real time customer information appropriate for an economy that's becoming increasingly real time. The newer media enables the creation of a flatter, more open company and an enterprise culture that is rapidly responsive. The successful call center managers will be considered experts at creating great value from information flow and we will see their compensation equal the most senior managers, directors and executives.

The executive that replaces today's call center manager will have strong business process knowledge and an ability to think beyond the technology to understand the business issues. Their responsibilities will be defined to include the implementation of strategic plans to leverage information technology to support business goals and not defined by metrics such as average speed of answer or average wrap-up time.

Breaking with the generally unacknowledged job safety found in being the only person who knows how to program the ACD or manipulate workforce management applications, the enterprise will recognize that it no longer has use for or the need for information overlords; rather they are looking for managers who have the combined interest and expertise in technology with powerful leadership skills, real business empathy and an intense ability to listen. An increasingly important skill in the call center manager's portfolio will be something akin to industrial psychology.

Smart call center managers know, for example, that the best ideas, concepts and constructs originate from the floor - from the agents themselves. In fact, astute managers realize that suggestions from agents should be the most valued because they know that the agent is the one with the closest contact with the customer and has the best, if not the only, opportunity to improve customer relationships.

Call centers will no longer be managed, they will be led. The highly paid call center manager will be the one who has developed the personal ability to build call centers, sell them and support them while sorting through a sizable number of problems, every one of which is influenced by the challenges of corporate culture (read: politics). This new breed of manager must be capable of successfully executing against a corporate strategy with a strong end user service orientation and have the proven capability to extend the customer service infrastructure to support every other part of the enterprise - both internal and external.

On the technical side of the equation, a side that most managers still must become proficient at, the new role will include being a system integrator. Instead of assembling components as an expertise, call center executives will become portfolio assemblers, pre-selecting and assembling multi-vendor solutions and then supporting those solutions. The trend that enables the call center managers is the evolution from managers of the bits and bytes of data to custodians of the most significant wellspring of enterprise knowledge.

To adapt to the needs and demands of the emerging generation of agents, customer relationship executives' new challenge will be to put into place the networks that manage the output of these agents; they, in fact, will be managing the processes and not the employees. It will be management by influence and not by direction. These executives no longer will "manage" people, they will lead them. The way one maximizes their performance will be by capitalizing on their strengths, experience and their knowledge, rather than trying to force them into molds.

According to Peter Drucker, what will motivate call center agents and the knowledge workers of the future will be the same thing that motivates volunteers. "Volunteers must get more satisfaction from their work than paid employees precisely because they do not get a paycheck. They work for challenge. They need to know the organization's mission and to believe in it. They need continuous training. They need to see results." If managers have done a good job of communicating the enterprise's mission and firmly believe in every agent's ability to participate and contribute to accomplishing the mission, they are well under way to being as evolved as the agents they manage.

One of the most significant (and appropriate) trends in call centers is to make agents responsible for their own training and development. This can manifest itself in many ways, but at a high level the best call centers identify and communicate growth opportunities to their agents and personalize growth plans. Then they encourage agents to be proactive in achieving their own growth plans. Imagine a call center where agents crave being monitored for their own personal achievement, not for conformity's sake.

Conclusion

More enterprises than not spend a lot of money on recruiting, training and nourishing agents only to place them in environments where they burn out quickly. This dramatically contradicts a new model focused on the agent as a more important piece of the call center than has been traditionally emphasized in the past. The technical intimacy approach to customer-centrisim means that there has to be a fundamental call center change, in fact an enterprise-wide change, in institutionally embedded behavior. You are either contributing or complaining.

In defining what the call center of the future will look like, Kelly Conway, the Chief Executive of the call center consulting firm, Technology Solutions Company, envisioned that, "Agents will find themselves called upon to handle a wider mix of transactions, complaints, service call management, marketing and even public relations tasks. Moreover a work day, which was largely routine will take on a much larger degree of 'emotional labor' typical of this kind of intensive customer contact, the work day will typically become either more exhausting, more exhilarating or both. Most call center will find themselves formulating changes in business rules and processes that allow them more discretion in customer interaction and also will involve more gray areas and greater risks."

Good service is just solving a problem – delivering what people expect to receive. Great service is getting below the surface of the problem and delivering what no one expects to receive. Every problem is different, every call is different. The enterprise can not prepare scripts to cover every situation, let alone every personality on the other end of the line.

The preferred skills of the new generation of agent will be with listening, learning, assessing and refining. Ultimately, great service requires sound judgements from the agents on the front lines. The only way to get better at answering customer calls is to get better at making judgement calls. Good judgement starts with deep knowledge, training. Great service is an art; a good call is subjective - literally a judgement call.

Successful enterprises today must recognize that customers are assets to be managed with a superior service bias. This bias will lead to greater retention and those retained customers will generate more revenues, at lower costs, than new customers will.

Knowledge may be power, but communication skills are the raw transport of the information age. Not being able to speak the language of the business is critical, as will be being able to understand the business issues and the role of the call center and the efficient use of technology tools as it becomes available.

It is important to understand that, for the gold-collar concept to be accepted, customer service chain executives must first convince themselves, their executives and ultimately their customers that it is with the agent that the most significant gains in call center efficiencies can be obtained. Imagine a customer base that has no concept or need to demand to speak to a supervisor because of an unsatisfactory contact.

While the trend has started to change recently, at least at a superficial executive discussion level, most customer service technologists tend to neglect the agent as a crucial and strategic piece of the customer technology picture. It is just easier to know how to program switches than to manage people.

It is in the technology of "humanware," the agents and customer service representatives, that customer loyalty battles will be won. The gold-collar worker is a new breed of articulate, educated, and responsible "agent." The role of management will be in enabling the remote environments they will work from, and the technologies that will empower them to be more effective and efficient. Their lifestyle demands are not the same as the demands of the executives that manage them and great skill will be required to reconcile these differing expectations. Balance will have to be struck between "over-enabling" critical service agents who are simply not prepared to use or take advantage of the expensive information technology resources at their disposal.

In conclusion it will, in all hope, be important to share a perspective contrary to the prevailing hype about the technical evolution of call centers.

The contrast between the white-collar sweatshop and the gold-collar worker represents a new concept in customer, employee and executive interaction - a philosophical change associated with the underutilized and underestimated intellectual resources available in the call center.

The intellectual application of the information available at the moment the enterprise is engaged with their customer, regardless of the medium, requires a new way of thinking. Information is the spoils of discovery. Where else can this discovery take place than at the moment of customer engagement and who else can enable this than the call center agent?

There is an African proverb that says, "If you know your history, the future will not trouble you." Changes from the discoveries of science, geography and customer service have required new tools, new technologies and new ways of thinking. Those customer service chain executives who anticipate and understand the fundamental nature of the changes ahead and actively reshape their business models to meet these inevitable changes will be best placed to exploit these opportunities. Those that do not will face a difficult transition from the legacies of the past to the intimate realities of the future.

The emerging technologies of customer service can support the sophisticated processes that in turn support enterprise strategies. But, fundamentally, customer service chain executives and leaders will have to make the key decisions that will shape the nature of their operations – information sweatshop or liberating opportunity.

The big returns are yet to come for those enterprises that learn to use agents - associates - as strategic tools. The enterprise may have the most current of the service technologies and its executives may be the most proficient in its implementation, but, as Nadji Tehrani succinctly says, "Treat good people well and they'll make your technology hum and sizzle like it was meant to. You'll be rewarded by outstanding revenue and enjoy a leadership role in your industry."

The fundamental determination of whether your enterprise is running a white-collar sweatshop or liberating gold-collar workers occurs at every moment that any agent (or manager) asks himself the question, "Am I a human being or a human doing?"

Don't negate the importance of technology, but also don't negate the importance of people. If there is one message about the strategic role of the call center in the enterprise's future, it is to look beyond the current technology based trends and select a long term strategy that views people, human resources, as the primary source of enterprise value. Only then can the enterprise evolve, adapt and change to embrace the new generation of knowledg-ified workers, their ideas, and their different view of work and working.

Chapter Seven
E-business and Customer Relationship Management

Introduction

According to Credit Suisse First Boston, there are about 7,100 new web sites created everyday. Every seven seconds someone in America turns fifty. Every four seconds someone creates and posts a new web site. Connect those trends! IDC estimates that two- thirds of the people, who will be on-line by 2002, are not yet. This year the worldwide number of internet users is expected to rise 28 percent to 147 million. On-line consumer spending in 1999 was $20 billion and by 2004 is project to be $184 billion. Business to business e-commerce in 1999 is $109 billion but will grow to $1.3 trillion by 2003, according to Forrester Research Inc. Andersen Consulting estimates that by 2007, from 8 to 12 percent of all package goods such as household products and groceries will be sold on the internet. This is a market of $60 billion to $85 billion! The world of e-commerce and e-business is in an evolutionary (or maybe revolutionary) learning mode, and while traditional customer telephone interactions won't disappear, they are certainly being supplemented or slowly supplanted by internet-based multimedia communications alterna- tives. The problem is that no one really knows exactly what the "customer" will do or expect in the new communications environment of the internet and information channels of the world wide web. Every consulting group in the world is doing market research to try to uncover the new truths and statistics to guide enterprise management on how to strategically exploit every new feature and function of multi-channel information and contact access.

The new communication technologies, particularly those associated with the internet and the world wide web, are not only changing how we make contact and exchange information, but are also dramatically changing the way we do business. While traditional enterprise customer care objectives for attracting, keeping and exploiting customers remain fundamentally the same for the successful growth of any business, the customer environments, needs and expectations, enterprise infrastructures, communication channels, tools, methodologies and metrics of evaluating operational effectiveness are all in the process of drastic change.

"Customer Relationship Management" (CRM) has become a catch-all buzzword that means different things to different people; sometimes referring to enterprise responsibilities for maximizing new sales opportunities, other times pertaining to keeping existing customers happy and "loyal" for future revenue generation. Since we now know about the Pareto customer, i.e., the relatively smaller percentage of "high value" customers that generate most of the revenue and profits, CRM can also include effectively differentiating the priorities and service levels for those more profitable customers from the rest of the customer population. Whatever the benefits to the enterprise, CRM is a set of policies and concepts—not a technology per se—that guides the enterprise in its day-to-day dealings with all types of customers in order to preserve or change the existing bond with such customers. These policies and concepts must be defined, then implemented and supported by computer and communication technology infrastructures, software tools and operational procedures. In the legacy technology environment of traditional telephone call centers, the opportunity to exercise CRM policies on a dynamic, realtime basis, was extremely limited, because ACD switches had virtually no database facilities, let alone built-in application smarts for "intelligent" call handling. They performed call control "functions," rather than "applications." It was only with the evolution of computer telephony, CTI and now, converged voice and data technologies, that CRM policies could start being exercised effectively and efficiently.

The overall CRM market will grow from approximately $2.55 billion in 1999 to $7.53 billion in 2003. This is the prediction made in the Yankee Group's July, 1999 report, CRM Megatrends. The CRM industry will reach $3.7 billion in revenue this year, a 60 percent increase from 1998. Growth is expected to continue at a rate of 49 percent to reach $16.8 billion by 2003, according to AMR Research in Boston.

Both technology providers and consultants in the call center industry have been using "CRM" to brand the latest technology products and services that can help an enterprise compete for business in the new millenium of e-commerce over the internet. In this context, new variables in the customer relationship model have surfaced, particularly with the new modes of self service information and transaction access and the new channels and media for two-way contact between the customer and the enterprise support staff. However, the availability of these new functional alternatives means that they have to be properly packaged within the context of the enterprise infrastructure and operational applications, along with the tools for measuring and managing their effectivity.

While all the functional elements of enterprise technology infrastructures are indeed important prerequisites for the implementation of CRM policies, i.e., the "front office" and "back office" software applications, the enterprise-wide database servers, and the internet Protocol (IP) network connections that provide universal access to information and people, etc., the most sensitive and perhaps most critical component will always be the software that directly controls and monitors the real world interface and interactions, the "touchpoints," with the customer. These touchpoints include:

Directional
- Contacts from the customer
- Contacts to the customer - solicited and unsolicited

Medium
- Face-to-face contacts
- Telephone voice contacts
- Email contacts
- Voicemail contacts
- Fax contacts
- Video contacts
- Web contacts

Purpose
- General information requests
- Transaction status inquiries
- Purchasing product/service assistance
- Customer problem resolution
- Proactive telesales
- Customer survey data collection
- General assistance

Customer Contact State*
- Waiting for access to enterprise

- Waiting for live connection
- Connected to live person
- Connected with enterprise automated function/application/messaging facility
- Waiting for response to a message request (message, callback, problem resolution)
- Not expecting any contact from the enterprise

   * The customer will be very sensitive to how his/her personal needs and expectations are met during these different contact states with enterprise touchpoints.

Touchpoint software is critical because it directly controls and can also capture what actually happens in the customer contact experience, including what the customer does, sees or hears, and the sequence of events in the logic flow of a customer interaction. Even when live assistance is involved to control the interface with the customer, there will still be touchpoint software in the form of programmed interaction guides and scripts for the customer support representative to ensure consistency in dealing effectively with customers. However, touchpoint software must also be responsible for the management tools to directly measure and evaluate the usage, procedure design and performance of every touchpoint process. "You can't manage what you can't measure," and CRM is no exception.

For most businesses, the importance of CRM is most directly tied to the elements of the "customer relationship chain," which includes:

- Customer satisfaction (or dissatisfaction)
- Customer loyalty
- Customer retention
- Customer value/profitability improvement

The ripple effect from customer satisfaction or dissatisfaction upon customer loyalty, retention and increased value highlights the critical role that customer contact/interaction touchpoints will have upon the enterprise customer. It is at these touchpoints that every enterprise is always vulnerable to the possible loss of a customer to easily accessible competition, along with related revenues and profits. While a comprehensive information and communication infrastructure is obviously necessary for CRM functions, it is not, however, sufficient for "intelligent," tactical management of enterprise resources at the customer touchpoints.

It is unfortunate that technology providers have a tendency to label their products and services with the latest buzzword acronyms, which may be confusing, misleading, and not functionally descriptive or accurate. We hear all kinds of technology being referred to as "CRM" products, implying that just by installing such software—voilà—you have "CRM"! The truth is that there is a lot more to implementing CRM policies than simply buying new technology and relabeling old functions with new names.

Reviewing Key CRM Concepts and Objectives

Depending on what you have read lately or which expert you have listened to, you will get different views of what "CRM" really is all about. Some people think it concerns new ways of advertising and doing business on the web. Others think its aim is to increase cost effective self service facilities for sales and customer support. Then there are those who like the idea of using live support staff to generate more revenue by "up-selling" and "cross-selling" new prospects and customers. Those are just some management perspectives for using technology that supports "CRM," and they are all right; it can be all of the above, depending upon the nature of the business and the type of customers involved. However, it may be more useful to first identify the characteristics and expected functional benefits that CRM facilities can offer before examining how the technologies can deliver such capability and how to implement them within a particular enterprise operational environment.

Satisfying the Customer—Selectively!

No matter which implementation approach is used, most everyone agrees that a key objective is "customer satisfaction" in dealing with a product or service provider. But that is a relative term that is different for various kinds of products and services, and also changes with the circumstances and needs of individual customers. It is different for a consumer sales situation, where the customer prospect needs purchasing advice to qualify his decision to buy something, as opposed to customer service, where the customer has a problem that needs to be corrected or a request that needs to be approved. In business-to-business commerce, there are numerous questions and issues that have to be resolved with different individuals within both the buying and selling organizations, and their resolution must be highly coordinated on both sides.

The starting point for "customer satisfaction" is often described as being achieved through fast, convenient access to enterprise information and people, timely enterprise responsiveness for resolution of customer problems and maintaining the interaction with the customer on an individual, personalized basis. Obviously, this means a basic requirement for an effective enterprise infrastructure, both organizationally as well as informational, to support these objectives. It is impossible, however, to always satisfy every customer expectation and still remain in business, so the pursuit of customer satisfaction must be tempered with "reasonableness" from the customer's perspective as a framework for enterprise customer support. What will be acceptable to the customer when his expectations cannot be met immediately? There is no pat answer for every situation and this is where CRM principles have to provide practical, dynamic guidelines for every customer touchpoint, and where the appropriate technology tools will enable those principles to be realized and controlled effectively by enterprise management.

Insight: Have you noticed that most people will have a fairly reasonable appreciation of the time associated with various kinds of efforts, e.g., how long it will take to customize something, how long it will take to deliver something, even how long it will take to find the right person to solve a problem? However, when it comes to being able to communicate directly with someone by telephone, they have very little patience. Whether the phone is always busy, or the phone rings unanswered, or they always reach an answering machine or voicemail, everyone's patience quickly wears thin. With voicemail and email, there is a similar expectation, where a "reasonable" response is expected by the next day. When these limits are exceeded, there is either a feeling of being personally ignored, or that the contacted parties are just not businesslike or responsive. In either case, the incident can be damaging to any relationship.

Enterprise-wide Consistency in Dealing With a Customer

A major source of delays and frustration experienced by customers is when different people or departments of the provider organization are not working with the same, up-to-date information. Such inconsistencies can show up in the following areas:

- General information
- Policies and rules
- Customer-related information and status
- Customer contact history data

Once the enterprise gets out of sync with the customer, confusion, extra time or effort and, worst of all, doubt and loss of trust can set in. In terms of customer contact and interaction, getting out of step with the customer means that the customer will have to explain things again and wait for information to be re-confirmed. The bottom line is that problem resolution takes longer and generates an annoying image of a poorly run, incompetent organization where the left hand and the right hand don't know what the other is doing. It is that kind of image or impression that creates dissatisfaction and triggers deterioration in loyalty, even though the business's product or service is satisfactory. It's not only a matter of maintaining an image of competency by the enterprise staff, but also doing the same for enterprise technology infrastructures that are involved. This is especially important when self service touchpoints for the customer are involved; no one likes dealing with dumb people or dumb systems. Both of these considerations are mainstays for establishing and maintaining trust in the enterprise organization as a whole, but particularly in the top management that is ultimately responsible for the actions of both individual employees and the technology being used. Think of technology tools as if they were human staff members of the organization. Like any new employee, they have be carefully selected, then trained (programmed), supervised, evaluated, given refresher courses (modified, upgraded), etc. to perform their ongoing and evolving responsibilities properly. When it comes to dealing directly with the customer, CRM principles demand that consistency be at the top of list, whether in employee procedures, technology application interfaces, or the thing they both must share in common— information about the customer.

Consolidated Customer Activity Information for the Touchpoints

Although customer information in database files has traditionally been relatively high level in terms of items like basic contact information, credit standing and product/service configuration status, there are now opportunities to go to a micro level of detail about relationship activity on the part of the customer, but on a more dynamic basis. The biggest potential source of "intelligence" for effectively supporting customer needs is in capturing and having immediate access to all relevant information about a customer for referencing during any "front-office" contact interaction or application process. Such consolidation can be accomplished through effective network access of information collected in various databases. One of the capabilities that e-commerce has enabled is the capture of new touchpoint communications and information access activities, including "mouseclick trails" that can provide detailed history and context information for more effective and personalized customer support in the future. These data not only let you know what the customer has done lately that will be most pertinent to the current contact/interaction, but with appropriate data mining tools and experienced insight, can help the enterprise to understand the customer's pattern of contact behavior and profile his needs and preferences.

Such consolidation of all customer interaction information will help bridge the critical gap between sales and service responsibilities within the organization; that is the essence of CRM objectives. Once an initial sale creates a new customer, the customer will always be a candidate for further sales, whether to solve a service problem or to satisfy a new customer need. The typical customer will be on the defensive when subjected to any kind of sales pitch, but on the offensive when service and support seems necessary. CRM policies are designed to effectively support and control the transition of the customer between these two mindsets and the enterprise technology infrastructure for activity data collection and retrieval technology for the touchpoints will be most important to personalizing all types of customer interactions.

Personalization of Customer Interfaces, Preferences and Priorities

The consolidation of customer information mentioned above will enable the personalization of customer interactions and contacts, based upon activity profiles and/or individual preferences. This benefit can be applied in a variety of ways, including "intelligent" call/message routing priorities and the selective exploitation of personalized automated self service functions for telephone (IVR) and web screen interfaces, as well as in application scripts displayed to Customer Support Representatives. Personalization increases both customer satisfaction and operational staff efficiency by providing immediate "intelligent recognition" of the customer and eliminating unnecessary or unwanted interactions. The positive, but subtle impact of personalization upon the customer is the feeling that the enterprise knows and fully understands all the necessary details of his/her needs and can therefore be relied upon to take care of the problem quickly. The reverse will also be true; if the support person or automated process doesn't recognize who you are, you get the queasy feeling that it will take a while to get things straightened out.

Flexible, Cross-media Accessibility and Communications

Nielsen Media Research report that during the past six months American households have come on-line at a rate of 550,000 per month, which is 18,000 per day and 760 per hour. The most popularized characterization of CRM associated with traditional call center operations is expanding its role in multi-channel communications between the customer and the enterprise beyond the traditional mail or telephone contact. This expansion includes messaging exchanges, both text, voice and fax, as well as telephone callbacks in response to messages. However, it's not just the new media alternatives that are significantly changing, but also the context of such communications, i.e., the information environment in which customer contacts will be initiated. Just because a customer is sitting down at a computer terminal while connected to the web in "typing mode," doesn't necessarily mean that text messaging is necessary or even desirable as a means of personal contact and interaction with live assistance. By the same token, just because a voice message is left, doesn't mean that the response has to be voice based (call back, voice message). Amazon.com recently announced that it will make customer access to its web site information convenient for wireless devices and wireless screenphones with browser interfaces will be good candidates for a practical mix of voice/screen input and output. What is really significant about e-commerce is that customers will be increasingly aware of new communication options—the best that technology can provide—and will have greater expectations for exploiting those options selectively, according to their personal needs, preferences, or circumstances. That means that the bar will be raised for every enterprise, particularly if involved with e-commerce, to support most of the logical communications alternatives for two-way customer interactions with the enterprise and vice versa. This doesn't necessarily mean supporting every single methodology, but the spectrum of realistic customer needs must always be covered.

Fortunately, the user interface for web applications can control the options made available to the customer, selectively directing customers in the direction preferred by management. Only what the customer is offered on the screen is what can be used. However, the lack of convenient contact access through the web could result in customers reverting quickly to familiar telephone access, generating more rather than less traffic for interaction center staff. If such convenient telephone access is not provided as an "escape hatch," dissatisfaction can quickly result.

A recent call to an airline's frequent flyer telephone number offered limited access to live assistance for certain kinds of information about applying for membership. Instead, the option was offered to mail or fax an address to which an application could be sent. A third option, i.e., to leave the address information was also offered, with the caveat that "voice messages will be automatically processed last" by the airline's staff, only "after faxes and letters are processed." Clearly, the most convenient option for the customer was given short shrift in favor of what was practical for the airline. As a consequence, customers who were not direly in need of such information might simply hang up. Checking the airline's web site wasn't much help either, since they did not offer online application forms. Is that a way to run an airline?

Increasing Customer Value

One of the major payoffs touted for using new technologies for CRM benefits is the opportunity to sell an existing customer something else, either up-selling or cross-selling. This may be done at the time of a customer-initiated contact for sales or service assistance or as part of a proactive sales campaign based upon mining comprehensive customer data. Generating such additional value from a customer is highly dependent on knowing what the customer might need, already has and doesn't have, as well as providing suitable incentives and value propositions pertinent to the individual customer's particular profile. Data warehousing and mining software are technology tools that can be used for proactive sales campaigns, but can also support reactive opportunities when the customer initiates a new contact, providing that up-to-date customer-centric information is immediately accessible at the time of contact. This means that it is not enough to have information just collected somewhere, or even properly consolidated in one place, but that information has to be made immediately available at the time of customer contact and in a form that applications can quickly utilize, either through a display to a customer support person, or directly with a customer's self service application (telephone or web page screen). So, the familiar principles of computer telephony integration and "screen pops" remain valid in the new world of e- commerce CRM.

Increasing Customer "Loyalty" and Retention by Avoiding Customer Dissatisfaction

A big pitch for using new technology to support CRM concepts is to protect the enterprise's existing customer base from the increasing threat of competition. This threat will not only come from new market needs that cannot be satisfied by existing products and services (e.g., e-commerce), but can also arise from bad experiences or failure to meet customer expectations for support. Customer loyalty can always be challenged by competitive marketing activities and any experiential situation that causes customer dissatisfaction. Therefore, to protect the current and future value of its customer base, any enterprise technology investment that will strengthen its ties with existing customers should be even more justifiable than those that will only reduce costs.

E-commerce has put "internet time" demands by customers on every on-line enterprise for efficiency and responsiveness. A recent study of on-line shoppers who spent over $2,000 on-line in the last six months at a web site, showed that 87% will desert that site for a competitor if they encounter "poor customer service," according to Socratic Technologies. 50% of the shoppers who spent less than $100 would do likewise. What did they think was "poor customer service?" Incorrect email replies, being forced to repeat or explain their questions more than once, or, worst of all, never getting an answer at all. In discussing a case study of an enterprise CRM "makeover," the technology provider reported that the key to increasing "loyalty" was really to reduce or eliminate the dissatisfaction that triggered customer departures. Once they found that dissatisfaction with waiting too long for the proper type of assistance by key customers caused most of the defections, they made sure that those customers needs were handled differently, directing them to a different access path that was more efficient with the customer's time. The customer defections dropped significantly.

Insight: The things that cause the greatest impression of "poor service" and, hence, dissatisfaction, are either caused by what the support staff does or doesn't do, or the lack of correct response content. Even if all the information required by the customer is available in the enterprise system, it is useless if there isn't a way to make the match to get it efficiently to the waiting customer. This means knowledgeable and available staff assistance, or idiot-proof interactive self-service applications, and the intelligence to route the customer to the proper

E-commerce is like a giant mall where customers can easily comparison shop for price, if they are buyers, or quickly find alternative providers if they feel frustrated by the customer support they get. However, "loyalty" and "stickiness," as opposed to "branding," are most applicable to existing customers who will provide repeat business to the provider they already know and love. Every industry is familiar with the various statistics that compare the cost of acquiring a new customer vs. retaining a current one, and whether it is twice as expensive or five times as expensive, it is obvious that retention will always be more cost effective. For this reason, whatever promotes customer loyalty also promotes customer retention, and is, therefore, a key objective for CRM strategies.

What Technology Can Do for CRM and What It Can't Do

Most of the CRM objectives described above are not really new. What is new is that there is a greater need to do something about these objectives on a practical, day-to-day basis. Not only is the need for something better for customer interactions becoming more pressing, but, fortunately, most of the relevant product and service technologies, ranging from information processing to telecommunications, have converged to make implementation more feasible and cost efficient. The public internet and world wide web are making it easier for enterprises to make information and people quickly accessible to customers and vice versa. What new technology is also enabling, including CTI and IP-based tools, is the ability to capture more detailed activity data about customer contacts and interactions. Not only is this data useful for data mining for strategic CRM planning purposes, but it is also vital to every contact with the customer for tactical CRM activities. You need to know the long term activity profile of a customer, but, perhaps even more importantly, what has the customer done lately that will be pertinent to the context of the current contact/interaction. Enterprise data networking and database servers enable customer information to be consolidated, distributed and synchronized on a realtime, dynamic basis across the enterprise so that up-to-date "intelligence" can be applied by both enterprise people and self service application processes at every sensitive customer touchpoint.

What technology tools cannot automatically fix are:
- Poor information content used by automated applications required to support customer needs,

- Poorly designed user application interfaces for both self-service and customer support personnel,
- Poorly qualified trained customer support personnel,
- Insufficient staff resources to support customer demands.

However, technology tools can help improve such problems and allow the best use of all available resources.

The main obstacles to implementing effective CRM policies within the enterprise infrastructure will start with management's traditional concern for protecting its investments in legacy technologies. The next obstacle is a universal need for more understanding and experience in effectively using, managing and supporting the new technologies that CRM relies on. While "CRM technology" tools and infrastructures may be useful in a variety of vertical markets, there will still be differences in the way application functions and user interfaces will be designed and implemented for individual enterprises that can't be "out of the box." CRM is not "plug 'n play"! Market studies have already shown that the bulk of implementation costs expended for "CRM" are not for the technology tools and infrastructures, but for the consulting expertise in analyzing business needs and designing and implementing customized solutions. Having the tools and infrastructure to create enterprise-wide databases and applications doesn't make it easier to define what data needs to be collected, stored, analyzed and applied at the customer interaction points to ensure effective CRM benefits. More importantly, whatever approach is taken initially has to be considered as a learning experience to find out what your customers really do and what will really work (cost effectively) for your enterprise.

The Tips of the Iceberg—What the Customer Feels Is What Counts the Most

Forget for the moment how CRM policies will be supported and look at how these policies will manifest themselves to the customer and what management responsibilities will be involved. To do this, we must take a "top-down" view of the interactions between the enterprise and its customers, the different ways they will happen, and, most importantly, what the customer will actually see and experience. Even though we know that there is a lot of technology and information infrastructure that goes into creating the interfaces between the customer and the enterprise, that complexity of effort doesn't get any applause from customers unless they can touch it and feel it and get the results they expect.

Is this something new? Not at all! It's just that the dramatic advent of individual users gaining access to information and services at "internet speed," along with the rapid evolution of network-based technologies, has made the application of these new capabilities more complex and more pressing. Before the internet, we relied on the telephone and voice as the fastest and most direct way for the enterprise to interact with the customer. You talked to them! This resulted in telephone call centers for live contacts and IVR for self service applications. To a limited extent, we used voicemail to take messages from the calling customer. (According to TCS: 51 percent of North American call centers have voice mail for their agents, but do they use it for customer?) Voicemail messages were limited for a number of reasons, including the fact that they had to be listened to sequentially (no screen information) in order to determine their content before routing the message to an appropriate person for processing. Also, because customers could not exchange voice messages from their voicemail system mailbox with other systems, this form of messaging was always "one way" (telephone answering) and there was no way to quickly "reply" by messaging as a practical alternative to a telephone call back. The best we could do for CRM policies before the advent of the internet, was to generate limited "screen pops" of basic customer information in a customer file, along with "canned" application-oriented scripts to guide the CSR in his interaction with the customer. This meant that the tip of the enterprise iceberg from the customer's perspective was mostly dependent on the knowledge and experience of the individual CSR assigned to take the call, or on the design of the IVR Telephone User Interface (TUI) for a self service application or function.

Now, however, the rules of the communication game are changing and we have added major new dimensions for customer interaction with the enterprise, web information and new ways for contact access. These changes have created new multimedia "tips" on the enterprise iceberg, i.e., new avenues of self-service information access and application transactions, two-way message exchange, and person-to-person voice connections from a web site. The explosion of e-commerce has generated the need to "web enable" traditional enterprise call center functions and added responsibilities to support and interact with the new capabilities offered by the internet and the world wide web. This convergence of telephone access and screen-oriented communications and information exchange requires different operational strategies and skills to be developed and deployed for more efficient and effective customer support. Most importantly, however, is that web-based, self service applications will require similar, but not identical, customer interaction "flow" designs that are just as sensitive, if not more so, as they are for telephone-oriented IVR applications. The challenge now for enterprise organizations is to do a better job in assigning responsibility for designing and managing such critical customer interfaces than they have done in the past with early IVR applications. It's not just a programming task; it's a management responsibility that must blend all customer interactions into a unified, enterprise-wide interface with the customer.

Becoming a Customer: Web Shoppers vs. Surfers, Interactive Advertising and CRM

The enterprise web site is usually multi-dimensional—a "portal" for a variety of access needs. It will not only support customers, but business partners, press contacts and anyone who wants to find out about the enterprise's business activities and interests. Intermediaries, who enter supply chains and implement web-based buying and selling processes, generated $12 billion in 1998 according to the Gartner Group. However, the web site is becoming the anchor for all strategic e-commerce initiatives, in terms of attracting new customers and supporting a variety of customer information and service needs. Even outbound "direct email" campaigns link the prospective customer, who responds or "opts-in," to the enterprise web site as the starting point for the customer relationship. The web site is also becoming the gateway for accessing live and automated assistance for new ways of dealing with customers.

The multimedia capabilities of web site interfaces, from animated graphics to sound, has generated tremendous interest and activity in the world of advertising, as enterprise marketing exploits these features to enhance information access and delivery to their visitors. The subject of "online advertising" has an important issue for application developers as well as in the curricula of university marketing programs. A recent article in the staid Communications of the ACM (Association of Computing Machinery), "Web Home Pages as Advertisements" (August, 1999) by S. N. Singh and N. P. Dalai from the Universities of Kansas and Oklahoma State respectively, discusses the subtleties of the "communication message" delivered by the design and content of an enterprise web page (home page, or special entry page linked to the home page) when viewed as a form of online advertising. They highlight the differences in browsing behavior between low-involvement "surfers" and high-involvement "searchers" (the latter includes serious shoppers) and the page design and content that will have the most impact on each. Since e-commerce will be heavily dependent on such "searchers," which can include both potential and existing customers, the article stresses the importance of traditional marketing principles for advertising design as prerequisites for attracting such visitors. However, the new capabilities of "interactive advertising" and the value of providing online customer assistance from the service and interaction center staff, particularly by an immediate voice/data connection, is a new factor for sales effectiveness that enterprise marketing must now seriously consider and plan for.

A Boston Consulting Group survey of on-line retailers found that only 5 percent of Web visitors become customers. Only 1.6 percent of visits result in purchases. Two out of three e-commerce customers, who fill out a shopping cart, will abandon them. A similar study showed on-line shoppers never complete 67 percent of their on-line purchases in a survey of top 25 e-commerce sites by Net Effect company. The study found that only 5 percent of these web sites offered on-line, real-time assistance although 90 percent of them offered some sort of self-help. Only 15 percent of e-commerce sites have a defined process of how to treat their customers on their web sites, and only 10 percent have web-based customer management systems. 40 percent of these same sites did have some sort of well defined process for dealing with e-mail. Early e-shoppers have already demonstrated their window shopping mentality by their propensity to load purchases into shopping carts, but then to abandon them before leaving the web site. "Buyer's remorse" can set in at "internet speed" whenever there is the slightest question in the buyer's mind and it is easy to "escape"! However, it is typically a lack of product information that triggers the buyer's insecurity after he expends a first effort in selecting a purchase, and it is at this point that further "browsing" is probably not an attractive option. The CRM solution is to bring in live assistance to supplement the self service stuff.

Clearly, the sales opportunity with e-commerce is NOW! This is true for both old and new customers, but it might be considered intrusive for someone to come online with the e-customer to ask why he didn't buy something he loaded in his shopping cart. However, if the customer really is interested and needs a quick answer that can't be easily found or understood on the web page, offering the option to get immediate assistance should be viewed as a contributing factor to basic customer satisfaction, not just closing a sale. Voice over Internet Protocol (VoIP) and Computer Telephony Integration (CTI) technologies support two contact solutions that can be deployed for such situations, i.e., "call-through" and (immediate) "call back" (these have already been discussed in Chapter 3). The first approach offers a number of benefits over the second, e.g., no second phone line required, "push" control of web pages to the customer's screen by the customer support person, etc. (The voice quality issue can still be a concern unless the connection utilizes a PSTN connection.) Such "web calls" can be handled by traditional call center ACD switches, where the CSR desktop PCs are also connected to the enterprise's application web server (Intranet).

CRM policies can be supported by technology in several ways here. Offering the option for immediate live assistance is the starting point. It is then followed by recognizing the priority of this type of call ("sales assistance") and associated skill requirements, queuing the call appropriately and coordinating a "screen pop" of customer information (if an existing customer), along with context information about the customer's current web page activity. Finally, live assistance for a web caller can be made more efficient and effective by enabling the Web Support Representative (WSR) to operate in a consultative mode, sharing the same information seen by the customer and directly controlling display of new information to the customer's screen, concurrent with a natural voice discussion about the customer's questions.

Proactive Telemarketing, "Spam" and CRM

How can we talk about the relationship with customers without mentioning the bane of the consumer market, the unexpected and often unwanted telemarketing phone call that comes at dinnertime, just to catch someone at home. From a CRM perspective, cold- contacting strangers is one thing, but pursuing existing customers and former customers is another. The invasion of individual privacy is, of course, serious business and continues to be the object of federal and state regulatory oversight. The abusive use of outbound contact technology in this area may often backfire and can cause the loss of a sale or even the loss of a current customer. There is no doubt that CRM policies can and should be judiciously applied to the technologies that support proactive marketing activities, including both campaign management for outbound predictive dialing or "opt-in" email promotions. Properly targeted email campaigns (as opposed to "spam") are a lot less costly to implement, more controllable for marketing management, and more quickly recognizable by a legitimate customer with potential interest than an invasive telemarketing phone call. Furthermore, with "click to talk" capabilities, the proactive email contact can easily lead to a productive live voice connection, if there is any positive interest at all by the customer. The creative ways for blending old and new contact technologies to support e-commerce are unlimited.

CRM and Access to Customer Service

The flip side of CRM's value to e-commerce is customer service. Although customer service actually begins during the process of making a first sale, post-sale customer service is where the future gold is. The Society for Consumer Affairs Professionals 1998 Customer Contact Study found only 86 percent of companies use toll-free numbers for customer service. Nineteen were open 24 hours a day, the average call mix is 59 percent inquiries, 24 percent complaints and twenty percent new business. The study also found that 61 percent of toll free numbers directed calls to an IVR system, which was most widely used for routing. The Yankee Group estimates that the customer service applications market will reach $1.2 billion by 2003. However, the logic of searching the web for a purchase in conjunction with order assistance doesn't necessarily hold true for customer contacts when a product or service problem arises. The need for immediate assistance will be as pressing as when the purchase selection is about to be finalized, but this time the customer is not necessarily going to be already logged on to the internet. Depending upon the nature of the support problem involved, the fastest and most convenient means of support access will often remain direct telephone contact. A major exception to this, however, will be when the problem happens to be directly related to online information that is being accessed from a web site, e.g., financial data, reservations, order status, etc., or help desk support about software that is being currently used online. The major benefit of problem resolution through concurrent web access is that relevant information can be conveniently shared or exchanged on-screen between the customer support staff and the customer in "consultative" mode. That's a hell of a lot better than asking the customer to describe what's on his screen and telling him what buttons to push.

Live Assistance vs. Self Service—The Impact of E-commerce

While competent live assistance is ideal for customer support, it is also expensive, accounting for 70 per cent of the costs of traditional call center operations. Then, too, there are many kinds of situations where the "assistance" needed is really just direct access to the same kind of information that a customer support person has. Finally, there is personal account information that the customer would just as soon get privately, rather than through a stranger, e.g., financial status information, medical results, even purchase order status for certain kinds of items. It would be a mistake to insist that CRM only applies to live assistance and all the traditional and new operational technologies that are involved in managing customer support staffing and task assignment activities. In fact, one noted expert in call center research has gone on record to claim that "Web-based CRM is...encouraging a high level of self service, reserving the telephone contacts for more complex customer issues handled by the best agents."

Insight: The traditional percentages for labor in the Service and Interaction Center are bound to increase dramatically as the increased skills necessary for web caller support drive up staffing costs, while communication access charges drop because of VoIP connections. With telecommuting ("Home Agent") staffing the costs of traditional site facilities can also be reduced significantly. All this means that the most sensitive area for CRM is still the humanware, and, since it will also be the most costly, it will have to be used more judiciously and strategically than ever.

Clearly, customer needs can best be satisfied with a flexible and dynamic combination of self service options and selective access to live assistance.

Sometimes, live assistance will be needed up front to guide the customer towards self service facilities; other times the customer will start with self service access and then request live assistance. The more fundamental question will be what mode of contact will be utilized by the customer, the voice telephone or the web screen? Both methods of access to the enterprise can initially start with self service functions and applications, followed by access to live assistance. With IVR applications, such access to a call center representative is usually made by pressing the "0" key on the telephone and the call is then transferred to a traditional call center waiting queue. With a web caller, the "click to talk" screen option discussed earlier can have a variety of responses depending on what the customer communications config- uration is, the context of the contact request and the availability of customer support staff. The biggest difference, however, will be the option for email alternatives for the web caller, as discussed earlier in Chapter 3.

Another issue for CRM is under what circumstances will it be more important to provide live assistance rather than self service? Again, there will be pressing circumstances where the customer has a big problem, doesn't want to waste time with complicated or time-consuming self service procedures, and needs the human contact and handholding that only live assistance can satisfy. This is where customers will want to pick up the nearest telephone (or similar future device) and talk immediately with a human and this is when CRM objectives will be most vulnerable. On the one hand such calls need to be screened, qualified and prioritized before being assigned to an appropriate enterprise resource, but it's also a situation where customers, who may not have had a problem for years, may be turned on or off by the current enterprise interactions and responses. The point is that customers won't care how the technology does it in the future, all they want is to follow the simplistic telephone model for immediate contact and efficient person- to-person interaction. So even if we have internet-based communications (VoIP), broadband, wireless access and new kinds of screen- based telephone devices for information and transaction access, the enterprise must still provide competent people at the other end to talk to the customers when needed.

While IVR self service applications have provided similar capabilities to the new kinds of online web applications, the greater efficiencies of screen-based information access will eventually shift much (but not all!) of this activity to multimedia internet access via PCs and the next generation of convenient web appliances and screen phones. The latter will eventually allow us to effectively combine the two media - voice and screen - in practical and more comfortable ways, e.g., making selections from the screen rather than voice menus, scanning informational text output rather than listening sequentially and using voice input rather than typing text. However, when it comes to person-to-person interactions, voice will still be the most efficient form of conversational dialogue. Even though there is a lot of discussion about the role of "chat" and "instant messaging" (IM) for interacting with customers, typing is still slower and error-prone for input and reading text output has little or no benefit over voice for personal conversations (except for spelling names, which may be "typoed" incorrectly anyway). Therefore, to effectively satisfy CRM objectives for all customer situations, the enterprise contact/interaction center will have to support both information/transaction access as well as person-to-person conversational voice forms of interaction.

Global, 24x7 Support and Web "Wrong Numbers"

46% of North American call centers are open 24 hours a day, 7 days a week according to TCS's International Benchmarking Study. More than 80 percent of call centers handle customer service. Aside from the issues of multimedia contact and information access, live assistance vs. self service applications, and sales vs. support situations, e-commerce on the internet and the world wide web have opened wide the Pandora's Box for cross-cultural, multilingual and 24x7 support of customers. For an operation running 24 hours per day, 365 days per year a decimal place can mean a big deal. When the availability is 99.9999%, the cumulative unplanned downtime per year is 32 seconds. 99.999%; 5 minutes. 99.99% is 53 minutes. 99.9% is 8.8 hours. 99% is 3.6 days. 90% is 36.5 days. Certainly this is not entirely new to the traditional telephone-oriented call center, but now the problem becomes exacerbated by easy access for anyone, from anywhere, and at anytime. Now there will be a greater need for live assistance to support customers who are dealing with information in a multitude of languages and from different cultures that may require different ways for handling problem situations, depending on the country of origin and the culture of the people. If we are concerned about the "customer," we have to be sensitive about the different ways we must deal with the people. It's not enough to have information. We have to use that information to exercise and control policies and rules that have been carefully designed on the basis of tested experience, not guesswork.

That's for openers for customers and shoppers who know what they are doing and what they want. We haven't yet seen the impact of people "lost" on a website, who will grab any opportunity to get live assistance for directions to get where they want to go. It's like the voicemail auto-attendant directory which asks the caller for a name or an extension, except here someone is looking for a particular information page and rather than search for it themselves, they hit the first "click to talk" option they can find, like pressing "0" for operator assistance. Or, maybe they are on an enterprise website and want to talk to a particular person and "click to talk" in order to be transferred to the individual they are seeking. People do this now with IVR systems, so why wouldn't or shouldn't they do the same from enterprise web pages?

The Rest of the Iceberg

And just what is "CRM technology?" Here again, there is mass confusion, because it's a buzzword that gives technology providers an opportunity to upgrade their old image of traditional call center software and hardware products. CRM competes with other acronyms that are popular in the IT domain, e.g., ERP, Enterprise Resource Planning, and more recently, ERM, Enterprise Relationship Management, which concerns itself with all enterprise interactions with people and organizations, other than just customers. All of these domains are heavily based upon suites of specific application software processes that integrate and differentiate the general workflow logic and database content from one industry to another and specific, heavily customized enterprise implementations. A Datamonitor report, titled "Call Centers in US Financial Services," indicates such companies spent $167 million on software for their call centers for nearly 23 percent of their budgets. One large bank's customer database has 30 million customers, 10 million households across five channels. By 2003, software will constitute 39 percent of call center budgets. This same report says that at the end of 1998 there were 183,000 agent positions in retail financial services and estimates that this number will grow to 215,000 by 2003. The worldwide market for such call center software will rise to $3.1 billion in 2003 from $580 million in 1998 according to Ovum. The question is, what kind of software is being developed to handle these tasks and functions? The components of such technology suites typically include:

- Application servers and workflow scripts
- Database structures and content
- Data communications access
- Communications access to people
- Desktop application software for customer support staff
- Activity recording for management and analysis

The big mistake here would be to treat customers in the same way that all other enterprise contacts are handled, both within the organization and with other business-to-business relationships. Not only are the needs different, but the "ties that bind" are not the same in form, logic, or content. While communication and information access and functions may appear the same or similar, the "application" context for utilizing those functions will be different, as will the priorities and rules for assigning support personnel to assist or respond to customers. So, just as a phone call from a customer must be handled differently than an intra- or inter-enterprise call, email from a customer must also be dealt with and accounted for more appropriately. Industry technology needs to provide better high-level tools for creating and managing such differences, rather than throw expensive "application" programming and consulting resources at the problem.

The "Intelligence" For CRM—Centralized/networked Databases

The Local Area Network (LAN) makes it possible to easily share access and responsibilities for information pertaining to customers. Such data are not fixed, but a living, growing repository that reflects everything about a customer that will be useful in understanding his needs and his value to the enterprise. Because such information is also of value to various enterprise departmental functions that interact with a customer, it needs to available and accessible holistically to all authorized enterprise users, rather than maintained piecemeal. Information must be maintained comprehensively, but used dynamically on a selective basis.

Information in and of itself, however, is static. Until a dynamic process applies rules to data, nothing will happen. This is where the different "applications" come in to play in supporting customer needs. However, until there is customer information along with the rules for using that information for various customer support functions, "intelligent" call/message handling tasks can't really be implemented. Therefore, a key prerequisite for CRM activities is the existence of a comprehensive customer data base infrastructure, and that it has useful, valid information content in it. So, while the database and its data are essential for CRM, it is nothing without the rules and processes of an "application."

Insight: Just because all the information about a customer is readily available, doesn't mean that it can be and should be used by enterprise personnel who are not skilled or authorized to make decisions based on that data. The idea of "universal agents" for handling all kinds of customer interactions, from service to sales in a Customer Interaction Center environment, may appear tempting because of the increased ease in accessing customer information and providing interaction guidance through pre-programmed call handling scripts. However, there are other skills and responsibilities that need to be included in the mix, before such tasks are assigned to the enterprise staff or to an outsourced service.

The Different Kinds of Data That CRM Needs

One of the reasons that we haven't been able to support CRM properly in the past is that we really didn't know everything there was to know about the customer. Old ACD systems that picked up incoming calls to a call center operation didn't even know who was calling, let alone what their contact history was, or the purpose of the current call. With additional information gleaned from Automatic Number Identification (ANI), customer identification and call objective from prompted caller input (using IVR technology), current call center technology supports basic elements of "intelligent" call routing. However, more information is needed to do a better job for CRM.

It is often not enough to simply know who the customer is, what his history and status as a purchaser of enterprise products and services is, the "value" of the customer, or even the nominal purpose of the current contact. That information will not tell you the state of mind of the customer, the reasons for that state of mind, or the context for most effectively handling the current interaction. This will be true not only for telephone call handling (inbound or outbound), but also for email messaging exchanges, initiated by customers from enterprise websites. The missing information is the audit trail of prior customer contacts and interactions, which tells you what the individual customer actually has already done and experienced. Some of that kind of information has been provided in limited form by IVR self service applications, that could tell the customer support person things like what menu options were selected and how long the caller was connected before being transferred to live assistance, etc. However, the comprehensive logging of all forms of contact, including the number of unsuccessful contact attempts in the past or the gory details of self service activities are now becoming even more important for customer activity taking place on the enterprise website, before connecting with live assistance. Like, were several emails and a voice message left that were not acted upon yet?

Data Collection at the Customer Touchpoints

The data that CRM needs is going to be generated or collected on an ongoing basis, whenever anything happens that affects the customer. Some of it will be generated by traditional "back office" application processes that maintain their own views and profiles of the customer; other data has to be collected whenever there is direct contact with the customer. The latter is particularly sensitive because that is when the customer is most vulnerable to problems with support needs which must be known and understood not only for both long range CRM analyses, but also for properly handling any subsequent contacts and interactions with that customer. Inbound telephone call and web call activities, outbound call interactions, web page application mouseclick actions, inbound and outbound email messaging and voicemail messaging are the sources for customer contact and interaction activity data collection. The processes that directly control these functions will be the ones to collect the data and deliver it to a centralized repository for use in interaction center routing logic, selective online referencing by customer support staff, or for future CRM data mining.

The important call routing processor "engine," will also be a source of valuable information about events that occur while the customer is "on hold" in an assignment queue, waiting for live assistance. This is a particularly sensitive customer touchpoint, since it is where the customer is noticeably wasting time in a non-productive mode and may abandon the contact attempt, select self service application alternatives, or other enterprise contact options (e.g., messaging). The "wait time" data, as well as the outcome of the customer's choices, will be important metrics for CRM evaluations.

Making Things Happen at the Touchpoints—Applications vs. Functions for CRM

CRM technology is not cheap, and averages $1,500 per seat. Ever since the early days of computers, software has been an enigma to everyone. It was what made computers do things and was written by "programmers" who knew the language of computers. But programmers didn't necessarily know what the software applications were supposed to do and so there always had to be an application "design specification" written by someone who knew what the input and output information would be in the real world. To complicate matters, there were all kinds of other software that had nothing to do with a particular application, but were necessary just to make the equipment work for any application. In the early days, the database information was defined in the application program, because they were never shared with other programs (in fact, early business computers operated in "batch" mode only. Only one application program at a time could run and it controlled everything).

We now have all kinds of software running simultaneously and not only sharing the processor chip, main memory, disk drives and other peripherals and processors, but also the user interface, i.e., the desktop PC screen. And this is where the continued confusion still reigns! The information that is shown on the screen can be retrieved directly from a networked database, using generic software tools and functions under the user's control, or it could be transformed into special formats and views and controlled through an application server. With customer contacts, there is a similar difference between "blind" generic call processing functions and "intelligent" enterprise application processes.

Telephony technologies have traditionally dealt with such call processing functions, but rarely could support applications. They would give you dial tone and a voice connection, but the rest was up to humans. Until CTI technology let computer applications direct and control switch and ACD functions, the "intelligence" for selective call handling was provided by call center agents, supported by separate software applications and information. The bad part was that the various applications and databases were separate entities, maintained and controlled by different departments, and the result has been that a customer contact could not always be handled by a single person, simply because the information or the application software was not accessible. That problem has been alleviated somewhat with LAN or Intranet-based enterprise-wide networks, where database information can be dynamically shared by both departmental groups and applications within the enterprise. While that is good for internal operations, it doesn't really do much for the customer directly. Now, with the world wide web and the convergence of voice and data technologies, this sharing of information and applications can be made accessible directly to customers (self-service) as well as to customer-serving enterprise staff. However, the real payoff for CRM policies will come from providing such shared information access to the heart of customer touchpoint activities with the enterprise, the routing "engine" for multi-channel contact/interaction. This is where the enterprise CRM policies and resources can be applied and controlled in realtime, when the customer is involved and needs them most.

Preferences and Priorities—Knowing Your Customers Better

Customer information is key to exercising effective Customer Relationship Management functions, using available resources to preserve a positive relationship with a customer in the best interests of the enterprise. This must be done every time there is a customer-impacting action, especially when in direct contact with the customer, through live assistance or through self service.

The basis for optimally supporting a relationship with a customer is to be fully aware of his needs and preferences in all areas of interaction with enterprise operations that are customer facing. It may also mean "personalizing" those interactions with the enterprise, so that the customer feels that his identity is not only recognized, but that the enterprise treats him or her as a unique individual, not just as an account number. The question is, how much can you know about your customer that will help you personalize those interactions?

There are two basic approaches that are typically used to profile a customer. One way is to simply ask customers questions about their needs and preferences, typically by surveying them periodically. The problem is that, aside from people not wanting to be bothered with such questions, they often just don't really know what they want. Also, individual needs are very circumstantial and the customer will usually not be able to define those situations ahead of time. Finally, it is more practical to track a customer's most recent transactions and interactions in order to realistically assess the present relationship and project its future.

What Have You Done for Me Lately? Actions Speak Louder Than Words!

A useful alternative to understanding the customer better is to monitor his contact behavior and in the context of what customers actually do, research the "why" of such behavior. If nothing else, tracking customers' behavior will help reveal their preferences and even their frustrations with interaction procedures and support experiences. More importantly, recognizing that the customer perspective of the enterprise will often be short term, where they'll remember the most recent bad experience rather than all the older good ones, it will be helpful to track such recent events and their impact on the customer, and, where necessary and appropriate, proactively compensate the customer with positive actions.

Although customer support personnel can make notes about their contacts with customers, it usually will be difficult to do so accurately without interfering with their primary task responsibilities and can often be very subjective. Logging various self service activities, however, either through IVR applications for telephone callers or web page mouse clicks, can provide useful context data for evaluating the customer's current experience. Coupling that data with post-contact survey questions, will be a way to catch customer satisfaction issues quickly and respond to them early. Thus, if a customer is detected as having a problem on a web site or has had to wait exceptionally long for a "callthrough" connection for live assistance, this information needs to be presented to the customer support person in order to immediately make apologies to the customer or research the cause of the customer's problem. Similarly, a telephone self service (IVR) application could detect delay, confusion, or repeated error actions, and not only capture the problem activity data, but also automatically transfer the caller to suitable live assistance. Most importantly, the captured activity data will be useful for both overall operational management, as well as providing input for the individual customer's history file.

It Will Never Be Perfect! —Managing the New Tradeoffs for Available Staff Resources

With all the information about customers and all the hot data and communications technologies, the keys to customer satisfaction will remain basically the same and when push comes to shove, it will be the human resources that will be the most important to support customers at the touchpoints of the enterprise. Timely responsiveness will be what is most visible to customers who need assistance that only humans can provide, but the problem of available staff resources will be a never-ending challenge for service and interaction centers of the future. Even with staffing strategies like "home agents," "overflow" groups, "blended" interactions assignments, etc., there will always be times when the traffic for responding to customer contacts will peak and customers will have to wait for assistance. Theoretically, the enterprise can always overstaff, but then the costs can seriously outweigh the value of supporting the customers.

E-commerce on the world wide web will enable new alternatives for customer self service applications and the practical exchange of messages, both text and voice, as a means of expanding enterprise methodologies for customer support and minimizing the impact on staffing resources. However, there will still be a need for direct human assistance, both by direct telephone access and by "web callers" initiating calls from the enterprise web site as well as indirect assistance in providing responses for customer-initiated email exchanges. The benefits of consultative sharing of information and navigation assistance for web callers and the media flexibility and cost efficiencies of VoIP have already been discussed, but the bottom line is that people and their various skills or responsibilities must still be selectively available to close the loop for the important touchpoints of customer relations.

Just as the waiting queue has been the backup alternative for realtime callers in traditional call center operations, it will still remain a necessary option for future realtime contact demands, whether for telephone callers, web callers, or messages. What will change, however, is the priority management logic that will control how available staff resources should most strategically be applied to waiting customers, from a CRM perspective. The enterprise contact routing "engine," often referred to as Skills-based Routing (SBR) discussed above, will not solve problems of understaffing or inadequate skills, but is designed to do the best it can under the circumstances, using CRM-based priority rules. Some interesting perspectives of the complex strategies and heuristics that can be exercised for routing decisions are discussed in greater detail in Chapter 8.

Chapter Eight
Taming Chaos: When Neural Networks Meet Customer Service

The Undeniable Persistence of the Old Way of Doing Things

A professor at the University of Texas recently wrote of the fascinating origins of the US standard railroad gauge – the distance between the rails – which today is 4 feet 8 inches. Most transportation experts would agree that there are more efficient widths of railroad tracks. Wider tracks could haul more cargo, but there is so much track laid at this precise width that it is implausible that any other gauge will ever be used.

In the mid-1800's, when the US began to build railroads, the only engineers that knew how to build them came from England. These Englishmen, quite naturally brought with them the tools, templates and measurements they had used to build trains and the trams used in England. The trams had used the same wheel spacing as the wagons of the day. The wheel spacing of the wagons coincided with the width of the ruts cut into the roads of Northern Europe. Had the spacing been any different, the wheels would have broken on the old, long distance roads built by the Imperial Roman army for the use of their war chariots. So, in fact, today we have railroad tracks based on the width of precisely two Roman war chariot-horse rear-ends.

We sometimes apply the character of "revolution" to indicate great changes in the ways we have done things. Certainly everyone has been affected by the "information revolution" and it is certainly obvious that the face of customer service has been changed drastically over the past twenty-five years by the information revolution. However, change is rarely as dramatic as we would want to believe. Super high tech trains, artificial intelligence-based routing logistics and computerized switching operations produce extraordinary efficiencies in today's modern railroad system; none of these advancements belie the fact that trains still run on tracks of widths consistent from the days of the Romans (the irony with railroads is that embedded beneath these very old tracks are the very new fiber optic pathways of the information superhighway).

The Y2K computer bug is another example of a "gauge," or standard, replicated to the point of being so imbedded that rooting it out has proved to be a significant challenge.

In every enterprise we can find examples of these deeply embedded, institutionally persistent ways of doing things, particularly in the customer service execution chain. A significant irony of technology is that, while the human resources of the enterprise are flexibly adaptive and evolve at the pace of revolution, it is the core technology and fundamental service processes that truly hinder the enterprise's ability to evolve and stay ahead of the competition.

Today, running parallel with information revolution, is the customer relationship evolution. The benefits and demands of the transformation from the spontaneity of mass adversarial marketing (for example, Nike's "Be Like Mike," or else) to marketing the lifetime value of the one-to-one relationships has not been lost on chief executives. Enterprise leaders, the C-level (CEO, CIO, COO, CFO, CKO, et al.) if you will, predominantly recognize that stimulating the future value of the customer now demands executing every customer service event with bias, preference, discretion and prejudice for both the customer and the enterprise's humanware resource. Forward thinking companies have gone as far as to establish a C-level advocate for the enterprise's customer identified as the Chief Customer Officer, the CCO.

While we have long recognized that not all customers should be treated equally, the technology to enable distinctions between customers is still very much derived from the practice of treating customers as though they were all equal. Out of the information revolution has come technology quite capable of applying a unique gauge of value for each and every customer and their related events. Unfortunately the true value of this knowledge can not be exploited or the benefits garnered as long as the technology of customer relationships is firmly rooted in treating all customers with parity and as equals.

If the average CEO could take a visual picture of the customers that are in line for service at any given moment and how they are being served, they would be stunned. He would immediately recognize that customers are shuffled, queued and moved around. Some customers are inappropriately given preference over others. These CEOs recognize that the enterprise is drastically over-serving the wrong customer. The service choices that customer service chain executives enable today are now resulting in consequences critical at the C-Level. Today's customer service technology fundamentally cannot support the sublime message being pushed down from the C-Level.

The C-Level is demanding that every customer engagement downstream reflect a service brand consistency as the company – not the customer service chain executive – would define it. Awareness of how service reflects and reinforces the brand expectation is accelerating and collapsing the distance between the boardroom and the call center. Increasingly, customer service chain executives will have to stretch up, not out, and effectively communicate about how the enterprise brand expectations are or should be met at the point of each and every customer engagement. Unfortunately, like railroads, old processes and technologies of customer service, predominately the ACD (Automatic Call Distributor), increasingly can not apply new models of service expectations.

The fundamental algorithms found in ACDs today, themselves more than twenty-five years old, were designed in the days when computer power resided in the pencil (Erlang tables were derived for telecommunications from work designed to calculate how many cannon balls were needed to demolish the opponents of Napoleon's armies). These algorithms were originally designed to efficiently match resources (telephone lines) to resource demands (callers). Like the railroad gauge, these fundamental rules of efficiency, based on the oldest customer waiting on hold for service, have persisted and permutated into quite successful accomplishments in efficiency and productivity.

Today many of the customer service functions of the enterprise still come down to making decisions based on the oldest customer waiting for service. Darwinian evolution now demands that the enterprise be smarter than taking the oldest customer call waiting – or perish.

Early call centers were designed to cut costs out of the business by efficiently matching resources (agents) with resource demands (customers). While awareness is growing in the call center, there has been little or no attitude of understanding that there is a lifetime value derived from a certain population of customers. The sensitivity we have toward customers today, such as what they buy, what they value and how they like to be served is entirely outside of the basic and fundamental assumptions on which ACD technology is built.

Until the call center breaks free of the persistent conventional wisdom of Erlang-ness, customer service chain executives can never walk into the enterprise board room and, with a straight face, enthusiastically say they are in fact meeting the relationship demand expectations of not only the C-Level, but of customers today. In fact, with enthusiasm and confidence, these very same customer service chain executives claim evolutionary progress, discretely ignoring statistics, facts and consequences that indicate otherwise.

The Fourth Generation Company

In the PWCoopers "Stages of Customer Evolution," IDEAS study discussed in Chapter Five, PWCoopers identified three stages in their model of the evolution of enterprises. The interesting facet of this study was not that 35 percent of North American companies surveyed were focused entirely on customer acquisition (the "Hunters"), nor that another 59 percent were focused on customer relationship management (the "Ranchers"), but that only 6 percent of companies actually embraced customer asset management as a mission (the "Farmers"). The PW Coopers definition of the stages of customer evolution may be simplistic, it may even be off by a few percentage points, even so it is an eye-popping and effective model when consideration is given to the fact that more than 50 percent of companies believe that they are actually in the top 6 percent!

These three stages certainly reflect the evolutionary transformation from a mastery at measuring event-by-event transactional efficiencies to an adeptness at engaging lifetime customer relationships. Since evolution never stops (it often stutters), we can anticipate the characteristics of a Stage Four or Fourth Generation enterprise.

A characteristic of the Fourth Generation company will be information and service parity; media independence. In other words, customers can expect to be served discriminantly based on their relative value and, regardless of the media they use, the information will always be consistent across media (is what your IVR or your web site responds with the same as what your agents tell your customers?).

Where creating incremental improvements in efficiency sufficed for PWCooper's Stages One through Three, it will not suffice for Stage Four and subsequent stage companies. In fact, one of the precise delineating characteristics segregating Stage Three's from Four's will be the characteristic of making resources allocation decisions based on, not only the call half of the equation (oldest customer waiting for service), but also the resource half (next best person becoming available) as well. As a note, for the purposes of this composition the author uses the word "call" with no distinction between a telephone call, an email, a web chat and so on. The word "call" is intended to define the event, not the specific media of a telephone call – although that is, and will remain for some time to come, the dominant engagement media.

To further explain the distinction between a Stage Three and a Stage Four company, let's use a restaurant as a simple metaphor. Imagine that you manage a restaurant and your staff just can't seem to get the right meals to the right tables in a decent amount of time and when they do, the food's cold. Customers are complaining about the service and business is declining. The owners decide that changes must be made and service improved. Their options are: a) make the menu longer and more complex (disguised as making it better) or, b) improve the kitchen operations. Option a) is what most every company does today; deciding that customer service, vis-a-vis the call center, can be improved by adding another layer of customer segmentation (gold and silver customers), more agent skills (your best waiters during rush hour) and more varieties of caller treatments (expanded menus).

However, more waiters, customers with gold cards and a longer, more complex menu will not make a poorly run restaurant better. Instead of focusing on creating efficiencies in the dining area with customers, Fourth Generation companies will focus on the kitchen – deciding which agent/waiter/chef does what work next, knowing what the overall demands placed on the kitchen are and what the patrons are expecting.

From another perspective, we are seeing the characterization of Fourth Generation companies shrouded in the expressions "front office" and "back office." The "front office" (the dining area) is where the convergence of call centers, sales force automation, product and price configuration tools and work-flow applications are converging. Still, what these programs, applications and processes have in common is an outward focus, aiming to improve the dealings with customers. The "back office" (the kitchen) defines applications which focus on streamlining the enterprise's in-house operations. The progress will be found at the point between the two.

The "leaky bucket effect" is an apropos descriptor for the phenomenon of customers who just never return to the restaurant with bad service. It is not that the owners of the restaurant do not recognize that the poor service they are delivering today is impacting the desire of customers to return later. In fact, they astutely have identified that the customer leakage is happening between the front office and the back office. However, most enterprises today, like restaurants, do not recognize that successes with the "front office" (customer acquisition - the goal of traditional forms of marketing) is masking significant losses out the back door.

A C-Level executive recently shared his view that the front door to their business does not need to be bigger, but that the back door must be made smaller. It is on those customers leaving discretely through the back door ("churn" in industry parlance) that every enterprise must now focus. There is a hole in the enterprise's boat, but too often the hole is ignored because it is on the other side. Like a Titanic, a hole in the boat ultimately affects the entire enterprise. The boat stays afloat because we have used technology to create tremendous efficiencies with the bilge pumps. Call centers have evolved to be extraordinarily efficient bilge pumps of the enterprise, but little is being done about the hole.

The persistence of old ways of doing things (railroad gauges), the substitution of complexity for better service (restaurant menus) and a "leaky bucket effect" (bilge pumps) are precise metaphors for the obstacles enterprises face as they stretch to evolve from a Stage Three to a Fourth Generation enterprise. However, be aware that the vault from Stage Three to Fourth Generation is over a far greater of a chasm than the jump over a ditch of a Stage One to Stage Two, or a leap from Stage Two to Stage Three.

To make this evolutionary "vault" will require changing the existing "gauge" of the thinking about who customers are, what they expect and how to best exploit every enterprise resource to meet the demands of the customer relationship revolution. A defining characteristic of the Fourth Generation company will be the realization that, in the call centers of customer relationship management, there are in fact two queues – customers and agents. First, we will discuss the territory that we are most familiar with, the efficiencies of dealing with customers and then move on to where greater opportunities lie, with the agents.

You Can't Beat the Bad Service Beast with the Technologies of Efficiency

Many call center managers and customer service chain executives have been successfully riding on the back of CTI (computer telephony integration), predominantly in the form of the transactional efficiencies created through IVR (Interactive Voice Response), screen pops and skills based routing. What CTI really allows enterprise agents to do is engage customers immediately instead of making the customer endure the clicks and "ah-ha's" of the agents as they enter in the relevant information necessary just to start the conversation. CTI itself has been sold on the efficiency and productivity perspective. The call center has justified technology that shaves a few precious seconds of each call because it creates more speed, hence convenience for the customer. By speeding up the response time to customers, we shorten the times the longest customer call has been waiting. This is the basic premise behind CTI's screen pop.

Because they have long been treated, although not necessarily thought of as cost centers, call centers have evolved into being adept at "talking" to other parts of the enterprise, particularly the accounting department. The discussion is almost always focused on in how efficiently the call center is operated, not in how effective customer relationships are.

Traditional metrics are important and they serve their purpose, but they don't give an accurate picture of what customer relationships are really all about. Traditional metrics do not reveal if the right choice is made consistently between serving one call or another. Abandoned calls are symptoms of a different kind of problem. We strive to lower the threshold of abandoned calls by increasing the number that don't abandon; we rarely ask why they abandoned in the first place.

When the C-Level asks call center managers today if they believe that they have beaten the bad service beast, they often reply, with a straight face, that they indeed have because some report says that they answered 80 percent of their calls in at least 20 seconds. They invoke the proverbial 80/20 rule like scripture. This call center person enthusiastically says, "we are exceeding traditional service quality thresholds like never before." The C-Level looks out at that 80/20 rule and immediately expresses that 80 percent is 20 percent utterly unacceptable.

What the C-Level realizes is that 20 percent of the time, for the wrong customer, is 100 percent of the time too much. And if you answer 80 percent of your calls in 20 seconds and 100 percent of those 80 percent are from your lowest value customers, you have actually done a dis-service. The C-Level correctly identifies that the call center flawlessly executes the right piece of work for the wrong customer and that the 20 percent of customers who abandoned just happened to be, as the C-Level realizes, your most valuable ones.

In Houston, Texas, because of coastline and geography, there is tremendous rainwater run-off. Every hundred years there is a flood called a "hundred year flood." Texans will see this level of water approximately once every one hundred years. I have recently experienced two "one hundred year" floods. During that time I got horrible emergency, police, gas, sewer and electric service from my county where I pay (too much) taxes. On average, the county tells me, they are prepared to handle 80 percent of all disasters. I pay a certain percentage more in taxes for flood control in the district where I live. During the floods, service from the Flood Control District switchboard was unavailable 100 percent of the time. Over one hundred year's period, on average, they do a great job. The Taxing District's track record is of no use to me if I am the one with a flooded house.

The cow path has been paved in the call center industry by the technology suppliers and vendors who have rallied around very binary terms such as Service Levels, Average Talk Time, Average Speed of Answer and Abandon Calls. Some binary arbitrary bar, standard or gauge is established. Against that criterion we ask, "Did we meet these standards, yes or no?" This is obviously not the paper to discuss philosophical tenets of customer service, but is "yes" 80 percent of the time really "yes?"

Binary measurement establishes a bar. If your enterprise is capable of jumping over the 16 foot level on a high jump but the bar is consistently put at nine feet, you will look like a hero of customer service every time. In call centers people place the bar at these arbitrary points and then slap each other on the back and exchange "high-fives" for being successful. Unfortunately, at the same time the complaint department is backed up and stacked up with letters about poor service.

These arbitrary bars of service levels are not true measurements of customer satisfaction today as the C-Level wants to define it. Increasingly, driven by concepts such as "World Class Service," "Best in Class," and "Olympic Class," the C-Level is insisting that the bar be raised– and call centers certainly comply – by claiming that they have gotten better, when "getting better" may mean only by five percent.

Like railroads, it has taken quite a bit of investment and capital to pave this customer service cow path. The C-Level has been led to believe that responsive customer service is very complicated and difficult to accomplish, requiring a lot of software, servers and systems integration experience. Call centers have become very adept at masking 20 percent failure rates through their expertise at creating reports and manipulating "acceptable" service thresholds.

Technology today has enabled a confusion between having very fast reflexes and meeting true service expectations from customers. Call center technology, for the most part, is designed around simply substituting activity for achievement. Even the designs for caller treatment, while more complex that ever, continually fail to achieve the desired results. Real time manual intervention in the call center is a perpetual and accepted practice in call center management, much like investing exclusively in fire-fighting equipment instead of investing in prevention such as with smoke detectors.

Relationship success can no longer be measured on a binary basis; it must be measured on an individual relationship basis. However, since we rarely have an opportunity to "clean-slate" it, the persistence of the binary service question can be extended into asking the question, "Are we accomplishing a 'yes' on a lifetime of customer transactions?"

Customer relationship management is not just about one engagement, but many engagements of any type. Customer relationship management is evolving into managing the effectiveness of the aggregate experience, not measuring the efficiency of each transaction. Efficiency does not equal effectiveness. Using averages, for example, means that, on average, all of your best customers will eventually have bad experiences. And in today's fast-paced world of the internet, they won't just tell one, six or nineteen people, they will tell 6,000.

The enterprise's C-Level increasingly realizes that understanding a customer's lifetime value requires changing from being exceptionally good at measuring transactional efficiencies to being exceptionally great at understanding effectiveness. Age, in seconds or minutes, not value, has been the defining characteristic of most every customer engagement. Lifetime value is what the customer service chain is directed to work toward; but given only technology tools that are great at understanding transaction metrics such as average speed of answer and average talk times, the challenge becomes clear.

Where Forecasting Fails

A brief disclaimer may be required here to avert a predictable misunderstanding about the authors' position on the importance of resource forecasting and simulation. There have been tremendous advances and successful companies built around applying the tools of forecasting and simulation in call center environments. There is no question that forecasting and simulation is an extremely valuable, useful and necessary tool.

Forecasting can be used to do many important "what-if" scenarios. However, at some point forecasting and simulation breaks down and has little or nothing to do with the actual execution of any particular customer's engagement event. Forecasting and simulation deals with the collective; customers must be treated as individuals.

Planning tools are not execution tools. As the enterprise gets closer and closer to handling the customer engagement event, every anticipated event is still only a hypothetical engagement. As the enterprise gets closer to the actual customer contact, you can still only make assumptions about the precise nature of the calls and resource demands.

We have gotten pretty good at refining and recreating those forecasts to the point that today's plans can be based on results that were developed this morning or as recent as thirty minutes ago. We even know how closely we can forecast; some application products can gain accuracy with as little as five percent variance over the course of the workday. And call centers base a lot on these forecasts, everything from daily staffing demands to long-term budgeting. In the call center today running operations two minutes behind schedule can be a very expensive proposition in the aggregate.

As you get close to handling any one call, the time span available for making decisions becomes compressed. The more focused on any interval you become, the more one can identify larger and larger gaps, variances and exceptions to the "forecast." Forecasting, at an event level, is an educated guessing game not extensible to execution.

There is a specific point in time where service moves from a planning stage to an executing stage. There is a line between potentiality and actuality that forecasting and simulation tools cannot cross. It is at this intellica (the Latin word for the point between potentiality and actuality) that the bursty of individual calls and events becomes apparent and chaos in the call center materializes. The true randomness and chaos of human nature can not, ultimately, be forecasted nor tamed only through good planning.

Taming Chaos; the Random Customer Event

Looking at the arrival of customer events is like looking at a coastline or mountain ridge; neither really runs straight or becomes more apparent the closer you move in. The input of customer engagements is ultimately neither a smooth sine wave nor a predictable bell curve. The difference in the order and the arrival times of any two customer events is always random.

In a retail store we could identify, on average, how many customers are expected and how much service they would require. What can not be identified is when any particular customer will arrive. So, how does one pick the highest value transactions out of the incoming stream of calls and events? Each customer event is placed into a queue of some sort and the challenge of the Fourth Generation enterprise will be in applying selective and deterministic logic to each event – as it occurs.

Traditional call center managers would have considered that this was impossible; that creating consistent service and engagement expectations breaks down at the call routing level. In actuality it does not because there is a fundamental moment of control that asks what work should I do next? People do this every day. When we walk into our offices and we see the list of emails that have come in, we certainly don't necessarily read the email at the top of the queue, or the one that just came in. Even when we look at our mail, we certainly do not look at postmarks to determine which one is the oldest piece.

Normal workflow processes show that we do not process tasks from the top down or oldest call first. You would not deal with every email, voice mail and snail mail in the order that they were received. The messages and events that you have between your customers, your boss, your CEO and your spouse are all treated in different ways, each being assigned a priority. You look at them and make one of three decisions: what do I have time to do, what would I like to do and which one provides the most value for my business? This is the type of intuitive decision that today's ACDs can not make.

A characteristic of the Fourth Generation call center will be the nature of applying selective logic to both the randomness of incoming events and the randomness of the availability of the resources to handle those events. Little consideration has been given to creating stability in the face of the true randomness of arriving events. A question of "what should we an agent do next?" is not the same thing as asking "what could an agent do next?" A "should" evaluation can encompass a wider range of considerations, from the individual caller value and urgency to knowing what agent is available now and which agents are likely to be available soon. This perspective overcomes randomness. A Fourth Generation call center will function like a machine where in one end is poured a random splattering of ingredients and out the other side comes an array of precise 3-inch squares with exact 6 inch separations. What is lacking in the technology of customer service today is the ability to insure consistent outputs of service from inconsistent inputs – truly taming chaos.

Imagine running your customer service operation like you would run a hospital emergency room.

Service Triage

First, we should agree that customer service probably does not have the same life-threatening drama as that of an emergency room. In fact, it is safe to say that, most every enterprise fastidiously avoids having anything to do with customers dying – there is no lifetime value to be gained from this consequence.

When the C-Level talks about the retention of customers and the segmentation of more valuable customers over others, we can identify these demands metaphorically with the critical care demands of emergency room patients. Unlike call centers, managing patients based on their order of arrival, is what we never do in hospital emergency rooms. Unless you have two identical sprained ankles sitting next to each other, a doctor would never ask, "Who was here first?"

Doctors have skills that they would use to look out across an emergency room full of possibilities and identify the most important situation to handle immediately. They would likely not treat a sprained ankle because they (actually the admitting manager) would apply selective logic and determine that if that sprained ankle isn't treated within the next several minutes, every one of the interns in the hospital can effectively treat that sprained ankle. The next available intern is likely to take that patient.

On average, is ten minutes a good or acceptable threshold wait time in the emergency room? For the most part yes, unless the patient arrives not breathing. In this case, ten minutes is at least six minutes too long. In the hospital triage environment, as in a call center, you have to understand and determine the amount of wait time a patient can reasonably and safely endure. If they are not breathing, that timeframe is very short; if they have a sprained ankle, it can be much longer.

The practice of triage understands the urgencies of need, length of reasonable wait and the skills of the available practitioner. Call centers handle callers with different needs, lengths of wait and have agents of various skills to handle the calls. Customers understand the similarity between the two and increasingly expect enterprises to know and understand how urgent their particular situation is. Not to mention that hospitals, too, recognize that if every patient had to wait five hours for treatment, customer relationship problems will ensue. Community percep-tion of a hospital's quality of service is formed by good execution across a variety of patients needing care on both busy days and slow days, at nights and holidays.

But, nooooo, according to the San Jose Mercury News, service discrimination is un-American.

Service Discrimination

In a January 10, 1999 article published in the San Jose Mercury News, Silicon Valley's paper, the writer essentially portrayed the idea of service discrimination based on customer value (or need, as in the emergency room) as inequitably un-American (SJMN 01/10/99 p. 1A, Deborah Kong, http://newslibrary.krmediastream.com). What the writer utterly failed to reflect is that service discrimination is absolutely permissible in free markets and that customers have never been treated equally. Doormen and maitre de's make these kinds of service discrimination decisions every night at clubs and restaurants. That it ignites the indignation of the media that CEOs are now making these very same type of customer-value decisions flaunts a certain kind of hypocrisy insignificant in its weight to change the shift of the customer service evolution.

An enterprise may want to talk to some people more, talk to others less and talk to some not at all, which is not a very accepted notion because it contradicts the traditional mass marketing notion that all customers are good. It's un-American to think of this as contradicting an old mass market-ing establishment that is designed to get as many customers as possible. The evolution of marketing to adapt to the one-to-one revolution and marketing's role in the Fourth Generation enterprise will define the role of marketing, not as endeavoring to garner new customers, but being good at retining the good ones it alrady has. Marketing's traditional job has been to throw big nets (TV). What is truly a more valuable enterprise opportunity – a 30 second, $1.5 million Super Bowl commercial or a four minute phone call between a valued customer and the call center agent?

The day has arrived that database technology has become capable of being precise and quick. We can understand our customers, quite literally, at a subatomic level.

We claim that our call centers are relationship centers, yet a customer can never be sure that he will get the same consistent experience when he checks in for service. Consider the similarity between a call center's queue and the line at an airport check-in counter. At the check-in line, a counter agent typically takes the next person in line (the oldest one waiting, except for cutters). When you have shown up at the airport and the flight is prepar-ing to leave in ten minutes, at some point, even if you are not the person at the front of the line, you are ready to go ballistic because you are about to miss your plane. Airlines are not dumb – they will have people who walk back through the line looking for those customers who need critical care because they showed up late. The value and effectiveness of this type of decision has not been lost on the airlines.

The new relationship model says that the agent shouldn't take the next person in line, he should take the most valuable person in line, which in the case of the airport is the person closest to missing his flight. This Fourth Generation enterprise will always look at the customer service line sideways, not straight-on. By limiting the view of the customer line from straight-on, the enterprise, always takes the next person in the queue, the one whom has been waiting the longest. Sideways, the enterprise can look across all of these opportunities and, just like selecting which email, voicemail or letter to answer first, applies a different kind of value determination to the queue of engagements.

The Fourth Generation enterprise will integrate software-based adaptive logic into their service process and use it to view horizontally which customers should be engaged and handled next. Ideally, we would want a human – like at the airport check-in counter – to make these "value" decisions. However, the pace of inputs into the call center and the variety of needs and media served makes it impossible for a human to make these judgement decisions to effect real-time operations.

Customer Service and Moving Vans

In spite of intended complexities of skills based routing today, fundamentally all ACDs execute call processing as though all calls – customers – are all created equal. We design and implement applications create distinctions among agents (which is the premise behind skills based routing). We can functionally identify and act on the fact that customers are not created equally. Why then put something in between – the traditional ACD – that treats them all the same?

Engaging the oldest waiting customer first is sufficient if every customer is considered equal. Are they equal in your enterprise? Most customer routing functions are based on aggregating processes, many callers queuing up to fewer agents. Currently, with most skills based routing, the incoming ACD aggregates callers (queuing) but at some point in the call queuing process a threshold is reached and all callers become the same. When this threshold is reached, queuing happens by "brute force." In the FIFO (first-in, first-out) model the enterprise ends up, regardless of customer value, with the human resource pool doing the right work for the wrong customer. A brain surgeon can certainly fix a sprained ankle, but it is the wrong customer if the brain surgeon is needed for brain surgery.

You don't want the brain surgeon answering low value or general information calls. In the traditional call center model, as soon as the chump change has been there longest, it gets prioritized to the top. At what threshold do 20 green card customers become as valuable as a single gold card customer? Are 20 bronze cards holding in line as valuable as making any gold card hold any time at all? At what point does the bad service to a green card outweigh the entitlement of gold card?

The intelligent adaptive-logic function of the advanced call center will act just as a master mover would apply logic to the packing problem of loading a moving van. You could , but wouldn't load a moving van in the strict order that items arrive. A call center traditionally only looks at the space available in the truck and does not turn around and look at the individual items stacked up on the lawn. The skilled mover looks up and down the line of furniture and box opportunities and logically prescribes these opportunities to the resources available which, in this case, are the spaces and holes in the truck. An experienced moving crew further discriminates by bringing out boxes and furniture in an advantageous order. The call center has little control over how the boxes, the calls, arrive, so the call center must be much more intelligent in how these randomly arriving calls are handled.

The Fourth Generation call center will manifest the desire to match valued customers with valued resources in the customer service chain. Adaptive logic is applied to customer service demands by looking ahead just as you would look ahead in a game of chess. In the old model of things, the enterprise would save a pawn but lose a king, just as in the hospital where the brain surgeon ends up treating sprained ankles when he should be saved for the brain surgery. From a resource utilization perspective, this isn't a balanced trade off. And the kings (and queens), not pawns, are where the value of the other half of the customer service chain equation lies.

People Are the Killer App

It was mentioned earlier that there are in fact two queues in the service enterprise. Call centers are about striking a balance between a surplus of calls and the surplus of agents. It is about understanding the demand, the supply and the operational goals at the same time, at any time. When an agent becomes available, you have a resource that can be used at that very moment. Like customer discrimination, agent discrimination, in the form of allocating call center agents as enterprise resources, will garner greater and greater attention.

Like railroad gauges, the old-fashioned typing pool serves as a perfect metaphor for defining how we will allocate the human resources of the customer service enterprise. In the days of typewriters (unless you were an executive lucky enough to have your own secretary), typing pools were where companies sent hand written documents and letters to be typed. Every typing pool had a manager who would have a stack of incoming letters and documents queued up in his/her job basket. Each of these typing projects had a different priority (needed this afternoon, needed tomorrow, needed next week, etc.). Some projects also had particular requirements that not every typist could fulfill. For example, a VP's paper must have no typos, or a paper may require a typist that can type formulas.

Like an ACD routing calls, the typing pool manager walks up, down and around the aisles (cubicles) farming out typing jobs (calls) as they come in, determining who gets what job and assigning a new job after a typist has finished the last. As in the call center, when a job (call) is completed, the typist (agent) walks up to the pool manager's desk, turns the work in and picks up a new job and, if a new job (call) is not ready, the typist waits for the next job (an idle agent).

Imagine yourself as a typing pool manager. Imagine, on average, every 20 minutes a VP sends down a "hot" letter that has to be typed and you know that, on average, you have three typists that can handle this VP's letter. You also know that, on average, these typists are only available every 40 minutes. As the typing pool manager you would not engage these particular typists on every first piece of work that comes in because the odds are that sometime during the next 40 minute period a "hot" letter is going to come down. In the meantime, the other jobs the pool typically gets can easily be handled by the less able typists.

Like the mover above, the typing pool manager not only walks up and down the aisle delegating jobs, but also looks or thinks ahead. They may, for example, identify a fast typist who makes very few mistakes (a highly skilled agent), just ten minutes away from being finished with the current job.

What is required in the technology of call centers today is a function, like that of the typing pool manager, to judiciously delay the start of one job in deference to a job that arrived more recently, or to keep the most able typist available for the jobs that garner the value of their respective talents.

In the traditional ACD's FIFO model, not only would the ACD take the best typist, but it would also take the agent that was the most efficient because he would become available more often. The faster you typed, the quicker you became available. The more work you got, the faster you typed, until eventually, the enterprise reaches the point where the best agent/typist burned out. Compound this with the fact that the busier agent has been designated as having some other particularly valuable skill as well, and the pace toward burnout increases rapidly. The agent leaves and now your second best agent becomes the first and so on. A cascading effect happens as your best people leave and what you are left with is the worst people being the best. The leaky bucket effect strikes the call center agent resource pool. It is not only the back door that the enterprise must make smaller, but the employee "exits" as well.

The human capital is the enterprise's most precious resource; people are the killer application. People have the unique abilities to apply judgements, discretion and intuition in customer engagements. Companies that are truly customer focused will also be equally focused on their agents and employees. When the value of the agent is characterized not as a unit for call processing, but as an ambassador for the enterprise, the care, comfort and retention of these ambassador-level resources takes on a different light. Most companies will spend tremendous amounts of money training agents only to put them in environments where they burn out quickly. An evolutionary shift in customer service must have an equal shift in the care of the human resources expected to engage with customers.

The relationship/service equation requires parity on both sides of the enterprise; customer and agent. The application focus of an advanced service company will be toward the issue of resolving best agent burnout and creating agent workload fairness. Short term gains derived from overwork shortchanges the long term contributions of the experienced agent. Qualified, functional and adept human beings are going to become more difficult to find and hence more valuable. Tools and technologies that fine-tune agents workloads are where significant progress will be seen.

Fine tuning agent workloads does not mean, in the context of this chapter, increasing the complexity of skills available in some skills based routing scheme. Bell Laboratories has done some significant, and under-publicized, call center traffic modeling and simulation research which has led them to believe that there is a fundamental and self perpetuating flaw in the application of skills based routing and the use of multi-skilled agents. The flaw is the load imbalance that skills based routing creates by delivering far more than the necessary amount of work to the more highly skilled agents while lesser skilled agents remain relatively idle. As in the typing pool, this "load imbalance" results in a faster burnout of the more skilled agents and, by default, a burn out of a call center's more expensive agents (those with more skills).

A Society Of Consumer Affairs Professionals (SOCAP) study identified that 68 percent of customers that leave a company leave because of reasons that have absolutely nothing to do with the price of service or product; they leave because of the perceived indifference of one individual. Pricing, service, technology and plumbing elements mean little if the enterprise's human interface is having a bad day, day after day.

For years now call centers have been designed to route calls into large common queues. While this arrangement yields pretty good overall resource utilization, the enterprise really has no way of knowing how "expert-ly" customer service is being delivered within that big pool if the pool gets too broad. How can you segment resources such that they each focus on their best work but are also included in the broader pool of resources for the sake of utilization – this is what skills should really be about. The intelligent use of resources eliminates the penalty of poor utilization even though resources are predominately segmented. In the Fourth Generation model, full utilization and very specific segmentation will occur at the same time.

The supra-proficiency basis of skills based routing will not be a characteristic of the evolved Fourth Generation service enterprise. Today's ACD technologies ultimately attach rules to the customer's call (adding items to the restaurant menu). The Fourth Generation enterprise will be characterized by invoking rules attached to the agents – deterministic rules invoked when the agent becomes available. Traditional ACDs permit little discretion with respect to influencing the order in which customers are served, particularly those customers that are identified for service by a particular agent based on some skills based routing scheme.

Earlier it was mentioned that there are in fact two queues in a call center; customers and agents. There is an important fundamental distinction that must be made between the two. When a customer event, typically a call, occurs, although it is certainly a real time event, it is often queued up for action. The call arrival creates a demand that can not be acted on until an agent becomes available. An agent's becoming availability is also a real time event. However, at the moment the agent becomes available the call center can do something. The question is what should the agent do.

The current technologies of ACDs are designed to achieve efficiencies by closing the latency gap between call arrival (any media) and response, but ACD technology has done little to gain efficiencies by leveraging the latency gap of the agent's availability. For example, one function of this evolved rules engine will essentially be to weigh the caller's expected wait time (EWT) with the expected availability time (EAT) of an agent with a specific skill set. It is important to understand that the concept of expected wait time is not only being applied to the caller, but to the agent as well.

The resource rules logic engine found in the advanced call center environment will perform a type of arbitrage; looking not only at customers queued, but at a predictable rate of availability of specifically skilled resources. In the Fourth Generation enterprise, and quite contrary to the traditional perspective, an agent becoming available is the most significant real time event occurring in the call center.

Are there any expert rules available when the agent becomes available? Not in today's call centers. Today if an agent becomes available, rules are invoked that are attached to calls. Nortel Networks and Lucent Technologies each have expert systems which are quite effective, but they are still fundamentally call oriented. This is the distinction between the agent focused expert engines found in Fourth Generation enterprises and the skills based routing engines found in traditional call center environments.

Event Arbitrage

Arbitrage is buying low from one place and selling higher to another. Call centers are nothing but event arbitrage. Although human at their core, arbitrage wasn't possible until the advent of faster and faster computers. Until the advent of technology powerful enough to track simultaneously all of the events that influence markets, arbitrage didn't work when things were done on paper; letters about events were not fast enough. Arbitrage only works when one can look at all markets at all times.

Now we have the ability to identify, evaluate and consider much more information relative to the real-time information of the call center operations that we have been able to in the recent past. In call centers, real-time decision making has been limited to identifying the highest skill preference, highest priority and oldest waiting call.

In the adaptive model, service availability is reevaluated at the execution of every single event. Some intelligent functions will look at the horizontal line and every time somebody steps into line, reevaluate work processing. Every action and event feeds the algorithm. If an abandoned call is experienced or additional agent resources log in, the adaptive model will instantly readjust the service engines to optimize the operation thorough each discrete decision.

The arbitrage of events, both customer and human resource, extends to every other media. These media include voice, fax, chat, email and even video. All these media are channels of events that can be prioritized – not by age, but by value and urgency. All have certain response conditions and different wait time expectations that can be established per media. For example, an agent may now have skill set definitions that may include voice and email. Where voice may be an immediate requirement, email may have an expected wait time of 24 hours.

Like voice, email has its own response expectations. When email is placed into a common service queue, application intelligence must be applied to insure that all email gets answered in, for example, eight hours. This intelligence sets off alarms as the email goes into hour seven of an eight hour service cycle without service. At this point, it may be worth it to have the next available agent, one who normally handles only voice calls, take care of that email.

Event arbitrage is about making the right real time decisions. The challenge with accomplishing the zero latency initiatives in the call center is making sure that the right engagement, event, media and customer is the next one we are handling.

Technology of Resource Arbitrage

ACDs have evolved into efficient systems for tracking agent productivity of both the agent individually or the call center in general. Where call center reporting generally fails is when new electronic transactions are added to the call center portfolio. The reporting applications of ACDs today do a poor job of reporting the entire breadth of media that can be involved in the workflow process of customer relationships and their transactions.

Successful event and resource arbitrage will require codifying human instinct. Like the manager of the typing pool, intelligent technology will be required to determine which one event gets served next.

Unfortunately, the C-Level has been given the notion that this is hard to do and that the data side of the enterprise is the only side capable of dealing with the perceived complexity. There is no question regarding the complexity of the applications and software required to arbitrage resources and events. However, the complexity of resource arbitrage (specifically the fundamental algorithms that support it) is analogous to the tip of the proverbial iceberg. Servers today can hold tremendous amounts of code and yet a simple GUI interface disguises the true number crunching going on. Have you looked under the hood of a car lately?

The military learned early on that at the speeds that supersonic jet fighters flew, too many pilots would grab the yoke (the steering device also called the "stick") at low altitudes. Unable to react in time to terrain changes, pilots with well intentioned actions often crashed very expensive airplanes. By the time flight information gets through the sensors, up on the screen, into the pilot's eyeball, down the optic nerve and to the hands, the plane has crashed. It does not matter how fast you get the information to the pilot, he is still not going to be fast enough to fly that jet without crashing at the speed of super service. The same principle applies in call centers (in the case of forecast and simulation, we often mistake the map for the terrain).

The fast pace of incoming calls and rapidly changing events in the customer service environment cannot possibly be managed by a human. How fast can it get? The SABRE booking service for airline, car and hotel reservations is the world's largest privately owned real time computer network and at moments has processed as much as 4,176 messages per second. Without the aid of terrain-avoiding radar, at some point a critical threshold is crossed and speed wobble, or worse, a crash, results. The strategy is to let go of the stick and let technology gain control of service.

There will undoubtedly be much debate over where this type of adaptive intelligence functionality should reside. Anticipate first seeing the technology, software and applications of resource arbitrage closely mated to the traditional PBX based ACDs and their peripheral servers. The driving influence for this will come from the institutionally embedded expectation of reliability and consistency that characterizes the traditional voice platforms. When reliability and consistency of service becomes an expectation, it becomes very difficult to retreat from the new (branded) standard you have established.

The ACD is a very good place to put an expert system because the fastest access to information about demand and resource is at the source of the data. In a call center environment the data source is the ACD itself.

As an example of the relevance of the proximity of information to the applications that process it, we can look at hotel reservations. When a traveler requires a hotel reservation, he typically calls the hotel's national toll-free number. Experienced travelers know that if they are unable to make a reservation through the national number, to call the hotel directly. Why? Because often calling the local hotel will give the caller an entirely different, "local" response made up of details not available at the national toll-free number (such as the local weather, bed availability or smoking rooms). The observation is that, although the national call center agents can make local reservations, they certainly do not have the depth of information available that the local hotel has, particularly if the hotel is full. In the case of the hotel being full (queue thresholds), it is the local reservation agent that has the most up-to-date information. This would likely, as the caller would hope, be expressed as, "Oh yes, we just had a cancellation, would you like it?" The closer the information resides to the decision engine, the faster it will be. And fractions of seconds become critically important when you fly call centers at the speed of jet fighters.

Making this intelligent arbitrage notion extensible to any platform in every customer service environment will occur. The evolutionary cycles of technology adoption dictates that, between here and there, will be the usual growing pains. We will first see the incubations of this concept in the form of some kind of Frankenstein's baby that could look like, in one hypothetical assimilation, one vendor's ACD system with its software compiled and running on an NT server with neural software, connected to a different vendor's ACD system over an ISDN CTI link or ATM backbone.

When Making Worldwide Decisions Is Too Slow

The trend toward the decentralization of not just call centers, but enterprises in general, is a paradox for many companies whose customer bases are growing and becoming more geographically dispersed. Conventional thinking would have one suggest that, as the enterprise and its customers grow, so must the number and location of customer contact points.

Scalability will occur in the network and these event and resource arbitrage applications will also have to function across networks of call centers. The challenge today with networking is with the latency of running service routing decisions over slow CTI links. The future customer service chain will see all of the remote switches connected by cheap bandwidth so that one location controls every other. The main brain will likely be connected over an ATM backbone. With single logic software remotely located anywhere in the world, the enterprise can eliminate all of the multiple site administration routines and overlaps of service.

Conclusion

No enterprise is immune from the demands to adapt to a competitive landscape evolving at an internet pace. Increasingly, the C-Level recognizes that the only way to compete is by influencing its customers in the way they are handled and serviced. Each and every transaction aggregately adds up to, or subtracts from, the overall business model. Delivering a branded experience requires the ability to execute precisely and consistently against expected levels of service and to minimize any deviation from that experience. The customer service environment must fundamentally insure that every interaction and engagement between the enterprise and its customers pays homage to what the enterprise brand stands for.

To this point in time enterprises have had little choice in the way they engage customers. Like Imperial Roman war chariots affecting the gauge of today's railroads, the technology of call centers works toward enabling the most efficient use of its resources. When the sophisticated software, applications and servers of call centers are peeled back away and the roots explored, you will indeed find a focus on the oldest call waiting and the longest idle agent – the traditional "gauges" of customer service.

Some of the biggest, most sophisticated enterprises in the world are dependent on totally archaic methods of utilizing their work forces. They get away with it because nobody is pounding them to do it any differently. There is no question that every company out there is constantly seeking improvements in its service endeavors. Unfortunately, even though the enterprise's C-Level demands that the call center comply with the vision of total customer care, the call center has little choice but to seek ways of increasing efficiencies because the fundamental technologies such as ACDs do little to enable effectiveness. In the old model, the possibility of angering the one wrong customer at any moment in time is all too real, on average. The defining characteristic of the Fourth Generation customer service enterprise will be that the company no longer risks, on average, angering anyone, customers and agents alike, at all.

At its core, taming the true chaotic nature of customer and agent events, both in the timing and media, requires new tools, application and technologies. These new tools and applications will be focused on the fundamental moment of control that exists when agents become available and customer events becomes queued. Executing the appropriate resource decision at that fundamental moment is where the enterprise's C-Level can look at their business's call center and feel comfortable that the relationship mission is being fulfilled and expressed with each and every transaction.

Customer service executives must recognize the inherent weakness when dynamic service demands are supported by obsolete, legacy and linear tools designed only to make binary decisions; then they will have made the next great leap along customer service's evolutionary path. Many customer service chain executives, deeply fearful of the revolutionary nature of evolution, may find comfort in the observation that neither revolution nor evolution is occurring here as much as it may be, as the Japanese call it, "kakumei". The Japanese word kakumei was, for many years, inappropriately used to describe the "revolution" of WW II. Kakumei more appropriately refers to a "renewal of rules and order."

The persistence of old rules and processes no longer fits the demands for providing consistent branded customer service to the right people every time. Positively stimulating the future value of the customer requires executing every customer service event, regardless of media, with prejudice and preference – not just for the customer, but for the agent and the enterprise's brand demands as well. The most evolved company, the most competitive enterprise has achieved a better balance where the customers win, the agents win and management wins: the board, the bread and the butter.

Chapter Nine
The Informal Call Center And
Relationship Communications

Introduction

"Informal call centers" are enterprise workgroups that supplement traditional "formal call center" operations, and the two will interact logically to complement each other's skills and availability. Thus, Skills Based Routing logic can still be used to direct calls or messages to either type of workgroup. There are therefore new challenges in configuring call center technologies and properly organizing the use of staff resources to support "informal call center" applications/functions. This chapter deals with the following issues and questions: What will be the impact of "informal call center" applications on callers and customers? Does the "informal call center" activity fit in with formal call center operations? Why will web activities, especially email, increase the need for informal traffic support, and change the role of "formal call center" operations? What call center technologies are particularly needed or not needed for "informal call center" operations? What will be different for call center management for informal call center operations?

Growth of the Small Call Center Market

The shift in call center technologies from expensive, proprietary, "closed" platforms to more flexible and economical "open" platforms, using software-based, client-server network infrastructures, has not only made possible improved distributed call center operations for the traditional centralized formal call centers, but has also opened the door to cost-effective call center operations for even the small business enterprises. This market segment is obviously large, and has attracted the attention of the traditional call center providers and a flock of computer telephony software developers who will integrate with small phone systems. In addition, the World Wide Web and eBusiness has made it possible for anyone to do business on the Internet inexpensively, but the price of doing so must include on-line access and live support via telephone (voice connections) and email.

In addressing this low-end of the market, the call center industry has recognized that small call center operations will be different in various ways, and have characterized these differences by referring to such operations as "informal" call centers. However, it is not "formality" that is really involved, but rather the operational procedures and supporting technology functions that will change because of the size, skills, and responsibilities of the call handling staff. These requirements are not limited to just small businesses, but will also be required even within large call center operations, where some of customer contacts will require one-on-one treatment by personnel with special skills or particular authority from within the enterprise organization.

A 1998 study conducted by the MultiMedia Telecommunications Association (MMTA) and Computer TELEPHONY magazine showed that enterprise organizations expect their call centers to become smaller and more de-centralized over the next two years. This is consistent with a finding in a recent study by the PELORUS Group on CTI in the Informal Call Center, that the average size of a "formal" call center operation is expected to drop from over 100 seats to between 50-60 seats, over the next five years. Also noted by both reports is the rapid growth in computer telephony products and services for the SOHO and Telecommuter market segments, both of which are excellent candidates for informal call center and unified multimedia call/message management technologies. The PELORUS Group reports that there were seven million telecommuters in the U.S. and 50 million SOHO workers in 1997, predicted respectively to grow to 25 million and over 78 million by the year 2000.

Defining the Informal Call Center

Most companies don't even know that they have a call center activity, according to a study by Versatility, Inc., let alone what to call it. Although only about 10% of responding companies will say they have a "call center," 60% say they do telesales and teleservices. What they really mean is they are not organized as a traditionally large, formal call center, nor do they have all the technologies that such formal call centers typically use.

The industry hasn't helped either, by using terms like "CTI" to describe call center technology and functions, and now we have "informal call center"! Talk about confusing names! I have seen such call center operations referred to as just small call center operations, a "partial seat call center," a remote or distributed call center, a "virtual" call center, an "unCallCenter," a "casual" call center, a departmental workgroup, a "help-desk", an "overflow" group, or just individual experts or specialists. That makes it pretty hard to figure out. One practical way to approach this topic is to start out by defining the Informal Call Center from the perspective of the people involved with call center operations. Specifically, this means the caller/customer, the call-handling staff, and the operational managers/supervisors who keep the activity moving properly. Then we can look at what it is not, relative to the formal, physically centralized call center.

Callers/Customers

Theoretically, a calling customer should not see a difference between the formal and informal call center operation, i.e., they should be getting the same required level of service from either one. The caller doesn't know what kind of technology is being employed, nor do they necessarily know whom they want to talk to. However, there may be a point at which the caller/customer will perceive a difference, and that is when a working relationship is established with a particular individual in the enterprise staff. At that point, the communication can become the basic person-to-person contact and the normal issues of making contact and exchanging messages come into play.

The reality is that when an incoming call ends up going to an informal call center workgroup, there will be a greater likelihood of a longer wait for service or the caller being offered a messaging option for a return call. This will be particularly true for "Web callers" who are initiating their voice calls from an enterprise web page. Such callers will be in a good position to initiate a message exchange and attach pertinent multimedia information data. However, handling such calls will require much more than a telephone set, and, in fact, should best be handled with both a web connection and a voice connection with the web support representative ("WSR").

Call Handling Staff

The biggest factor in contrasting an informal and formal call center activity is the call-handling staff. The implications for the informal call handling staff originate from a combination of skill requirements, availability for call handling tasks, and the size of the group that can support the amount of traffic for such types of calls. These considerations make it very obvious that an call center group can very well be part of a larger, formal call center operation, and is not restricted to being viewed as the only call center activity in an enterprise.

Functionally speaking, the "call center" is a local or wide area communication network for controlling and supporting customer access to information, transactions, and, most importantly, providing call and message management for access to enterprise personnel. From that perspective, the informal call center will perform similar functions, with a major difference when it comes to the skills, responsibilities, and authority of the enterprise personnel that will interact with customers. Such differences will also be reflected in the level of communications management functions involved, which will shift from varying degrees of supervised controls and automated call/message routing assignments to more autonomous, individually controlled, person-to-person levels of call/message management by the enterprise staff.

Staff Size

Certainly, the most obvious and commonly accepted characteristics of the Informal call center is that it is not a large, heavily supervised workgroup, sitting in one big room, dedicated to nothing but taking phone calls from people they don't know personally. Being a small workgroup doesn't necessarily mean "informal" either; however, being small does reduce and even eliminate a lot of the responsibilities, chores, and the overhead of managing and supervising the larger staff of call handlers found in traditional formal call center operations. Right there, the informal call center operation must be viewed differently from the perspective of typical call center technology requirements, like scheduling software, performance monitoring tools, predictive dialers, etc.

The small enterprise is statistically a big target for call center technology, but has traditionally been attacked with simple, basic communication tools like telephone key systems, voicemail auto attendants, IVR applications, and simple forms of call distribution like hunt groups. As more sophisticated computer telephony-based personal call management software for the individual user desktop becomes available, its role for relationship management at the person-to-person level will complement traditional call-handling activities at the enterprise call center level.

If we include the SOHO operation as a valid segment of the informal call center marketplace, then we will find a significant number of applications that fall under the classification of the "Call Center of One."

Dedication to Taking Calls

Although the line may be somewhat fuzzy about dedication to call handling, staffing for the informal call center will typically be determined by other job responsibilities and priorities. This means that taking an incoming call may not necessarily be the highest priority for the call-handling individual, as it would be in traditional formal call center environments. These other responsibilities and priorities, coupled with the relative staff sizes, limit call-handling capacity. From a scheduling perspective, there would be no guarantee of staff availability, and this will impact the interface with the caller/customer and the options they should be given.

When there is no guarantee of adequate staff availability, the usual alternatives must come into play, including self- service applications, "callback messaging" (leaving a message for a return phone call), or just waiting in queue. What we are talking about here is, in reality, a "blended" activity, where call-handling is interleaved with some other task responsibilities, and, depending on the relative priorities, call handling traffic needs may have to be met with these alternatives. If that's not acceptable, then you will need to use dedicated staffing.

"Gold Collar" Staffing – Specialists, Knowledge Workers, and Sole Decision Makers

As the traffic from simple customer questions and transactions increasingly shifts over to convenient 7x24 self-service call center applications, either via interactive voice response (IVR) or web desktop interfaces, the use of live assistance will also shift to supporting more critical or complex customer needs, such as resolving problems, making approval decisions, or giving expert opinions. Although client-server and LAN technologies will help empower call center personnel to do more for callers by enabling access to enterprise-wide information, there will always be some situations which can only be resolved by a very small group of high-level specialists, and, in some cases, even by only one particular person. In the last case, we are talking about a single point of access, with absolutely no guarantee of immediate availability, and the only practical alternative will be non-real-time responses such as callbacks or message exchanges.

Such call-handling individuals may or may not have other responsibilities, but the bottom line is that they will not be able to accept all calls immediately, and will therefore fall into the framework provided by the "informal call center." Furthermore, once the one-on-one relationship is initiated, it may remain at the person-to-person level over the course of an entire transaction interchange. This means enabling direct connections to that support person, leaving messages in the support person's individual mailbox, and even enabling direct consultative multimedia informational exchanges between the two parties.

Insight: What we are really seeing now, is that everyone in the enterprise can theoretically be part of "call center" operations, but only some will be dedicated or supervised as part of the "formal" activity. However, in evaluating the outcomes and effectiveness of call center strategies and policies, both formal and informal activities must be considered.

Account Ownership

Another major source of "informal call center" activities will involve those situations where there is account "ownership" by specific sales or customer service staff. Under such circumstances, any contact with the customer/caller must be handled by the owner of the account, rather than anyone who is available. Skills based routing defaults to the owner of the account as the criterion for call assignment, although there could be specific backup alternatives as well. In the simplest case, the situation becomes similar to the "expert" assignment to a call mentioned above, except that the assignment is not based just upon the specific purpose of the individual call, but also on the identity of the caller.

Account ownership can activate call center inbound routing rules to send calls from the workgroup level to the individual call management level, where the personalized rules of the "Call Center of One" prevail. Such calls would be directed to a particular individual's extension number, where the call could be immediately picked, forwarded to another wireline or wireless phone, or give out information and caller options for making contact or leaving a message for a return call.

For outbound activity, the use of predictive dialing software for initiating outgoing calls is not typically exploited in the informal call center environment, either because there is usually too small a staff for a pacing algorithm to initiate calls ahead of time, or because there is specific ownership of the accounts and all calls related to those accounts, such as salespeople with assigned prospect lists. Message processing, e.g., email processing, is implicitly an outbound function, because it an incoming message will almost require a outbound reply, even if it is just a confirmation of receipt. However, other forms of automating a response to email are required rather than just call placement, and these will be as applicable to the informal environment as in a formal environment. As a matter of fact, message response processing will be discussed later on as a primary reason for an increasing shift to informal operations.

Call Routing/Assignment

Perhaps one of the most debatable issues regarding the "informal call center", is how calls are actually assigned to specific call-handling individuals. The question here is whether calls will be routed by some "intelligent" call distribution software logic, such as Skills Based Routing rules, or is it going to be done through manual selection by a member of the call handling staff. From a conceptual standpoint, the call routing logic should be the same as that found in the big formal operations, where we identify the caller, the caller's purpose in calling, evaluate the availability of suitable skills to take the call, and make the assignments. This is a traditional "push" scenario for call center operations.

However, some low-end products for the small, informal call center simplify the approach significantly, by presenting information on all incoming calls waiting in a queue to an available staff member who is ready to take a call, and letting them select or "pull" the call of their choice to be processed, or even route the call to someone else. This decision is based on the same kind of information that an up-to-date ACD systems would use, including ANI data, a "screen pop" of the caller's database file, how long the caller has waited, other waiting calls, etc. For someone who knows their callers intimately, this is a viable strategy, but it does require the call handler to also act like a (silent?) switchboard operator.

The Coexistence of "Formal" and "Informal" Call Center Activities

A leading industry publication recently featured a cover page story on the technology requirements for "casual" call centers, under the assumption that such activities had nothing to do with a formal center operation. Their observations are appropriate for the many enterprises that have very small call-handling staffs. Even as such small enterprises expand by doing eBusiness on the web, email message processing will be where much of the added activity will take place, relative to telephone call traffic. However, they missed the boat in assuming that existing formal call center operations won't require similar informal call center staffing for certain kinds of calls. Nothing could be farther from the truth!

Legacy call center technologies provided special terminals, station sets, and desktop software for call handling personnel, while specialists usually were able to take a transferred phone call. With new computer telephony features for personal call management at the desktop, call center management should rethink the way calls will be handled by informal call center staff. What we have is the convergence of two enterprise communications technologies, one for the enterprise call center staff, and one for individual, personal communications; the former works with calls and messages in assignment queues, while the latter, the "Call Center of One," doesn't try to queue up more than one call at a time ("call waiting") and relies heavily on caller messaging (voicemail) and a personal "mailbox." The interface between the two deals with the transfer of call/message processing responsibilities between the call center work groups and the individuals comprising the informal call center. In particular, the management of messages in a call center environment, will require mailboxes where new messages that can be both individually controlled, as well as monitored and accessed by call center management if necessary.

Now that industry-standard, "open" platforms are being used for all telephony functions, such platforms could theoretically house all computer-telephony functions. However, issues of scalability and manageability make a distributed, networked system much more practical for all but the smallest systems. So we will probably still find a call server (switch), an "intelligent" call management/routing "ACD," an Automatic Message Distribution ("AMD") and processing system, an email (multimedia) messaging system, and what we describe as a Personal Call/Message Management server. The last item is familiarly known as a "unified messaging" system.

"The Call Center of One"

"Informal Call Centers" emphasize the more personal aspects of the call handling in their support to enterprise knowledge workers who are empowered to resolve issues with customers. It is different in several respects from the formal call center operation; it incorporates individual, communications control, and person-to-person interactions for the "Call Center of One." This involves unified call/message management, which includes personalized call screening, message filtering, unified message notification and delivery, and fax to the desktop, all elements of what is today being incorporated under the label of "unified messaging."

Every individual in a workgroup/call center environment needs several communication "views" and interfaces. They represent the enterprise to callers by their workgroup responsibilities, their individual task responsibilities to the workgroup and the enterprise, and, finally, their personal accessibility for family, friends, etc., from outside of the work environment. Management of all these levels of communication must be consolidated within a consistent framework of relative priorities from the individual's perspective relative to the organization.

The communications of the individual are very similar to that of a workgroup or call center group, with the primary difference that the individual may have more control, i.e., "pull" over communication tasks, rather than the "push" of an ACD or Predictive Dialer. In addition, the individual knowledge workers or specialists normally do not use communication "scripts", and are supervised or monitored directly on their performance or procedural skills as are "formal call center" agents.

Self-service Applications and The Informal Call Center

Self-service applications, both for the telephone caller (using IVR facilities) and web callers (web server applications) are equally important to customer support in both formal and informal call center environments. Although it is usually necessary to have some form of immediate "escape" to live assistance from such automated services, there have been many applications where only the self-service application was provided, with no direct access to live backup. In some self-service applications, the only "escape" provided is via messaging, voice or email, because there may be no real pressing need for assistance to be immediate, or such staffing just could not be provided (e.g., after hours).

As we see convenient access to information dramatically increase through self-service automated telephone and web access, the need for live assistance will decrease. But, we can expect the need for live assistance to become more specialized and with higher skill levels. Such demand will increase the need for the communication and staffing strategies offered by informal call center technologies, including two-way messaging discussed below.

Call Center Messaging

Messaging, as a powerful new means of communication between the enterprise and its individual customers, falls into two basic categories; "informational messaging" and "relational messaging." For the most part, informational messages can be generated and processed by automated applications, and as such, can satisfy some of the needs of a customer, but not all. These can be answers to specific questions, an account statement, a document or personalized report, product literature, a fax document, data files, etc. However, when it comes to supporting and reinforcing relationships with customers, person-to-person communication rules, including conversational exchanges and responsive messaging etiquette, are critical to the effectiveness of any information exchange. This factor is perhaps the biggest differentiator between the traditional IT perspective of information exchange and the telecommunications heritage of real-time communications.

Aside from the mechanics of automated message routing and processing, the "blending" of calls and message handling is an ideal marriage for enterprise personnel who are not completely dedicated to handling real-time telephone calls. Such staff activities support two-way email messaging and callback messaging that form the essence of the informal call center concept. Rather than being committed to handling just incoming phone calls (or predictive dialing outbound calls), the informal call center personnel make themselves available whenever their other responsibilities permit. When either particular expertise or assigned responsibilities requires "ownership" of all enterprise communications with a particular customer, we have "relational" communications and messaging, traditionally known as "person-to-person" correspondence and phone calls. Unified messaging technology and "universal" mailboxes, however, will further empower informal call center staff to exploit both multimedia and cross-media messaging and information exchange, and still maintain the interpersonal relationships where needed.

The Implications of Call Center Messaging for the Informal Call Center

We mentioned earlier that a caller who can't be serviced by a live person would typically be given the option of leaving a callback message. Furthermore, we indicated that "Web callers" may well choose to leave an email message/form ("Webmail") rather than wait for live assistance, especially if a data attachment is required as part of the message. Finally, the response to the caller's Webmail message may well be a response message either as text or voice, since we now have direct Internet access to a personal mailboxes. All of these possibilities suggest an increased use of messaging for call center interactions.

Messaging is an interruptible activity, unlike incoming calls. As such, messaging activities are logical candidates for "blending" with other task responsibilities, especially if they are also interruptible. Therefore, depending upon the traffic flow of incoming messages that require human attention, the message processing tasks can be distributed to various individuals and groups who normally could not efficiently handle normal incoming calls. In this way, the increased use of messaging will foster greater use of informal call center groups and the specific technologies that such activities will exploit. These include multimedia messaging (attachments), cross-media messaging, callback messaging (voice and email), personal call management, and automatic message distribution ("AMD").

Message Management and Individual Mailboxes for the Informal Call Center

The management of incoming messages, whether voice or email, poses other issues from a management perspective. Once messages leave the domain of the call center queue and enter the individual mailbox of the knowledge worker, there will be a need to track the disposition of the message. If necessary, message-handling responsibility may have to be manually reassigned, when response time deadlines expire or other circumstances so dictate. This suggests management access to an individual's mailboxes that can be monitored for throughput of enterprise message handling, which is not the same as a traditional personal mailbox and its need for privacy. Such mailboxes can be accommodated by call/message systems that provide for flexible classes of service.

Operational Management for Informal Call Centers

Depending upon which definitions you use for your "informal call center" operations, there will be different ways of managing its traffic and its support staff. However, there are main characteristics that will impact the operational management of an informal call center.

Small Center

If the staff is small but adequate for traditional inbound or outbound telephone traffic, most of the same requirements of the formal call center operations can be applied here. Obviously, scheduling, staff performance monitoring and evaluation chores will be simple enough to eliminate the need for elaborate software tools. Depending upon the types of callers and the role of self-service applications, the call routing logic can also be extremely simple, requiring little management involvement.

"Gold Collar" Staff

Clearly, high-level knowledge workers cannot be tightly scheduled, nor supervised in the same way as less skilled call center staff, but there are other metrics that may be brought into play. There is an increasing trend towards measuring "outcomes," which would be more appropriate for higher-skilled staff that manages their own availability, priorities, and time. This introduces another area of information convergence, where enterprise performance can be linked to the involvement of specific individuals in the customer service chain.

Another area involves training and skill categorization. Where do these specialists come from? How do they get trained on an ongoing basis? How are they evaluated for their particular expertise and areas of responsibility? Clearly, these issues and responsibilities cannot be handled by traditional call center management, but belong to various enterprise departments, whether it is sales expertise, product technology expertise, or financial accounting problems. However, these sensitive interactions and transactions will flow though the informal call center facilities, and must be tracked, logged, and managed through those facilities as well.

Message Traffic Management

Message traffic becomes a new area of responsibility for the management of an informal call center, without the critical concern for real-time staffing and trunking resources that call-handling traffic imposes. However, the throughput of messaging traffic, as it pertains to response time and processing priorities by enterprise staff, is a dynamic that can't be neglected. Even with high-level enterprise personnel, the throughput must be tracked for level of service issues, wherever there is interaction with the customer.

Messaging Quality Control

As mentioned elsewhere, messaging responses must be as automated as possible, where the interchange is "informational, rather than "relational" in order to cost-efficiently support message processing. This will include use of web and voice forms, rather than freeform email and voicemail messages, "content scanning" of messages (voice and text) to identify the purpose of the messages for routing and processing, automated canned responses from a knowledge base, and "cut and paste" options for manual responses. Where human judgement is required, including the use of "cut and paste" or manually created responses, management responsibilities for quality control become a concern. The challenge here is to allow this to be done cost-effectively, whether by sampling techniques, or reactively only when problems are noticed. With higher-level staff, issues of privacy may become a problem as well.

Summary

Traditional call center operations are becoming distributed, not only geographically, but also in terms of access to everyone with an enterprise organization, as well as using different modes and media of information exchange and personal interaction. The impact of this trend is that communications management technologies must support customer access and interactions with both traditional call center workgroups (large and small) and individuals with special skills and responsibilities. Furthermore, this flexibility must also provide "intelligent routing" for the seamless transition of any real-time customer contact to the most appropriate of these call-handling resources or process that is required.